VALI NASR

THE DISPENSABLE
NATION

American Foreign Policy in Retreat

Doubleday | *New York London Toronto Sydney Auckland*

Copyright © 2013 by Vali Nasr

All rights reserved. Published in the United States by Doubleday,
a division of Random House, Inc., New York, and in Canada by
Random House of Canada Limited, Toronto.

www.doubleday.com

Book design by Michael Collica
Jacket design by Emily Mahon
Jacket illustration © Stefano

Library of Congress Cataloging-in-Publication Data
Nasr, Seyyed Vali Reza
The dispensable nation : American foreign policy in retreat / Vali Nasr.
pages cm.
Includes index.
1. United States—Foreign relations—Middle East. 2. Middle
East—Foreign relations—United States. 3. United States—Foreign
relations—Islamic countries. 4. Islamic countries—Foreign relations—
United States. I. Title.
JZ1670.N37 2013
327.73056—dc23   2012043100

ISBN 978-0-385-53647-9

MANUFACTURED IN THE UNITED STATES OF AMERICA

1 3 5 7 9 10 8 6 4 2

First Edition

To Richard C. Holbrooke, a tireless champion
of American leadership in the world

There is a tide in the affairs of men,
Which, taken at the flood, leads on to fortune;
Omitted, all the voyage of their life
Is bound in shallows and in miseries.
On such a full sea are we now afloat,
And we must take the current when it serves,
Or lose our ventures.

—William Shakespeare,
Julius Caesar

CONTENTS

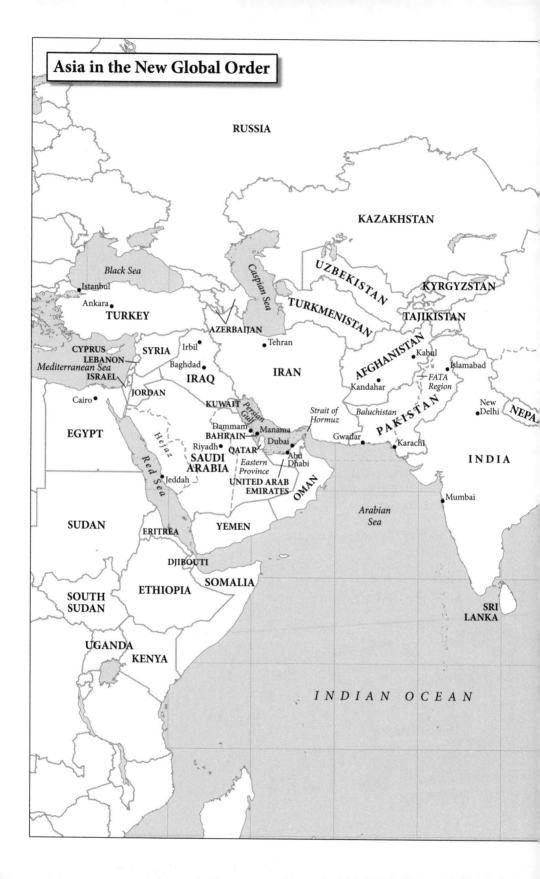

Asia in the New Global Order

RUSSIA

KAZAKHSTAN

Black Sea

UZBEKISTAN

KYRGYZSTAN

•Istanbul

TURKMENISTAN

TAJIKISTAN

Ankara•

Caspian Sea

TURKEY

AZERBAIJAN

•Tehran

CYPRUS

SYRIA   Irbil•

AFGHANISTAN   •Kabul

•Islamabad

Mediterranean Sea   LEBANON

Baghdad•

IRAN

Kandahar•   —FATA
Region

ISRAEL

IRAQ

PAKISTAN

New
•Delhi   NEPAL

JORDAN

Cairo•

KUWAIT

Persian Gulf

Baluchistan

Dammam•   •Manama

*Strait of
Hormuz*

EGYPT

BAHRAIN   •Dubai

Gwadar•

Karachi•

Riyadh•   QATAR

Hejaz

SAUDI
ARABIA

Abu
Dhabi

INDIA

*Eastern
Province*

UNITED ARAB
EMIRATES   OMAN

•Jeddah

Red Sea

•Mumbai

*Arabian
Sea*

SUDAN

ERITREA   YEMEN

DJIBOUTI

SOUTH
SUDAN

ETHIOPIA   SOMALIA

SRI
LANKA

UGANDA

KENYA

INDIAN   OCEAN

THE DISPENSABLE NATION

INTRODUCTION

This book tells the story of my two years working in the Obama administration on the problems of the greater Middle East. I thought long and hard about writing it—I didn't want it used as a political bludgeon. My goal instead is to shed light on the making of American foreign policy during the Obama years and explain what its consequences will be for the greater Middle East and for us.

The book tells three stories simultaneously.

The first is the story of an administration that made it extremely difficult for its own foreign policy experts to be heard. This book will describe how both Hillary Clinton and Richard Holbrooke, two incredibly dedicated and talented people, had to fight to have their voices count on major foreign policy initiatives. Holbrooke never succeeded; Hillary Clinton did—but it was often a battle, and usually happened only when it finally became clear, to a White House that had jealously guarded all foreign policy making and then relied heavily on the military and intelligence agencies to guide its decisions, that these agencies' solutions were not, and could never be, a substitute for the type of patient, long-range, credible diplomacy that garners the respect of our allies and their support when we need it. In other words, when things seemed to be falling apart, the administration finally turned to Hillary because they knew she was the only person who could save the situation, and she did that time and again.

One could argue that in most administrations, there is an inevitable imbalance between the military intelligence complex, with its offerings of swift and dynamic, as well as media-attracting, action, and the foreign

policy establishment, with its slow and seemingly plodding delibera-
tive style. But this administration advertised itself as something different. On the campaign trail, candidate Obama repeatedly stressed that
he wanted to get things right in the Middle East, reversing the damage
that had been done by the previous administration's reliance on faulty
intelligence and its willingness to apply military solutions to problems
it barely understood.

Candidate Obama said he would engage the Muslim world, not just
threaten to attack it. He would work to change the standing of the United
States in the region. He would show leadership by listening, not just
by talking. While the American Right was belittling the benefits of his
community-organizing background, I thought to myself that the Middle
East could use a little community organizing. In fact, the more I thought
about it, the more I felt that American leadership in building and nurturing economic and political ties, rooted in regional and international
institutions that would bring stability in a chaotic place, was just what
was missing in the region. It is why I joined the administration.

The imbalance in influence between the military and the foreign
policy establishment was cause enough for concern, but the president's
habit of funneling major foreign policy decisions through a small cabal
of relatively inexperienced White House advisers whose turf was strictly
politics was truly disturbing. The primary concern of these advisers was
how any action in Afghanistan or the Middle East would play on the
nightly news, or which talking point it would give the Republicans in the
relentless war they were waging against the president. That the Obama
administration has been praised during the 2012 election season for
its successful handling of foreign policy has, I believe, less to do with
its accomplishments in Afghanistan or the Middle East than with how
American actions in that region of the world were reshaped to accommodate partisan political concerns in a way unimaginable a few decades
ago.

By September 2012, when violent anti-American protests swept
across the Muslim world, claiming the lives of four American diplomats
and dozens of demonstrators, two things were clear: first, that we had
got the Middle East badly wrong and the administration's policies had
been off the mark. And second, that retreating from the region given the

direction it is moving in would be disastrous. This book will explain all this.

The second story this book will tell is what happened when those of us in the foreign policy establishment were told to go out and sell often stunningly obtuse proposals to our allies in the region. Many Americans hold a picture in their head of Middle East leaders as militaristic thugs, corrupt political operators, narrow-minded connivers, or American stooges. And there are no doubt people who fit those descriptions in positions of power there—and elsewhere. But over the years, especially the past eleven years, the leaders of the Middle East have developed exquisitely fine-tuned ears to the potential consequences of U.S. actions for their own nations. They greatly fear our military power because they feel we use it recklessly, and they know they have few defenses against it. And they are no longer willing to sit back and nod in agreement when we propose plans that require their cooperation, plans they know won't work and put their nations at risk, plans they have good reason to believe we will abandon when push comes to shove, and sometimes even before that, leaving them to deal with the mess we have made.

I will describe in detail what it was like to sit through these kinds of negotiations, first with Richard Holbrooke at the head of our side of the table, and later with Hillary Clinton. I will also relate what world leaders and foreign policy professionals I have known for years have seen and heard in these settings. For many Americans this will be an eye-opening view of how their country presents itself in world councils. It will give voice to those who call the shots in the Middle East and ask whether their responses to our plans are worth hearing and perhaps heeding. For the American public has to understand that when your grand plans for a region persuade no one but yourself—not your friends, not your "frenemies," not your collaborators, and certainly not your enemies—it's time to start asking some hard questions back home.

But perhaps the most important story this book tells is this one: the story of the price the United States will pay for its failure to understand that the coming geopolitical competition with China will not be played out in the Pacific theater alone. Important parts of that competition will be played out in the Middle East, and we had better be prepared for the jousting and its global consequences.

The American people are tired of war, rightly so, and welcome talk of leaving the region—not just packing up the soldiers but closing up shop altogether. Indeed, the president has marketed our exit from the Middle East as a foreign policy coup, one that will not only unburden us from the weight of the region's problems but also give us the freedom we need to pursue other, more pressing, initiatives to address significant national security concerns.

Ending the wars in Iraq and Afghanistan, not to mention the broader ill-defined "war on terror," is, I agree, a very good idea, provided it is done properly without damage to our interests or the region's stability. But we should not kid ourselves that the rhetoric of departure is anything more than rhetoric; we are bringing home our troops and winding down diplomatic and economic engagement, but leaving behind our drones and Special Forces. We should not expect that the region will look more kindly on drone attacks and secret raids than they did on broader U.S. military operations. But the more important point is that none of the issues that brought us to the Middle East in the first place have been resolved—not those that existed at the end of World War II, when Britain handed over to us the role of the great power in the region, not those that have kept us there for over sixty years, and certainly not those that attracted our attention after 9/11. If anything, the region is less stable and more vulnerable to crisis than ever before. And its importance to commerce and global order has not diminished.

Here is what America's leaders and the American public cannot afford to miss. The near- and even long-term prospects for the Middle East are not difficult to predict. Either some outside power will have to step in and impose order on the region or it will collapse into chaos and instability, becoming the stage upon which untold numbers of nonstate actors, each with a different script, will attempt to wreak havoc upon us. China would love to play the role of great power in the region, and, one might argue, is preparing to do exactly that. Just as we pivot east, China is pivoting farther west. And it is doing so through its close and growing economic and diplomatic relationships with the Arab world, Pakistan, Iran, and Turkey. Indeed, while we scratched our heads about how to turn Pakistan our way during my tenure in the Obama administration, Chinese leaders were serenading Pakistan with reassurances that

Sino-Pakistani relations are "higher than the mountains, deeper than the oceans, stronger than steel, and sweeter than honey."[1]

Will we be comfortable having China pull the Middle East into its sphere of influence? Letting China manage al-Qaeda or Iran's nuclear ambition? Or try to resolve Arab-Israeli conflicts? Of course not. The Middle East will once again become the region where a great rivalry is played out, with China now playing the role of the Soviet Union.

These past four years presented us with an unrecognized opportunity to build regional economic, political, and military institutions to help the region resolve its many crises and allow it to manage on its own without constant new infusions of American lives and dollars. We could have simultaneously reduced the threat of al-Qaeda and strengthened the push for democracy, and figured out a way to draw Iran into the fold and minimize China's influence in the region, not to mention saving the lives and money spent on yet another surge whose ultimate benefits remain questionable. But there is no equivalent to NATO or ASEAN in the Middle East—no organization anchored in an economic and security alliance with the United States. Nor does the Obama administration, despite its own claim to engaging the region and building comity and community, show any indication of understanding the need for such institution building. This, of course, would be even truer of a Republican administration. And so instead, after China further strengthens its position in the Middle East, we will find ourselves on the back foot, having to play catch-up with money we don't have or will have to borrow from China.

But it is not too late. It is still possible to look ahead and deal with the problems in the region before they become another major crisis. This is why I have written this book.

—Vali Nasr, November 1, 2012

PROLOGUE:
"A WEEK IN SEPTEMBER"

Once a year, in mid-September, dozens of heads of state and many more foreign ministers fly into New York City for the annual meeting of the United Nations General Assembly. Generally speaking, it is not the speeches that draw these diplomats to New York. It is the chance to see and be seen, to exchange ideas and compare notes, to talk shop and even gossip. And it is an ideal place for a diplomat looking to drum up support for his country's plans to get things done.

That's what Richard Holbrooke intended to do in September 2009. Seven months earlier, he had been appointed by the president as his special representative to Afghanistan and Pakistan. During the campaign and once in office, the president had made clear that getting Afghanistan right would be a high priority for his administration. I knew how seriously Holbrooke took that charge. If we get Afghanistan right, he told me when he brought me on board as his senior adviser, it will be the end of America's wars in the Muslim world, and if we get it wrong, the "forever war" will continue, well, forever.

By late summer of 2009, the final plan for Afghanistan—more troops and serious nation-building—was clear enough for Holbrooke to inform some of our most important allies where we were heading. He told me he intended to start by meeting with a half dozen of those allies in New York during the UNGA meetings and that he wanted me to go with him. It was a week I will never forget.

Our very first meeting was with Egypt's foreign minister, Ahmad Abu Ghaith. He was Holbrooke's longtime friend and could not have been more gracious in his greetings. Holbrooke launched into his presentation of our plans for Afghanistan—defeating the insurgency and building democracy, a vibrant economy, a large army, and a strong civil society. He spoke with enthusiasm and grace, and Abu Ghaith nodded gently throughout. But whenever there was the slightest pause on Holbrooke's part, and sometimes even before Holbrooke had quite finished his thought, Abu Ghaith interjected in rather blunt, borderline-rude terms that everything Holbrooke was saying sounded a lot like our plans for Iraq, none of which worked out as we had hoped. When Holbrooke finished, the foreign minister immediately launched into his own presentation, certainly not one we were expecting.

"Richard," he began, "of course we will support you, we always have. But why do you want to get mixed up in another war? This will only help the terrorists. All the talk among our youth now is of going to Afghanistan for jihad against the Americans."

Abu Ghaith was not altogether correct; many of Egypt's youth were then dreaming of democracy. But the correlation between U.S. attacks and Arab (but also Pakistani) youth packing up to fight America was surely correct. Still, it was not just the words he used that came through loud and clear to us. It was his dismissiveness and frustration at having to once again support a plan that made no sense to him and that was being presented as a near fait accompli.

Reactions only worsened after that. At our next meeting with an Arab foreign minister, we sipped tea and nibbled on dates as Holbrooke went through his talking points, this time giving a long, glowing description of what America hoped to accomplish in Afghanistan. By this time he had a good idea what the reaction would be, but Holbrooke was always a loyal soldier. It was his job to sell our plan. And he tried.

Once again the diplomats on the other side of the table made it painfully clear that they thought we were way off in la-la land with our talk of building democracy and a strong civil society and everything else we were offering.

And when it was their turn to talk, they said just that. "It is much better you buy local warlords to keep al-Qaeda out of Afghanistan," our host responded. "I figure that will cost you $20 billion, which is what, one fifth of what you spend every year in Afghanistan? Spend that and then just go home!"

I had to repeat those last words to myself—just go home!—to have the meaning sink in. It was such a stunning rebuke that for a moment neither side said anything. It wasn't as if the foreign minister was trying to put us down; you could tell from the way he spoke that he truly believed that we didn't understand and that he was doing us a favor. Once again it was not the response we were looking for, but perhaps it was a response we should have listened to. About a year later, Rajiv Chandrasekaran of the *Washington Post* reported that in the parts of Afghanistan that experienced the least violence, credit went to American-backed local warlords.[1]

Between this meeting and the next, I asked Holbrooke about the responses we had encountered. I could see that he was deeply disturbed by how dismissive our interlocutors were about America's ability to do good in the region. At first he said little, fumbling for an answer. Then he managed the rejoinder that the doubters did not understand our strategy. Our problem was communication—we had to exorcise the ghosts of Iraq before we could create new hopes for Afghanistan. And then, after a pause, he came clean. "They have a point," he said.

Next on our list was another Arab foreign minister. I could have closed my eyes and thought I was in the previous meeting. In fact, had there been more time between the two meetings we could have concluded that the two foreign ministers had compared notes. As Holbrooke went through the same talking points—which, I have to admit, had lost a little oomph by now—our host fidgeted, as if he were impatient for Holbrooke to finish so he could bring the discussion back to reality. When his turn came, he jumped right in.

"You can pay to end this war," he began. Then he moved to the edge of his seat and raised his index finger in the air and said, "One billion dollars. It will cost you one billion dollars, no fighting needed." He put out the number as if he were giving us his best discount price!

Then, as if he were talking to someone who clearly had little to no understanding of the dynamics in the region, he told us we were fighting the wrong war. "You should talk to the Taliban, not fight them. That will help you with Iran." Then he gave us a big, knowing smile. Since the Iraq war, Persian Gulf countries have been worried about the rise of Iran's influence in the region, and are especially worried about its steady march toward nuclear capability. They wanted America to focus on Iran—even if it meant playing nice with the Taliban.

King Abdullah of Saudi Arabia couldn't have agreed more. "You have to look to the root of the Taliban problem," he told Holbrooke. And what did the king think was the source of our problems in Afghanistan? Iran, of course.

Holbrooke was correct when he referred to the ghosts of Iraq diminishing our credibility in the region. As far as the leaders of the Middle East were concerned, we didn't understand the difference between defeating an opponent on the battlefield (which we did quickly enough) and psychologically breaking his will to resist. We'd been flummoxed by—and totally unprepared for—what came after military victory in Iraq, a long-simmering but predictable outbreak of Sunni-Shia violence. What our allies understood—even if we couldn't admit it to ourselves— is that after ten years of war, Iraq was a country broken into dozens of pieces held together by a few pieces of Scotch tape. The tape started to come off the moment we left. Should it really have come as a surprise to us that there was no more confidence in our wisdom regarding Afghanistan than in the delusions that got us into Iraq?

When the week was over and we returned to Washington, Holbrooke dutifully reported what our allies thought of our plans for war. He did so carefully, in terms that would not make it seem as if he were scoring points. For his part, Holbrooke was concerned enough to caution against doubling down on war. But his counsel was dismissed as overblown and outdated. "When I talk about counterinsurgency and Vietnam at the White House," he once said, "those guys roll their eyes as if I am from another planet."

Six weeks later, on December 1, 2009, with no further discussion of the clear reservations on the part of the allies in the region whose cooperation we needed to make our plans work, President Obama announced his much-anticipated decision about the war in Afghanistan. It was reported that he spent hours and hours, indeed months, considering all the relevant information before sending another 33,000 American troops to continue the fighting there. The world held its breath for a new vision, one that would not be a mere reiteration of the familiar impulse to turn to the generals to fix a vexing foreign policy problem. But Obama did just that. There would be no attempt to restore diplomacy to primacy in foreign policy. To the American people it seemed that Obama had shown resolve, telling the world that America would fight the war to victory. But those whom America had to work hardest to convince of its wisdom were unimpressed. They did not think our strategy would work, and at any rate, they did not believe we would stick with it for long.

The drumbeat of skepticism continued. Almost a year later, in October 2010, during a visit to the White House, Pakistan's army chief, General Ashfaq Parvez Kayani, gave President Obama a thirteen-page white paper he had written to explain his views on the outstanding strategic issues between Pakistan and the United States. Kayani 3.0, as the paper was dubbed (since it was the third paper Pakistanis gave the White House on the subject), could be summarized as follows: You are not going to win the war, and you are not going to transform Afghanistan. This place has devoured empires before you; it will defy you as well. Stop your grandiose plans and let's get practical, sit down, and discuss how you will leave and what is an end state we can both live with.

Kayani expressed the same doubt time and again in meetings. We would try to convince him (as we did other regional leaders) that we were committed to the region and had a solution for Afghanistan's problems: we would first beat the Taliban and then build a security force to hold the place together after we left. He, like many others, thought the idea of an Afghan military was foolish and that we were better off negotiating an exit with the Taliban.

In one small meeting around a narrow table, Kayani listened carefully and took notes as we went through our list of issues. I cannot forget Kayani's reaction when we enthusiastically explained our plan to build up Afghan forces to 400,000 by 2014. His answer was swift and unequivocal: Please don't try to build that Afghan army. "You will fail," he said. "Then you will leave and that half-trained army will break into militias that will be a problem for Pakistan." We tried to stand our ground, but he would have none of it. He continued, "I don't believe that the Congress is going to pay nine billion dollars a year for this four-hundred-thousand-man force." He was sure it would eventually collapse and the fragments of the broken army would resort to crime and terrorism to earn their keep. That after all was pretty much what happened when the Soviet Union stopped paying for the Afghan army it had built—sixty days after Soviet cash dried up the Afghan army melted away and Kabul fell to the insurgents. Memories in the region run long, much longer than ours.

Kayani's counsel was basically "if you want to leave, just leave—we didn't believe you were going to stay anyway—but don't do any more damage on your way out." This seemed to be a ubiquitous sentiment across the region. No one bought our argument for sending more troops into Afghanistan, and no one was buying our arguments for leaving. It seemed everyone was getting used to a directionless America. The best they could do was to protect themselves against our sudden shifts and turns.

Bill Clinton famously called America the "indispensable nation," the world's leader by default, destined to solve problems large or small the world over.[2] Americans like this image of themselves.[3] That is why Obama harkened back to Clinton's famous phrase, telling the American people in his January 2012 State of the Union address, "America remains the one indispensable nation in world affairs—and as long as I am President, I intend to keep it that way." America—dragged by Europeans into ending butchery in Libya, abandoning Afghanistan to an uncertain future, resisting a leadership role in ending the massacre of civilians in Syria, and then rolling back its commitments to the region to "pivot" to Asia—hardly looks indispensable.

In the cocoon of our public debate Obama gets high marks on foreign policy. That is because his policies' principal aim is not to make strategic decisions but to satisfy public opinion—he has done more of the things that people want and fewer of the things we have to do that may be unpopular. To our allies, however, our constant tactical maneuvers don't add up to a coherent strategy or a vision of global leadership. Gone is the exuberant American desire to lead in the world. In its place there is the image of a superpower tired of the world and in retreat, most visibly from the one area of the world where it has been most intensely engaged. That impression serves neither America's long-run interests nor stability around the world.

AFGHANISTAN

The Good War Gone Bad

In late 2011, fighting in Afghanistan and frozen relations with Pakistan were endangering the president's plans to wrap up the Afghan war. The administration decided that it could use China's help. After all, the Chinese should want a stable Afghanistan, and should be worried about Pakistan, too. Beijing had made fresh investments in Afghanistan's mining sector, which appeared set for massive growth after the 2010 discovery of vast new mineral riches.[1] And China had long and deep economic ties with Pakistan. So the administration asked a veteran diplomat, an old China hand, to reach out to the Chinese leadership. The diplomat made the rounds in Beijing, meeting with the Chinese president, premier, foreign minister, and a host of other political players. Their answer was clear and unequivocal: "This is your problem. You made this mess. In Afghanistan more war has made things much worse, and in Pakistan things were not so bad before you started poking around. We have interests in this area, but they do not include pulling your chestnuts out of the fire. We will look after our own interests in our own way." In short, "You made your own bed, now lie in it." Once they were done pushing back, they invariably asked, "What is your strategy there, anyway?"

Afghanistan is the "good war." That was what Barack Obama said on the campaign trail. It was a war of necessity that we had to wage in order to defeat al-Qaeda and ensure that Afghanistan never harbored terrorists again.[2] Obama took up promoting the Afghan war at least in part as an

13

election-year tactic, to protect himself against perennial accusations that Democrats are soft on national security issues. Branding Afghanistan as a "war of necessity" gave him cover to denounce the Iraq war as a "war of choice" that must be brought to an end.

Obama's stance was widely understood at home and abroad to mean that America would do all it could in Afghanistan—commit more money and send more troops—to finish off the Taliban and build a strong democratic state capable of standing up to terrorism.

Four years later, President Obama is no longer making the case for the "good war." Instead, he is fast washing his hands of it. It is a popular position at home, where many Americans, including many who voted for Obama in 2008, want nothing more to do with war. They are disillusioned by the ongoing instability in Iraq and Afghanistan and tired of eleven years of fighting on two fronts. They do not believe that war was the right solution to terrorism and have stopped putting stock in the fearmongering that the Bush administration used to fuel its foreign policy. There is a growing sense that America has no interests in Afghanistan vital enough to justify a major ground presence.

It was to court public opinion that Obama first embraced the war in Afghanistan. And when public opinion changed, he was quick to declare victory and call the troops back home. His actions from start to finish were guided by politics and they played well at home. But abroad, the stories we tell to justify our on-again, off-again approach to this war do not ring true to friend or foe. They know the truth: that we are leaving Afghanistan to its own fate. Leaving even as the demons of regional chaos that first beckoned us there are once again rising to threaten our security.

When President Obama took office, the Afghan war was already eight years old. America went to Afghanistan in October 2001, less than a month after 9/11, to eliminate al-Qaeda. A quick victory made it possible to imagine a hopeful future there after more than two decades of civil war.

With international help, Afghanistan got a new constitution, a new government, and a new president whom the West celebrated as an enlightened partner in the effort to rebuild the country. President Hamid Karzai cut a dashing figure, debonair and progressive, the avatar of America's goal to free the Muslim world from the clutches of extremism. Even the designer Tom Ford had something to contribute, anointing Karzai "the chicest man on the planet today."[3]

Meanwhile, the Taliban and al-Qaeda had retreated to Pakistan,[4] seeking refuge in the country's northwesternmost region: the Federally Administered Tribal Areas (FATA), an uncertainly governed and ruggedly mountainous region the size of Massachusetts that is home to about 4 million Pashtun tribespeople. Consequently, while Washington was looking to build a new democratic and forward-looking Afghanistan to act as a bulwark against terrorism, it also relied on a close relationship with Pakistan to hound al-Qaeda in its FATA lair. Billions of dollars went into Afghanistan and Pakistan during the Bush presidency, supporting not only counterterrorism efforts but also democracy promotion, schooling for women and girls, and rural development.

But the investment failed to pay the hoped-for dividends. Long before President Obama took office, things had begun to change. By 2006 the Afghan government's stride had slowed, and there was little doubt that war and instability had returned. In that year the number of attacks by returning Taliban and al-Qaeda fighters rose 400 percent and the number of those killed in such attacks was up by 800 percent.[5] In June 2006 more international troops died in Afghanistan than in the Iraq conflict, more than in any other month since the war started.[6] The Taliban were making a ferocious comeback against what they saw as an American occupation and a vulnerable puppet government in Kabul.

By 2008 the fighting had morphed into a full-blown insurgency. The United Nations used to issue security maps for aid workers on which green marked safe areas and yellow those areas with some security problems, and red was used for dangerous areas under insurgent control. By 2008 large areas of the maps were in red. Many Afghans thought that the Taliban looked poised for victory, and when it comes to insurgencies, what the locals think often dictates the outcome. One Western observer back from Kabul in mid-2008 said every shopkeeper in the city (the most well-protected part of Afghanistan) thought that Taliban fighters would be in the capital by the year's end. Afghanistan was fast slipping into chaos.

Everything about Afghanistan was a challenge—its rugged geography, its convoluted ethnic makeup, labyrinthine social structure, and jealous tribalisms, its byzantine politics, and the bitter legacy of decades consumed by war and occupation. But the biggest problem lay across the border: Pakistan.

The Taliban operated out of the FATA, but its leadership had set up shop farther south in Quetta. They used the Pakistani city's relative safety to regroup and orchestrate the insurgency in Afghanistan. Taliban commanders recruited foot soldiers from seminaries across Pakistan's Pashtun areas and ran training camps, hospitals, and bomb-making factories in towns and villages a stone's throw from the Afghanistan-Pakistan border.

Moreover, since the Taliban's formation in 1994 the insurgent organization has maintained close ties with Pakistan's intelligence agency and received financial and military support from Islamabad. Pakistani support sustained Taliban military offensives throughout the 1990s, and even after the U.S. offensive broke the Taliban's hold on Afghanistan that relationship continued.

Pakistan has viewed the Taliban as a strategic asset that could keep India out of Afghanistan and under Pakistan's control. That makes the Afghan insurgency a regional problem. It is hard enough to fight an insurgency, but one that has a safe haven to retreat to within a sympathetic population and can rely on the financial, intelligence, and military support of a neighboring country is a tougher challenge still, by orders of magnitude. The Taliban and al-Qaeda would fight in Afghanistan, and when things got too hot, they would hasten south across the border to tend their wounds, recruit and train fresh fighters, and plan for more war. Indeed, the collective leadership of the Taliban became popularly known as the Quetta Shura, after the city where it met. The Afghanistan fight was starting to eerily resemble Vietnam, with Pakistan acting roughly like Laos, Cambodia, and Maoist China all rolled into one. The war was taking on a new, expensive shape, one that needed urgent attention.

By the time President Obama moved into the Oval Office, the Taliban juggernaut looked unstoppable. They had adopted a flexible, decentralized structure that reported to the leadership in Pakistan, but organized locally. There was a national political infrastructure in place too, with shadow governors and district leaders for much of the country. In some cases, this Taliban presence was nominal—the Taliban are almost exclusively a Pashtun phenomenon and do not reach into every corner of multiethnic Afghanistan—but elsewhere the Taliban were in control.

The Taliban had a strength that belied their numbers. The U.S. government estimated that in 2009 the Taliban were no more than 35,000 strong. Of these, only a core of at most 2,000 were battle-hardened veterans of Afghanistan's earlier wars. A larger number, maybe 5,000 to 10,000, were in the fight to avenge government abuse or the death of kith and kin in U.S. raids and aerial bombings. The largest number of fighters, 20,000 or more, were mercenaries, in it for a few dollars a day.

The Taliban had become politically more savvy and militarily more lethal.[7] Gone was their objection to pictures and music, and in came the use of both in their recruiting videos. In their statements, the new Taliban claimed to be open to women going to school. Talk of chopping off hands and lopping off heads in public was put aside.

Other beliefs, more ominously, were put aside as well. Steve Coll, the journalist and longtime observer of Afghanistan, writes that in the 1980s, when Afghan warriors were battling Soviet occupation, the CIA was desperately seeking someone to set off a massive vehicle bomb inside the 1.6-mile-long Salang Tunnel. The tunnel is a crucial north-south link running beneath a difficult pass in the towering Hindu Kush mountain range, and blowing it up would have cut the main Soviet supply route. In order to be effective, the bomb would need to go off mid-tunnel, meaning certain death for its operator. In effect, the CIA was looking for an Afghan suicide bomber.[8] No one volunteered. Suicide, said the Afghans, was a grievous sin, and quite against their religion. And yet, fast-forward to 2009, and there had been more than 180 suicide bomb attacks in Afghanistan.[9] The Taliban had evolved to make Afghanistan an even more dangerous place.

Shortly after he took office, President Obama appointed Richard Holbrooke as his point man on Afghanistan—his special representative—to help him quickly gauge the situation in that country and come up with a strategy to deal with it. At the time the military was urgently lobbying the new president for more troops, needed to hold the line against the Taliban while Washington thought through the problem. Obama asked for a quick strategy review—a quick read of the situation—and tapped former CIA and Clinton White House Pakistan point man Bruce Riedel to lead the effort.[10] The review took sixty days, and its findings (popularly known as the Riedel Report) argued for beefing up American troop presence in Afghanistan, "fully resourcing" counterinsurgency operations there, and getting tough with Pakistan. Holbrooke, who served on Riedel's commission, disagreed. He did not favor committing America to fully resourced counterinsurgency and thought America would get more out of Pakistan through engagement.

Riedel met the president alone to brief him on his report's findings. Holbrooke thought the president should have heard from more people. Absent a proper debate on the report's findings and recommendations, thought Holbrooke, the president moved too quickly to deepen the war.

In February 2009, Obama announced that he was sending 17,000 more troops to Afghanistan, buying enough time for the president and his advisers to determine their next steps. Soon after, he also asked his commander in Afghanistan, General Stanley McChrystal, to review the war strategy and outline what we needed to do to win.[11] As General McChrystal prepared his review, the National Security Council (NSC) pulled together facts, figures, opinion, and analysis from across the government (mostly from the Pentagon, State Department, CIA, and U.S. Agency for International Development) in order to prepare the president to evaluate McChrystal's recommendations. The goal was to place before President Obama a set of clear options from which he could choose.

The Obama administration was facing a bedeviling two-headed problem. Even as the Taliban were regrouping and growing more formidable, our local partner, the Karzai government, was proving to be weak and ill suited for the task of democracy building.[12] The shine had come off Hamid Karzai even before Obama took office. In the administration's and Congress's minds the smartly dressed, enlightened leader of a new

Afghanistan had somewhere along the line been reduced to a venal, corrupt, and unreliable partner, and as such a chief reason why the Taliban were doing so well. Whatever the "new" Afghanistan was supposed to look like, in the real, existing Afghanistan, clans and extended families mattered. Karzai's clan, unfortunately, looked a lot like the Sopranos. The president's brother Ahmad Wali was actually the fixer in Kandahar, a Taliban stronghold. He worked notoriously with both the CIA and the Taliban and had his hand in every deal and all the political wrangling in that wayward city. Karzai also patronized an array of corrupt local grandees with ties to the drug trade. They bolstered his rule and he gave them the means to line their pockets while abusing the local population.[13]

Aid workers, members of Congress, ordinary Afghans, and ordinary Americans alike were angry and frustrated, but the situation regarding corruption tended to be misunderstood. Yes, there was waste and graft, and millions were embezzled. But it was also true that Afghanistan was still a tribal society in which tribal leaders and local bigwigs saw it as their duty to take from the state resources for their community. Karzai felt the need to satisfy that demand to survive at the top. That sort of corruption is not alien to politics, and certainly not in Afghanistan.[14]

Did Karzai's corruption really matter to the ebb and flow of the insurgency? Yes, but not in the ways that we might think it does. There was never evidence that most who joined the Taliban did so in protest against the corruption of Karzai's ministers. The problem was local. The corruption that really mattered, that angered the small peasant and drove him to pick up a gun and join the Taliban, was being shaken down by local police and government officials. We treated Karzai as if he was head of an independent sovereign government, but in reality his was no government at all. He was holed up in the capital, reliant even there on foreign protection for his physical security, and had a writ that could not run much of anything without U.S. help. Karzai was (as he remains) no more than a glorified "mayor of Kabul."

His government was poorly designed, too. On paper it was overcentralized—the central government controlled the purse strings and made every decision on education, health care, or development. Yet in practice it was absent from large parts of the country, and where it was present people did not welcome it but wished that it would go away.[15] The economy was a shambles, too. Infrastructure remained inadequate and industry nonexistent, and agriculture barely dented endemic poverty in the countryside. The country's economy was a sum of the drug trade plus the money that international aid and military operations sloshed around.[16]

Afghans blamed the sorry state of the economy on Karzai's failings and on America, his main backer. In growing numbers, they were lending the Taliban a hand to take back the country.[17] The situation was particularly bad in the Pashtun heartland of southern Afghanistan, which had served as the Taliban's power base in the 1990s. Southern Pashtuns felt excluded from Karzai's government. They viewed the December 2001 Bonn Agreement—the result of an internationally sponsored conference to decide the shape of Afghanistan's constitution and government—as having favored their enemies, the Uzbeks, Tajiks, and Hazaras of the Northern Alliance. They felt that Karzai, though a Pashtun of the Durrani tribe himself, had never done much to address their concerns. Feeling disenfranchised, many had thrown their lot in with the Taliban.

The Obama administration's initial reading of the crisis in Afghanistan was to blame it on the spectacular failure of the Karzai government, paired with wrongheaded military strategy, inadequate troop numbers for defeating an insurgency, and the Taliban's ability to find a safe haven and military and material support in Pakistan. Of these, Karzai's failings and the need to straighten out the military strategy dominated the discussion. Above all, the Afghan conflict was seen in the context of Iraq. The Taliban were seen as insurgents similar to the ones whom the United States had just helped defeat in Iraq. And what had defeated the insurgency in Iraq was a military strategy known as COIN.

COIN, shorthand for counterinsurgency, was not new, and it had a checkered past. The British had adopted it while fighting rebellious Boers in South Africa at the dawn of the twentieth century, then used it again in Malaysia in the 1950s. The French had employed a version of it at around the same time with less success, in Algeria, and America had tried it, disastrously, in Vietnam. COIN strategy recognizes that a rebel group does not always organize into regular military units or hold on to territory. Insurgents avoid fixed positions and hide among the people, denying them to the adversary. An insurgency wins by controlling people. Its center of gravity is not a place on the map, but its support base among a sympathetic (or at least cowed) population.

To defeat an insurgency, therefore, you must secure the populace. They must be shielded from insurgent violence and their trust gained. Only then will they stand against the insurgency and help with its defeat. The keys to COIN are small, socially and politically aware units; local cultural and linguistic knowledge; and good relations with civilians, whose loyalties are the real prize.

In Iraq, American troops had fanned out into districts and villages, setting up small posts from which they could mount patrols, see to security and governance at the local level, and squeeze the insurgency out of villages, towns, and entire districts in restive Anbar Province.[18] It worked. As more and more places were freed from insurgent control, community leaders asserted their authority and joined hands to form the so-called Sons of Iraq. They took over local politics and security, and, with American financial assistance, rebuilt the local economy. American troops protected these leaders, but eventually it fell to Iraq's own American-trained security forces to provide that security and help local leaders finish off the insurgency.

Success in Iraq crowned COIN as America's military strategy of choice for winning "asymmetric" wars against terrorists, tribes, and what used to be called guerrilla fighters in failed, or failing, states. The relevance of Iraq to Afghanistan seemed self-evident. COIN had won Iraq; it was the right choice for Afghanistan.

Still, COIN requires governance, and governance requires a government. The Afghan government did not have the means (or the will) to follow the marines into areas cleared of Taliban to provide governance, and thus COIN could go only so far and no more. President Karzai would prove singularly instrumental in dashing America's hopes of anything good coming out of Afghanistan. But in early 2009, Washington was hopeful it could knock some sense into him. Failing that, Afghan presidential elections in the fall of 2009 might return a better partner.

The strategy review proved torturously long. The president sat with his national security team through ten meetings—twenty-five hours—over the course of three months, hearing analysis and debating facts. There were many more meetings of those advisers and their staffs without the president present to dig further into the relevant issues, and go through stacks of folders, each one the size of a phone book, answering every question that came down from on high. At SRAP (the office of the Special Representative for Afghanistan and Pakistan), we managed the State Department's contribution to the paper deluge. We worked long hours preparing memos and white papers, maps and tables, and then summaries for each. The Pentagon and CIA had their own stacks. In fact there was a healthy competition between the agencies over who did a better job of producing more.

Early in the process, Holbrooke came back from a meeting at the White House, called us into his office to give us an update, and said, "You did a good job, the Secretary [Clinton] was pleased with her material but wants her folders to be as big as [those of Secretary of Defense Bob] Gates. She wants color maps, tables, and charts." Clinton, continued Holbrooke, "did not want Gates to dominate the conversation by waving his colorful maps and charts in front of everybody. No one reads this stuff, but they all look at the maps and color charts." Everyone in the office looked at him. "So who does read all this?" I asked him, pointing to a huge folder on his desk. "I'll tell you who," he said. "The president reads them. He reads every folder."

The amount of time spent on the process seemed absurd. Every time Holbrooke came back from the White House, he would say, "The president has more questions," and warn us that we should be ready to go to work the minute formal instruction came from the White House. Frustration was written all over Holbrooke's and Clinton's faces as the process dragged on. The White House attributed this to Obama's meticulous probing and the degree of thought and analysis that went into this historic decision. But increasing numbers of observers and participants began to worry that the delay was not serving America's interest. President Obama was dithering. He was busybodying the national security apparatus by asking for more answers to the same set of questions, each time posed differently.

Holbrooke thought that Obama was not deciding because he disliked the options before him, and that the NSC was failing the president by not giving him the right options. The job of the NSC, Holbrooke would say, is not to make policy for the president, but to give him choices. The NSC was not doing its job, and hence the president was not making his decision. The decision-making process was broken. To make his point, Holbrooke took to handing out copies of Clark Clifford's description of how the NSC works from Clifford's 1991 memoir (on which Holbrooke had collaborated), *Counsel to the President.*

What Holbrooke omitted from his assessment was that Obama was failing to press the NSC to give him other options. As a result the process had come down to a slow dance in which the president pushed back against the options before him but neglected to demand new ones, and his national security staff kept putting the same options back in front of him.

At the end of the day, President Obama had two distinct choices. The first was "fully resourced" COIN, which meant more troops and more money to reverse the Taliban's gains and put in place the kind of local security and good government that would make it unlikely they would come back.[19] It would be Iraq all over again. But the president was not sold. He did not think a long and expensive counterinsurgency campaign was the way to go, particularly as his domestic advisers were telling him that public support for the war was soft (and getting softer), and especially when the economic news at home was bad. So Obama kept kicking the tires on COIN and kept asking questions. The military's answer every time was the same: Fully resourced COIN is the way to go.

The night before General McChrystal was to release the report outlining what he needed to fight the war, Holbrooke gathered his team in his office. We asked him what he thought McChrystal would request. He said, "Watch! The military will give the president three choices. There will be a 'high-risk' option"—Holbrooke held his hand high in the air—"that is what they always call it, which will call for maybe very few troops. Low troops, high risk. Then there will be a 'low-risk' option"—Holbrooke lowered his hand—"which will ask for double the number they are actually looking for. In the middle will be what they want," which was between 30,000 and 40,000 more troops. And that is exactly what happened, along with the "high-risk" and "low-risk" vocabulary.

All along Vice President Biden had pushed for an altogether different approach. This was in effect option two. Biden noted that we had gone to Afghanistan to fight al-Qaeda, but that al-Qaeda was no longer in Afghanistan; it was in Pakistan. The CIA's estimate was that there were as few as a hundred al-Qaeda operatives left in Afghanistan.[20] Biden thought that over time there had been mission creep. Fighting terrorism (disrupting, dismantling, and destroying al-Qaeda and its affiliates, as the president defined the mission) had evolved into counterinsurgency and nation-building, and the Taliban had replaced al-Qaeda as the enemy we organized our strategic objectives against. We don't need COIN, a functioning Afghan state, or the billions poured into rural development and local security, Biden argued, to allay America's fear of al-Qaeda. In fact, for that we did not need Afghanistan at all. We could protect ourselves and advance our interests through a stepped-up counterterrorism effort—which was quickly dubbed "CT-Plus"—mostly directed at al-Qaeda's sanctuary, the wild border region of Pakistan. We could use unmanned drones and Special Forces to check al-Qaeda activity from bases in Afghanistan, and achieve all the security we needed for a fraction of the money and manpower that COIN would require.

Biden's argument favored using the resources of the CIA over those of the Pentagon, and was seen at first as an outlier, too far-fetched in assuming you could win without boots on the ground. But Biden's view had its sincere supporters in Congress and pragmatic ones among White House domestic advisers who thought the American public was tired of the war. Holbrooke, too, thought COIN was pointless, but was not sold on CT-Plus. He thought you could not have a regional strategy built on "secret war." Drones are no substitute for a political settlement.

There were other criticisms of COIN. In November 2009, America's ambassador in Kabul, Karl Eikenberry, who had once led American forces in Afghanistan as a three-star army general, wrote in a cable titled "COIN Strategy: Civilian Concerns" that Afghans would have no incentive to take responsibility for government and security in their country if we kept putting more troops in. Karzai was not an "adequate strategic partner," wrote the ambassador, and "continues to shun responsibility for a sovereign burden."[21] A troop surge would only perpetuate that problem. Holbrooke thought Eikenberry had it right.

During the review, there was no discussion of diplomacy and a political settlement at all. A commitment to finding a political settlement to the war would have put diplomacy front and center and organized military and intelligence operations in Afghanistan to support it. Holbrooke wanted the president to consider this option, but the White House was not buying. The military wanted to stay in charge, and going against the military would make the president look weak.

CT-Plus, too, looked risky—too much like "cut and run"—and there was no guarantee that CT-Plus could work without COIN.[22] In Iraq, Special Forces had taken "kill and capture" missions to industrial scale, decimating the ranks of al-Qaeda and the insurgency, and yet this did not turn the tide of that war. Counterterrorism, unlike COIN, did not win territory or win hearts and minds of the local population; CT merely amplified the impact of COIN on Iraq.

So President Obama chose the politically safe option that he did not like: he gave the military what they asked for. Months of White House hand-wringing ended up with the administration choosing the option that had been offered from day one: fully resourced COIN. But he added a deadline of July 2011 for the larger troop commitment to work; after that the surge would be rolled back. In effect, the president told both Karzai and the Taliban that our new strategy was good for a year.

Fully resourced COIN, however, failed to achieve its objective. There were ambitious pushes into Taliban territory, but gains were temporary. A much-ballyhooed counterinsurgency operation in the spring of 2010 failed to pacify Marjah.[23] In mid-2010, six months after 30,000 troops were sent, an internal intelligence review presented the White House with a dire account of the security situation in Afghanistan. COIN was not bringing safety and security to Afghans as promised; more of them were dying.

COIN's success requires expensive nation-building. To win you have to provide good government and ample social services to wean the population away from the enemy. The Obama administration did much more in this area than its predecessor, but it was not enough. The State

Department was put to work on civilian aid and assistance programs. Holbrooke the diplomat was turned into a development warrior, organizing development projects and deciding on budgets and personnel to support them. He was particularly keen on putting more agricultural workers on the ground, and became a veritable spokesman for Afghanistan's pomegranate farmers. He would say that in a country where eight out of ten people depend on agriculture you are not going to get anywhere unless you revive the agricultural economy.

Unfortunately, economic logic would not drive American development assistance. Aid was used to serve COIN. The harder American troops had to fight to win territory, the more money they poured into development projects in the neighborhood—and not all of it wisely. Only 1 percent of Afghans live in the Helmand province, but in 2010 nearly all COIN efforts (both troops and aid money) went to Helmand.[24] Or consider that in 2011, although only 6 percent of all Afghans had electricity, the United States spent $1 billion to provide electricity to mere parts of Kandahar.[25]

COIN was at best a game of whack-a-mole: when U.S. troops poured into a district, the Taliban packed up and went somewhere else. Security improved where Americans were posted, and deteriorated where the Taliban moved. There were not enough American soldiers to be everywhere at once, and the Afghan government did not have forces that could relieve them, so the insurgency stayed alive.

But the military told a different story. It focused on the favorable statistics for where American soldiers stood, and used that to tout COIN's success. These claims of success gave Obama a basis for turning the tables on COIN. He was able to declare victory and ditch the policy that he did not like and that (more importantly) was not working. In June 2011, standing before the Corps of Cadets at the U.S. Military Academy in West Point, New York, the president declared that the situation in Afghanistan had improved enough to talk of troop withdrawals. By 2014, the Afghan war would be no more. COIN had won, so we did not need it anymore.

It was a stunning shift. COIN was over, not just in Afghanistan, but also as America's strategy of choice. America no longer needed to win counterinsurgencies or put its shoulder to nation-building, Obama seemed to be saying; it just had to focus on decapitating terrorist organizations. CT-Plus was quietly supplanting COIN.

This was more than a shift in strategy. It announced a new set of American priorities. Fighting terrorists and fixing the failed states that they might use as bases were no longer an American priority. We had won not just in Afghanistan, but more broadly against terrorism. Now we could go back to addressing global issues. And our military strategy would reflect that.

Obama announced the new American stance in a January 5, 2012, speech on trimming the military budget. The president referred to "the end of long-term nation-building with large military footprints." He announced that the U.S. military would be shifting gears and changing its focus to East Asia and the Pacific—a region where the higher-tech, lighter-manpower "blue" services (the navy and air force) will naturally take the lead as compared to the way boots-on-the-ground "green" services (the army and marines) bore the brunt of land combat in Iraq and Afghanistan. In a follow-up to that speech, the administration also announced an expansion of the Joint Special Operations Command (an endorsement of CT-Plus), and reiterated that America would not do any more nation-building of the kind that it had tried in Iraq and Afghanistan.

Switching strategies on the quick like this—announcing our imminent departure from Afghanistan—had a devastating impact within the region. Americans were not the president's only audience. Power players all over the Middle East were watching carefully as America experimented with strategic plans and troop numbers, showed a will to fight, and then quickly tired of the whole affair. What they had seen had not impressed them. The dizzying pace of change in policy presented America as indecisive and unreliable. It also suggested that we really had no strategy or long-term goals. Our only goal seemed to be getting out, first of Afghanistan and then the whole region, under the cover of talk about a "strategic pivot" toward Asia.

The Norwegian historian Geir Lundestad writes that in the 1960s German leaders defended the Vietnam War before protesting German students because they thought America was doing the right thing by sticking with its strategy and its South Vietnamese ally. It sent the right message; when the time came, America would stick by them too. "It came down unavoidably to the question if one could generally trust America."[26]

From Obama's arrival in power in 2009 through 2011, our only leverage with the Taliban, and also Pakistan, had been the sense that we would stand behind our strategy.[27] It is arguable that we should never have embraced COIN, but once we did, we should not have ditched it so quickly. After the president announced our withdrawal we lost our leverage and with it our influence over the final outcome in Afghanistan. What is more, who will now believe in our intentions or our commitment? Can CT-Plus alone work in the long run without our troops, or cooperation, trust, and support from our friends and fear from our foes? Not likely. The Taliban know that once our troops are gone they will not come back—the cost would be too high. If they press us then we would more likely fold our CT-Plus operations rather than deploy more troops to protect them.

President Obama did not have good options during the strategic review, and ultimately decided that it would be better to reverse course and end COIN before its failings became evident and its costs mounted. Better to cut one's losses, especially if one can claim some sort of victory by quoting the military. Had he had better options before him— had he *demanded* those options, as should be expected from the chief executive—then perhaps America could have avoided the costly COIN shuffle to start with.

The option that the president did not consider, and which could have spelled a very different outcome for the war and how it reflected on the United States, was the diplomatic one.

AFGHANISTAN

Reconciliation?

It was close to midnight on January 20, 2009, and I was about to go to sleep when my iPhone beeped. There was a new text message. It was from Richard Holbrooke. It said, "Are you up, can you talk?" I called him. He told me the president had asked him to serve as his envoy for Afghanistan and Pakistan. He would work out of the State Department and he wanted me to join his team. "No one knows this yet. Don't tell anyone. Well, maybe your wife." (It was on the *Washington Post* Web site the next day.) He continued, "Nothing is confirmed, but it is pretty much a done deal. If you get any other offers let me know right away." Then he laughed and said, "If you work for anyone else, I will break your knees. This is going to be fun. We are going to do some good. Now get some sleep." Before he hung up I thanked him for his offer, and said it would be a treat to work with him (which it was—the ride of a lifetime, as it turned out) and an honor to serve in government.

I met Richard Holbrooke for the first time in 2006 at a conference in Aspen. We sat together at one of the dinners and talked about Iran and Pakistan. Holbrooke ignored the keynote speech, the entertainment that followed, and the food that flowed in between to bombard me with questions. We had many more conversations over the course of the next three years. I met him for lunch or visited him at his office in New York; and after I joined him on Hillary Clinton's presidential campaign in 2007 we spoke frequently by phone.

Holbrooke was a brilliant strategic thinker in the same league as such giants of American diplomacy as Averell Harriman and Henry Kissinger. He looked at a problem from every angle and then planned how best to tackle it. He knew what bureaucrats would say, how politicians would react, what headline would lead in the media, what the public reaction would be, and how history would render its judgment. He was a doer; that was his ambition—to *do*, not to *be*.

Holbrooke held fast to American values. He was an idealist in the garb of a pragmatic operator. I never ceased to be astounded by his energy and drive; he was tireless in pursuit of his goals and relentless in standing up for American interests and values. In the words of his close friend and veteran diplomat Strobe Talbott, he was the "unquiet American," who believed that America was a force for good in the world.[1]

Fixing America's broken foreign policy and correcting its jaded view of the Muslim world were the most important foreign policy tasks before the new president. Holbrooke told me that government is the sum of its people. "If you want to change things, you have to get involved. If you want your voice to be heard, then get inside." He was telling me to "put your money where your mouth is." He knew I preferred to work on the Middle East, and in particular on Iran. But he had different ideas. "This [Afghanistan and Pakistan] matters more. This is what the president is focused on. This is where you want to be."

Holbrooke was persuasive, and I knew deep down that we were at a fork in the road. Regardless of what promises candidate Obama made on his way to the White House, Afghanistan now held the future, his and America's, in the balance. Holbrooke was seeing clearly into the future, well beyond where the rest of the administration was looking.

The first months in the office of the Special Representative for Afghanistan and Pakistan (SRAP) were a period of creativity and hope. Holbrooke had carved out a little autonomous principality on the first floor of the State Department, filling it with young diplomats, civil servants, and outside experts. Daily, scholars, journalists, foreign ambassadors and dignitaries, members of Congress, and administration officials walked in to get their fill of how "AfPak" strategy was shaping up. Even Hollywood got in on SRAP. Angelina Jolie lent a hand to help refugees in Pakistan, and the usually low-key State Department cafeteria was abuzz when Holbrooke sat down for coffee with Natalie Portman to talk Afghanistan.

SRAP was an experiment in what Holbrooke called the "whole of government approach to solving big problems," by which he meant doing the job of the government inside the government but *despite* the government—an idea that for obvious reasons did not sit well with the bureaucracy.

But Secretary Clinton liked the idea and embraced SRAP. Had she become president she would have likely given Holbrooke the same kind of broad purview in the White House or as secretary of state. Rumor had it that she favored Holbrooke as her deputy secretary of state, but the White House said no. Creating a new office that cut across government agencies to formulate effective policy was the next-best option. The office worked very closely with her during my two years there. We met with her frequently, briefed her on the latest developments or what we were planning, got her input, and wrote memos and white papers that represented the State Department's position in White House debates. She came to rely on SRAP, trust its judgment, and appreciate its work— SRAP came through for the State Department time and again at critical junctures. Clinton spent more time with SRAP than with any other bureau in the State Department, getting to know more of its people well.

The idea of coordinating AfPak policies across government was also popular around the world. At a meeting at NATO headquarters in Brussels, Finland's foreign minister teased Holbrooke, telling him, "Nowadays everywhere I go someone comes up to me and introduces himself as 'some country's Holbrooke.' " And soon there were many such Holbrooke equivalents, some three dozen by the time Holbrooke died. He started getting them together regularly, every six months, for consultations and to coordinate their activities—it was key to managing allies around the world. Hamid Karzai was impressed with the concept, and told Holbrooke that every Muslim country he could bring on board was worth ten NATO ones. And so soon there were Holbrooke counterparts in several Muslim countries. He did not live to attend a gathering of his counterparts in Jeddah, Saudi Arabia, in the spring of 2011, hosted by the Organization of the Islamic Conference.

SRAP was then full of energy and ideas. It had an entrepreneurial spirit, a bounce in its step. People started early and worked late into the night, making sure the trains ran on time, so to speak, but also to develop new ideas like how to cut corruption and absenteeism among the Afghan police by using mobile banking and cell phones to pay salaries; or how to use text messaging to raise money to help refugees in Pakistan; or how to stop the Taliban from shutting down cellular phone networks (which they did every night) by putting cell towers on military bases. Many of these ideas were eventually used to address problems in other areas of the world. SRAP then felt more like an Internet start-up than the buttoned-up State Department.

Holbrooke encouraged the creative chaos. Soon after I joined the office he told me, "I want you to learn nothing from government. This place is dead intellectually. It does not produce any ideas; it is all about turf battles and checking the box. Your job is to break through all this. Anyone gives you trouble, come to me." His constant refrain was "Don't get broken down by government routine, forget about hierarchy; this is a team. You are as good as the job SRAP does." On his first visit to SRAP, General David Petraeus, then commander of CENTCOM (the U.S. Central Command), mused, "This is the flattest organization I have ever seen. I guess it works for you."

Holbrooke knew then that Afghanistan was not going to be easy. There were too many players and too many unknowns, and Obama had not given him enough authority (and would give him almost no support) to get the job done. It is an open secret that, oddly enough, after he took office, the president never met with Holbrooke outside large meetings, never gave him time and heard him out. The president's advisers in the White House were dead set against Holbrooke. Some, like General Douglas Lute, were holdovers from the Bush era who thought they knew Afghanistan better and did not want to relinquish control to Holbrooke. Others (those closest to the president) wanted to settle scores for Holbrooke's tenacious support for Hillary Clinton (who was herself eyed with suspicion by the Obama insiders) during the campaign; and still others begrudged Holbrooke's storied past and wanted to end his run of successes then and there. There were times when it appeared that the White House was more interested in bringing Holbrooke down than getting the policy right. The sight of the White House undermining its own special representative hardly inspired confidence in Kabul or Islamabad.

But still Holbrooke kept attacking the problem the president had assigned him from all angles. It was as if he was trying to solve a Rubik's

Cube; to get all its colored rows and columns into perfect order. In his mind he was constantly turning the cube, trying to bring into alignment what Congress, the military, the media, the Afghan government, and our allies wanted and how politicians, generals, and bureaucrats were likely to react. Just before he died, in December 2010, he told his wife, Kati Marton, that he thought he had finally got it; he had found a way out that might just work. But he wouldn't say what he had come up with, "not until he told the president first"—the president who did not have time to listen.

The die had been cast earlier, and there was not going to be too much out-of-the-box thinking or debate over grand strategy. The generals wanted a military solution to Afghanistan, and the president's advisers thought the political fallout of going against the military would be too great. Holbrooke thought the impulse to hand over foreign policy to the military was a mistake; there was going to be fighting in Afghanistan, but diplomacy alone could bring that war to a satisfactory end.

Holbrooke was no starry-eyed pacifist. He believed in the use of force: not as an end in itself, of course, but as a means to solving difficult problems. In the Balkans, he had wielded the threat of U.S. air power to compel the recalcitrant Serbian president Milosevic to agree to a deal. On one occasion he walked out of a frustrating meeting with Milosevic and told his military adviser to roll B-52 bombers out onto the tarmac in an airbase in England and make sure CNN showed the footage. Later, at a dinner during the Dayton peace talks that ended the Bosnia war, he asked President Clinton to sit across from Milosevic. Holbrooke said to Clinton, I want Milosevic to hear from you what I told him, that if there is no peace you will send in the bombers. Holbrooke was seasoned in the business of war and diplomacy.

In Afghanistan, too, Holbrooke believed that the U.S. military had a key role to play—*a* role. But what the president was considering in the fall of 2009 was something altogether different. He was being pushed to sign on to a military solution to the conflict. Holbrooke was convinced then that such an effort would fail, and that in trying to avoid that outcome, America would deepen its military commitment, doubling down on a failing strategy in what might turn into a dangerous repeat of the Vietnam debacle that Holbrooke had witnessed as a young Foreign Service officer. Or we would end up abandoning Afghanistan in strategic defeat.

It is the job of diplomats to end conflicts like Afghanistan, to solve big strategic problems facing America. Military might is supposed to be an instrument in the diplomat's tool kit. That is how it worked in the Balkans, and that is how it had eventually played out in Vietnam. That war was waged on the battlefield for decades, but it ended around a negotiating table in Paris. Total battlefield victory is rare, and when it has happened, for instance at the end of World War II, it has required a level of commitment that is above and beyond what America was willing to give in Afghanistan. Iraq stands out as a rare case of a quick battlefield victory, an end to a war that did not happen around a negotiating table. But was Iraq really won? That proposition is yet to be tested by the departure of American troops.

But diplomacy was conspicuous by its absence in the 2009 White House strategy review. Diplomacy was then seen narrowly as a useful tool for getting governments around the world to contribute soldiers and money to the Afghan war. It was not a solution to war, but its facilitator.

This, Holbrooke thought, was a fundamental problem. The military was by its nature simply not the institution to define and run America's foreign policy. I remember his reaction when General David Petraeus affectionately referred to him in an interview as his "wingman."[2] Holbrooke chuckled and said, "Since when have diplomats become generals' wingmen?" In the same interview Petraeus had dismissed a role for diplomacy in ending the war, saying, "This [the Afghan war] will not end like the Balkans."[3] This imbalance at the heart of American foreign policy was Obama's to fix, and the strategic review would have been the place to do it.

From the outset, Holbrooke had argued for reconciliation as the path out of Afghanistan. But the military thought talk of reconciliation undermined America's commitment to fully resourced COIN. On his last trip to Afghanistan, in October 2010, Holbrooke pulled General Petraeus aside and said, "David, I want to talk to you about reconciliation." Petraeus replied, "That is a fifteen-second conversation. No, not now." The commanders' standard response was that they needed two more fighting seasons (two years) to soften up the Taliban. They were hoping to change the president's mind on his July deadline, and after that convince him to accept a "slow and shallow" (long and gradual) departure schedule. The military feared that Holbrooke's talk of talking to the Taliban would undermine that strategy. Their line was that we should fight first and talk later. Much later. Holbrooke thought we could talk and fight, and in fact that you should fight in order to make your foe find talking more appealing (not the other way around). Reconciliation should be the ultimate goal, and fighting the means to facilitate it.

The Taliban had been ready for talks as early as April 2009. At that time, Afghanistan scholar Barnett Rubin, shortly before he joined Holbrooke's team as his senior Afghan affairs adviser, traveled to Afghanistan and Saudi Arabia. In Kabul he met with the former Taliban commander Mullah Abdul Salam Zaeef, who told Rubin the Taliban were ready to break with al-Qaeda and talk to America. He laid out in detail a strategy for talks: where to start, what to discuss, and the shape of the settlement that the United States and the Taliban could agree on. Zaeef said the Taliban needed concessions on prisoners America held in Guantánamo and wanted the removal of some Taliban names from so-called black lists developed by the U.S. government and the United Nations sanctioning terrorists. Rubin went to Riyadh from Kabul, and there he met with Prince Muqrin, the Saudi intelligence minister, whose account of conversations with Taliban go-betweens lined up with what Zaeef had told Rubin.

Back in Washington—on the day he was sworn into government service—Rubin wrote a memo regarding this trip for Holbrooke. That afternoon the two sat next to each other on the US Air shuttle back to New York. Holbrooke read the memo, then turned to Rubin and said: "If this thing works, it may be the only way we will get out." That was the beginning of a two-year campaign to sell the idea of talking to the Taliban to Washington: first to Secretary Clinton, then to the White House and President Obama.

Reconciliation meant a peace deal between Karzai and the Taliban that would end the insurgency and allow American troops to go home. The military had opposed the idea from the outset. The Pentagon thought that talking to the Taliban—and even talking about talking to the Taliban—was a form of capitulation to terrorism. The CIA, too, was not enthusiastic, believing that the Taliban were not ready to talk. Reconciliation, for them, was a Pakistani ploy to slow down the American offensive in Afghanistan and reduce American pressure on Pakistan.

Those attitudes scared the White House, ever afraid that the young Democratic president would be seen as "soft." The White House did not want to try anything new, nothing as audacious as diplomacy. It was an art lost on America's top decision makers in the White House. They had no experience with it and were daunted by the idea of it.

While running for president Obama promised a new chapter in American foreign policy, especially when it came to managing thorny issues in the Muslim world. America would move away from Bush's militarized foreign policy and take engagement and diplomacy seriously. Talking and extending a hand would be his priority. But when it came down to brass tacks in Afghanistan and Pakistan, Hillary Clinton was the lone voice making the case for diplomacy. The White House had decided early on to walk in lockstep with the military. Clinton elevated the State Department's profile, but without the White House's backing its influence was no match for that of the Pentagon and CIA.

During the 2009 strategic review Clinton held her cards close to her chest. In the many meetings I attended with her on various aspects of the war she asked a lot of questions, and on one occasion said she did not believe in cut and run. So it was not a surprise that in the end she supported sending more troops to Afghanistan. However, she was not on board with the deadline Obama imposed on the surge, nor was she for hasty troop withdrawals in Iraq and Afghanistan. Clinton thought those decisions looked a lot like cut and run and would damage America's standing in the world. Add this to where she came out on a host of other national security issues, including pushing Obama to go ahead with the Abbottabad operation to kill or capture Osama bin Laden and breaking with the Pentagon to advocate using American air power in Libya, and it is safe to say she was, and remains, tough on national security issues.

But Clinton does not see American foreign policy as a zero-sum choice between hard power and diplomacy. She shared Holbrooke's belief that the purpose of hard power is to facilitate diplomatic breakthroughs. America is not going to fight its way out of one crisis after another; it has to deftly use all elements of its national power, military might as well as diplomatic, to find its way out of vexing conflicts like Afghanistan.

During many meetings on Afghanistan and Pakistan (and separately on the Middle East) I attended with her, she would ask us to make the case for diplomacy and then quiz us on our assumptions and plan of action before evaluating how it might work. At the end of this drill she would ask us to put it all in writing for the benefit of the White House.

Holbrooke and Clinton had a tight partnership. They were friends. Clinton trusted Holbrooke's judgment and valued his counsel, counsel that Holbrooke happily provided on a variety of issues, and not just on Afghanistan and Pakistan. They conferred often, and Clinton protected Holbrooke from an obdurate White House. The White House kept a dossier on Holbrooke's misdeeds, and Clinton kept a folder on churlish attempts by the White House's AfPak office to undermine Holbrooke, which she gave to the national security adviser, Tom Donilon. The White House tried to blame Holbrooke for leaks to the press. Clinton called out the White House on its own leaks. She sharply rebuked the White House after an article in *The New Yorker* mentioned a highly secret meeting with the Taliban that it was told about by a senior White House official.

Holbrooke went to battle first, getting battered and bruised. Then Clinton would take up the charge, lobbying with her counterparts in the Pentagon and CIA. And whenever possible she went to the president directly, around the so-called Berlin Wall of staffers who shielded Obama from any option or idea they did not want him to consider.

Clinton had regular weekly private meetings with the president (sometimes the two of them met alone, and at other times they were joined by a few of the president's key staff). She had asked for the "one-on-ones" as a condition for accepting the job of secretary of state. This way she made sure that once she was on board, the White House would not conveniently marginalize her and the State Department. Clinton used this time to talk to Obama about ideas that his staffers would keep out.

But even then she had a tough time getting the administration to bite when it came to diplomacy. Obama was sympathetic in principle but not keen on showing daylight between the White House and the military.

Talking to enemies was a good campaign sound bite, but once in power Obama was too skittish to try it.

On one occasion in the summer of 2010, after the White House had systematically blocked every attempt to include reconciliation talks with the Taliban and serious regional diplomacy (which had to include Iran) on the agenda for national security meetings with the president, Clinton took a paper SRAP had prepared on the subject to Obama. She gave him the paper, explained what it laid out, and said, "Mr. President, I would like to get your approval on this." Obama nodded his approval but that was all. So his White House staff, caught off guard by Clinton, found ample room to kill the paper in Washington's favorite way: condemning it to slow death in endless committee meetings. A few weeks after Clinton gave Obama the paper I had to go to an interagency meeting organized by the White House that to my surprise was going to revise the paper the president had given the nod to. I remember telling Clinton about the meeting. She shook her head and exclaimed, "Unbelievable!"

Clinton got along well with Obama, but that did not mean that the State Department had an easy time dealing with the White House. On Afghanistan and Pakistan at least, the State Department had to fight tooth and nail just to have a hearing there. Had it not been for Clinton's tenacity and the respect she commanded, the State Department would have had no influence on policy making whatsoever. The White House had taken over most policy areas: Iran and the Arab-Israeli issue were for all practical purposes managed from the White House. AfPak was a rare exception, and that was owed to Holbrooke's quick thinking in getting SRAP going in February 2009 before the White House was able to organize itself.

The White House resented losing AfPak to the State Department. It fought hard to close down SRAP and take AfPak policy back. That was one big reason why the White House was on a warpath with Holbrooke—he was in their way and kept the State Department in the mix on an important foreign policy area. Holbrooke would not back down. He would not cede ground to the White House, not when he thought those who wanted to wrest control of Afghanistan were out of their depth and not up to the job.

When Holbrooke died in December 2010, Clinton kept SRAP alive, but the White House managed to take over AfPak policy, in part by letting the Pentagon run the policy on Afghanistan and the CIA on Pakistan (which escalated tensions with Pakistan). Clinton wanted John Podesta, an influential Democratic Party stalwart who had served as Bill Clinton's chief of staff, to succeed Holbrooke. But Podesta was too influential (including with the president) and too high profile, and that would have made it difficult for the White House to manage him and snatch AfPak policy back from the State Department. The White House vetoed the choice. Turf battles are a staple of every administration, but the Obama White House has been particularly ravenous.

Add to this the campaign hangover. Obama's inner circle, veterans of his election campaign, were suspicious of Clinton. And even after Clinton proved she was a team player they remained concerned with her popularity and approval ratings, and feared that she could overshadow the president.

Admiral Mike Mullen, chairman of the Joint Chiefs until spring 2012, told me, "She [Clinton] did a great job pushing her agenda, but it is incredible how little support she got from the White House. They want to control everything." Victories for the State Department were few and hard fought. It was little consolation that its recommendations on recon-ciliation with the Taliban or regional diplomacy to end the Afghan war eventually became official policy after the White House exhausted the alternatives.

The White House campaign against the State Department, and espe-cially Holbrooke, was at times a theater of the absurd. Holbrooke was not included in Obama's video conferences with Karzai and was cut out of the presidential retinue when Obama went to Afghanistan. Accord-ing to Rajiv Chandrasekaran, on one occasion the White House's AfPak team came up with the idea of excluding Holbrooke from the president's Oval Office meeting with Karzai and then having Obama tell Karzai, "Everyone in this room represents me and has my trust" (i.e., not Hol-brooke). Clinton foiled that ploy and would go on to foil others.[4] None-theless, the message to Karzai was: ignore my special representative.[5]

At times it looked as if the White House was baiting Karzai to com-plain about Holbrooke so they could get him fired. After Holbrooke died, the White House quickly changed its attitude. It signaled to Karzai that it would no longer welcome criticism of the president's special representative and that it expected Kabul to work with SRAP. Obama told Karzai in a video conference that Ambassador Marc Grossman (Holbrooke's replacement) enjoyed his trust and spoke for him. That helped Grossman in his job, but it did little to change the perception that American policy was scattered and confused.

The White House worried that talking to the Taliban would give Holbrooke a greater role. For months the White House plotted to either block reconciliation with the Taliban or find an alternative to Holbrooke for managing the talks. General Lute, who ran AfPak at the White House, floated the idea of the distinguished UN diplomat Lakhdar Brahimi leading the talks. Clinton objected to outsourcing American diplomacy to the UN. Pakistan, too, was cool to the idea. The "stop Holbrooke" campaign was not only a distraction, it was influencing policy.

The president's national security adviser, General Jim Jones, would travel to Pakistan for high-level meetings without Holbrooke and would not even inform the State Department of his travel plans until he was virtually in the air. Again the message was "ignore Holbrooke." This sort of folly undermined American policy. It was no surprise that our AfPak policy took one step forward and two steps back.

During one trip General Jones went completely off script and promised General Kayani, Pakistan's top military man, a civilian nuclear deal in exchange for Pakistan's cooperation. Panic struck the White House. It took a good deal of diplomatic tap dancing to take that offer off the table. In the end one of Kayani's advisers told me that the general did not take Jones seriously, anyway; he knew it was a slipup. The National Security Council wanted to do the State Department's job, but was not up to the task.

Nor were Afghans and Pakistanis alone in being confused and occasionally amused by the White House's maneuvers. They also baffled people in Washington. The White House encouraged U.S. ambassadors in Kabul and Islamabad to go around the State Department and work with the White House directly, undermining their own agency. Those ambassadors quickly learned how easy it was to manipulate the White House's animus for Holbrooke to their own advantage. In particular, Karl Eikenberry, the U.S. ambassador to Afghanistan, became a handful for the State Department. In November 2010 Obama and Clinton went to Lisbon for a NATO summit and planned to meet with Karzai there. Eikenberry asked to go as well. Clinton turned down his request and instructed him to stay in Kabul, but, backed by the White House, he ignored the secretary of state and showed up in Lisbon.

Even at the State Department reconciliation was not without its critics, some on Holbrooke's team. Rina Amiri, Holbrooke's other senior Afghanistan adviser, thought the whole idea of negotiating with the Taliban was a betrayal of the hopes and aspirations of the Afghan people—it would condemn them to relive their horrible Taliban past. She reminded Holbrooke at every turn that the Taliban could not be trusted. They had not abandoned their narrow view of Islam and draconian attitude toward women, they were relentless in visiting violence on the population, and only wanted America out of the way to take Afghanistan back where they left it in 2001. She insisted that most Afghans were wary of reconciliation—we should at least allay their fears by talking to them about the idea before moving ahead. Otherwise, women, civil society groups, and non-Pashtun minorities (Hazaras, Tajiks, and Uzbeks) who had fought against the Taliban in the Northern Alliance would never back a deal with the Taliban, and in a worst case, that could mean civil war. It was foolish to think Karzai could sell reconciliation to Afghans— he was not even consulting them on the idea. She thought America should convince him to make the case.

Others echoed Amiri's concerns and added that Pakistan had already tried reconciliation with its Pakistani Taliban and the outcome was hardly reassuring. The Taliban there had used truces to establish brutal theocracies and then resume fighting when they were ready. The Taliban were crafty interlocutors with an agenda. They too knew how to realize their goals by fighting and talking.

Holbrooke listened to all these views, probed them, and debated their merits. But he concluded that we were not going to win the war, and we were not going to fight forever. We were going to leave at some point. Without a deal, we would still leave, only later, and with Afghanistan even worse off for years of fighting. In a deal we could address some of the issues the critics raised; without a deal, their worst predictions would come true. He thought we had to push ahead with reconciliation, but we had to design the process and structure a final deal accounting for some, if not all, of the dangers Amiri and others had alerted him to.

Pursuing reconciliation was difficult against the combined resistance of the Pentagon, the CIA, and the White House. It took a massive toll on Holbrooke. He knew it had to be done delicately and against strong resistance. Rubin provided the intellectual capital, arguing in ever greater detail that evidence showed the Taliban would come to the table; Karzai and many Afghans favored talking to them. A deal that would sever ties between the Taliban and al-Qaeda and bring peace in Afghanistan was within reach. Holbrooke asked Rubin to put his ideas into a series of memos that Holbrooke then fanned out across the government. After Holbrooke died Rubin put all those memos into one folder for the White House. Then, in early spring of 2012 in a meeting at the White House, Clinton pushed the White House one more time to consider the idea. National Security Adviser Tom Donilon countered that he had yet to see the State Department make a case for reconciliation. So Clinton asked Rubin for every memo he had written on reconciliation going back to his first day on the job. The three-inch-thick folder spoke for itself. It took over a year of lobbying inside the administration to get the White House to take seriously the idea of reconciliation. It was close to eighteen months after Rubin wrote his first memo that Clinton could finally, and publicly, endorse diplomacy on behalf of the administration, in a speech at the Asia Society in February 2011.

Reconciliation involved more than Karzai and the Taliban, however. Holbrooke thought that a political settlement between them was possible if Afghanistan's key neighbors (Iran and Pakistan) and other important regional actors (India, Russia, and Saudi Arabia) could be induced to support it. Iran had backed the last political settlement in Afghanistan, the Bonn Conference of 2001. Pakistan had not been a part of that deal, but its acquiescence was bought afterward with generous American aid. This time Iran was not part of the equation, but Holbrooke hoped that Pakistan would go along much as Iran had done at Bonn if Washington actively engaged Islamabad. You needed at least one of the two—Iran or Pakistan—for a settlement to have a chance.

It was important to tackle the problem from the outside in because all these countries had vital interests in Afghanistan, and unless they endorsed the process and its outcome, it would fail. In addition, America would eventually leave, and then it would be up to those neighbors and regional actors to keep the final deal in place. They would do that only if they had been included in the process all along and saw their interests protected in the final political settlement. America's job was to get the region on board with a peace process and commit to protecting its outcome. That perspective never grew roots in Washington. Even when the White House warmed up to the concept of talking to the Taliban it saw diplomacy as hardly more than a cease-fire agreement with the Taliban.

But there were deep divisions between Pakistan and India, Iran and Saudi Arabia, and less visible but equally important disagreements separating Iran and Russia, on the one hand, from Pakistan on the other. During the Taliban period in the 1990s, these countries had supported different warring factions, and they would do so again, scuttling any final settlement unless they were on board with what Karzai and the Taliban agreed on.

Holbrooke thought that, as varied as the interests of these regional actors were, it should nonetheless be possible to bring them into alignment. He imagined a Venn diagram in which all the circles would intersect; the small area where they all overlapped would be where the agreement would have to happen. His approach was reminiscent of how Nixon thought of diplomacy with China. Before he got to Beijing in February 1972, Nixon took a pad of paper and jotted on it: "What do they want, what do we want, what do we both want?" Whatever he thought the answer was to that last question was where he anchored his China diplomacy.[6]

The most obvious area of overlap regarding Afghanistan was that no one (not even Pakistan), regardless of what other interests they wanted to protect there, wanted to see chaos and extremism reigning in the country. The logical thing to do was to get everyone to agree on the principle of an Afghanistan at peace with itself and its neighbors. You could build on the consensus that Afghanistan should never constitute a threat to any of its neighbors, and that its neighbors in return should not use Afghanistan to wage proxy wars against one another. These were broad principles that could serve as the basis for concrete agreements. For instance, Pakistan might well demand formal recognition of the Durand

Line as its border with Afghanistan—a recognition that the Afghans have never agreed to accord this ill-marked international frontier.[7] The positive security implications of such recognition would give Islamabad a reason to agree to a lesser role in Afghanistan. Pakistan's meddling in Afghanistan (supporting the insurgency and interfering with U.S. COIN strategy) has been in plain sight for all to see, but not so Afghanistan's refusal to abandon claims to Pakistani territory, claims that form one motivation for Pakistan's desire to meddle in Afghanistan.

Holbrooke pursued this idea of bringing the Afghans and Pakistanis to see mutual benefit with a vengeance, which is one reason why Kabul looked at him with suspicion and accused him of favoring Pakistan. On one occasion, he pressed Pakistan's top military man, General Kayani, on what it would take for his country to give up on the Taliban. The general did not want to acknowledge that Pakistan was supporting the Taliban but nevertheless took the bait. He put it hypothetically and listed a few conditions. Right after "Afghanistan should not be an Indian base for operations against Pakistan" came "Pashtuns in Afghanistan should look to Kabul, and Pashtuns in Pakistan to Islamabad," by which he meant that Karzai (or any future Afghan leader) should stop posing as the "King of all Pashtuns" and Afghanistan should abandon its irredentist claims to Pakistan's Pashtun region.

That all sounded reasonable. Pakistan was waging a preemptive war of sorts in Afghanistan. Islamabad wanted Kabul on the defensive and Pashtuns under the thumb of its friend the Taliban lest Afghanistan start causing problems in Pakistan.

The next stop was Kabul. In several meetings with Afghan ministers, Holbrooke went off script to talk about the Durand Line. He got no takers. In one meeting, after Afghanistan's interior and defense ministers and intelligence chief were done complaining about Pakistan, Holbrooke told them General Kayani had said that if Afghanistan recognized the Durand Line, then Pakistan would have no reason to invest in the Taliban (he embellished Kayani's promise, but it was close enough). The three Afghans were caught off guard. They were accustomed to complaining about terrorist-sheltering Pakistan, but not being on the receiving end of a Pakistani complaint. Amrallah Saleh—Afghanistan's seasoned spymaster and most lucid strategic thinker—leaned forward, looked Holbrooke straight in the eye, and said, "That is not politically feasible, no Afghan government would do that." But to Holbrooke, that was an opening.

Saleh had just confirmed to Holbrooke that the core issue between the two governments—and hence a major driver of the insurgency that we were spending billions to contain—was a diplomatic matter. There was a diplomatic solution to this war. Of course a resolution would not be easy or immediate, but there was a path to a diplomatic resolution of what motivated Pakistan's destructive game in Afghanistan. Diplomacy could create an overlap in the Afghanistan-Pakistan portion of the Venn diagram.

Of course, Holbrooke could not start with the border issue. That was not on Washington's radar, and there had to be a few smaller agreements between Kabul and Islamabad before you got to the border issue. Kabul thought that America would control the Afghan border as a part of COIN, and Pakistan resisted COIN precisely because it would eliminate Islamabad's trump card without resolving one important issue that got Pakistan into the Taliban business in the first place. Where he could start talks, however, was with a discussion on trade and commerce.

During a three-way meeting between the United States, Afghanistan, and Pakistan in Washington in 2009, Holbrooke sat through a discussion on trade. He learned that there was a market for Afghan goods in India, but Afghan trucks and produce could not cross Pakistani territory because there was no transit-and-trade agreement between the two countries (in fact there were hardly any treaties between the two countries). The two had started negotiating a trade-and-transit agreement in the 1960s but had let the matter drop and never resumed it. Finishing that deal became something of an obsession for Holbrooke. He spent hours going over every detail in it and tapped his chief economic adviser, a tireless and talented young diplomat named Mary Beth Goodman, to work on the issue.

Over the next year, he talked trade with the Afghan and Pakistani foreign ministers every chance he got. They were tired of hearing him make the case for a treaty that they thought had no chance of being signed. They were happy to use the idea as happy talk about the future or to point to each other's malfeasance, but neither foreign minister was really eager to roll up his sleeves and negotiate a deal. But then, they had no idea how persuasive and tenacious Holbrooke could be.

The two foreign ministers by turn brought excuses or came up with myriad reasons it would not work, and would then make outlandish demands. The Afghan foreign minister brought India into the discussion hoping that Pakistan would back out, but Holbrooke found a way around that by asking the Indians to reject the Afghan request. Holbrooke lobbied Karzai and Kayani, and then got Clinton to lean on them as well. Eventually both sides, to their own surprise, said yes. That he got the Pakistan military to give its okay (given that the deal would connect Afghanistan and India economically and would require Pakistan to open its border to India) was a mighty achievement.

But it was not a treaty until both sides showed up for a signing ceremony. Holbrooke used Clinton's visit to Islamabad in July 2010 to corner both sides into signing the treaty. Ambassador Eikenberry flew the Afghan finance minister to Islamabad and waited there until after the signing to fly him back (so there would be no excuses citing the alleged difficulty of travel). Holbrooke told Goodman to get the two ministers in the same room: "Don't let them out before they are done; don't go in, but stay right outside in case they need technical help." It worked. Afghanistan and Pakistan signed the first treaty between the two countries in decades (in fact, no one could remember when they had last inked one together). It was a giant step in creating trust and momentum to tackle the bigger border issues.

Now, on any day of the week, you can go to the Wagah, the border crossing between Pakistan and India that sits a short distance from the center of the Pakistani city of Lahore, and you will see a mile-long line of trucks loaded with fruit and other produce, both fresh and dried. Much of this cargo waiting to cross into India comes from Afghanistan. It is legitimate, productive trade, and Holbrooke made it possible.

After Holbrooke died the State Department promoted the idea of a New Silk Road to give Afghanistan an economic anchor after American troops left. It conceives of Afghanistan as a trading hub for the region.[8] The Transit Trade Agreement made this idea possible, and if it ever comes to fruition it will have to be based on what Holbrooke and Goodman negotiated.

A little over a year after Holbrooke died, in April 2012 India and Pakistan opened their border to trade. The Transit Trade Agreement had given both India and Pakistan reason to expand beyond the Afghan trade connecting the two countries. Pakistan now saw it was possible to trade with antagonistic neighbors. Pakistan would grant India most favored nation (MFN) trade status; Pakistan and India literally lifted entire clauses and passages out of the Transit Trade Agreement to craft their own trade agreement. If all goes well they will get to a transit-and-trade agreement of their own. The Transit Trade Agreement had done good for the region; America had built the foundation for something positive that impacted daily lives.

Holbrooke was elated when the trade deal was signed. Clinton congratulated him for once again pulling a rabbit out of the hat. But the White House was silent. This kind of diplomacy was not part of their game plan. They did not know what had happened, or why it would matter to the war. In those days, achievements such as this did not endear Holbrooke to the White House. Instead, the president's staff treated the accord as a nuisance. Or at least they did until a few weeks later when, hard-pressed to show any progress in Afghanistan and Pakistan, they suddenly discovered the Transit Trade Agreement. But they still remained oblivious to the potential of diplomacy.

Holbrooke was undeterred, however. He thought that, in time, the White House would come around and then would be glad to find that all the pieces were already in place. So he started talking to all the countries that mattered, and made repeated requests to be allowed to talk to Iran as well. He crisscrossed the region, and in every capital asked his hosts to lay out their interests in Afghanistan, explain how they saw the region's future, and let him know what they thought of reconciliation. Then he focused on how to create the overlap of interests. He talked about all this with Clinton and had her support, though the rest of Washington either didn't know or didn't care.

The thorniest issue was India. India and Pakistan had distinct interests in Afghanistan and were deeply suspicious of each other's intentions. They had backed opposite sides during the Taliban's war on the Northern Alliance in the 1990s and continued to see Afghanistan's future as a zero-sum game that could change the balance of power between them.

India had invested more than a billion dollars in the development of Afghanistan and was keen to keep its foothold there. Pakistan thought that any Indian presence in Afghanistan would inevitably give India a base in its strategic rear. Indians complained about Pakistan's support for terrorism and the Taliban; every conversation with Pakistanis on India's role in Afghanistan seemed to end with charges that India supported Baluch separatists operating out of Kabul.

Still, Holbrooke thought that it was possible to get past mutual recriminations and focus the two on an Afghan settlement that both could live with. He did not want to solve everything between India and Pakistan—he knew that he would never get a visa to Delhi if he touched the third rail of Kashmir. Concessions on that territorial dispute, over which India and Pakistan in 1999 fought what so far is mercifully the world's only ground war between two nuclear-armed states, were definitely not on the table. But he thought there must be a sliver of mutual interest in Afghanistan, extremely narrow though it may be, enough to keep both India and Pakistan on board with a diplomatic outcome. So every chance he got, Holbrooke pushed his Indian and Pakistani counterparts to explain their red lines, revise them, and explore the potential for engaging one another on Afghanistan.

After a lot of back and forth, Holbrooke persuaded General Kayani to agree in principle to talks with India over Afghanistan and Afghanistan only. Holbrooke took that concession—which was not much but enough to work with—to Delhi. The Indians had said all along that they would talk to Pakistan if talks remained focused on Afghanistan and did not include other issues. I remember Holbrooke talking through how India and Pakistan could arrive at their sliver of Venn-diagram overlap during dinner with his Indian counterpart at La Chaumière, his favorite French restaurant in Georgetown. It was December 6, 2010, less than a week before he died of a ruptured aorta. He looked haggard and not in his usual form, but he was about to pull another rabbit out of the hat, a diplomatic coup of serious consequence.

His counterpart was intrigued. He asked Holbrooke, "How do you envision this happening?" Holbrooke replied, "It will have to be 'variable geometry,' some bilateral talks, sometimes three (including the U.S.), and at times a larger conference that would include Afghanistan and even others." "Diplomacy," he was fond of saying, "is like jazz, improvisation on a theme." He was improvising himself, all on the paramount theme of reconciliation.

At the end of the dinner his Indian counterpart said he would have to talk to Prime Minister Manmohan Singh directly and would have an answer for Holbrooke within a week. After dinner, I walked with him back to his apartment. He switched on the TV to see the Jets play the Patriots on *Monday Night Football*. He was pleased. The Indians seemed to be moving in the right direction. We talked through possible next steps. "Be ready to go to Delhi at the drop of a hat," he said to me. "I may not be able to go, it draws too much attention. Then we go to Islamabad—I will have to work on Kayani—and then maybe back to Delhi. Tomorrow we will go see Hillary and brief her." Clinton was pleasantly surprised with our account of the meeting and supportive of the hard-earned success. Holbrooke was worried that Christmas vacation could disrupt things. But he was energized and in his element. He intended to be involved every step of the way—in the room when possible, standing outside the door when not.

Holbrooke had created momentum out of thin air. Even Pakistanis and Indians were surprised at how far he had managed to bring them along. But the India-Pakistan conversation never happened. Holbrooke collapsed at the State Department on December 10, and a few days later he died. Holbrooke was still fighting for his life when Clinton called his counterpart in Delhi to tell him that she would be personally seeing through what he and Holbrooke had agreed on. Shortly thereafter, a message came from Delhi that Singh had given the green light. But progress would be superficial. Both the Indians and the Pakistanis already knew that Clinton was too highly placed to get into the details of their nascent diplomatic opening. She could champion talks, but with the administration's most tenacious champion of diplomacy out of the picture, the slim opening would close, not just between them but everywhere else the Venn diagrams intersected.

The problem all along was that Holbrooke had been forced to freelance. He had never received the authority to do diplomacy. The White House failed to endorse his efforts. He pursued them anyway in the belief that diplomacy alone could save America from this war and its aftermath. If he could lay the foundations and point the way, then perhaps the White House would warm to the idea, and when it did it would not have to start from scratch. But the White House—more so than the Indians and Pakistanis—remained resistant to diplomacy and blind to its potential in Afghanistan, and the region as a whole.

Holbrooke thought that Iran was singularly important to the endgame in Afghanistan. Iran had played a critical role at the Bonn Conference of 2001, which gave Afghanistan a new constitution and government. Iranian support also accounted for that government taking root. Iran had become a surprising force for stability in Afghanistan by investing in infrastructure and economic development and supporting the Afghan government in Kabul and in provinces with ties to Iran. It was a counterweight to Pakistan's destabilizing influence. Holbrooke thought that America should bring both Iran and Pakistan on board to successfully end the war and leave behind a peace that would last. Ironically, he also thought that we would have an easier time winning Iran's support than Pakistan's.

Iran has deep cultural, historical, and economic ties with Afghanistan. Iranian influence was ubiquitous in Afghan politics. It was especially strong among the former Northern Alliance forces. Many Tajiks and Hazaras, absent Iranian prodding, might well balk at any deal with the Taliban and plunge Afghanistan back into civil war instead.

The Iranians were worried by the Taliban and what its return to prominence might mean for the regional balance of power. They had been happy to see the end of the Taliban regime in 2002 and had supported the Karzai government since. The Taliban pushed an extremist version of Sunni Islam that is brutally and even murderously hostile to Shiism. Pakistani Sunni extremists who are spiritual brothers to the Taliban like to send suicide bombers into that country's Shia mosques during Friday prayer services when they know the largest number of Shia worshippers will be available for slaughter. And as the book and film versions of *The Kite Runner* dramatized for a global audience, the Taliban enjoyed persecuting their Hazara countrymen, partly on ethnic grounds of Pashtun chauvinism, but also because Hazaras are mainly Shia. In 1997, Taliban forces had overrun the Afghan Shia cities of Bamyan and Mazar-e-Sharif, massacring thousands of Shias and killing eleven Iranian diplomats and journalists. Iran mobilized 200,000 troops on Afghanistan's border but in the end decided going to war with a neighbor would prove costly. It is the only time since 1859 that Iran has contemplated attacking a neighbor.

Iran also worries about chaos in Afghanistan. There are as many as 3 million Afghan refugees in Iran already. If the Taliban were to conquer Kabul, Herat, and Mazar-e-Sharif again, that number could rise, with untold economic and social consequences for Iran. Chaos also means drug trafficking. Iran has one of the world's largest populations of addicts, and its eight-hundred-mile-long border with Afghanistan makes policing drug trafficking next to impossible. Finally, the Iranians well know that Pakistan is the Taliban's sponsor, and that Pakistan has always acted to extend the influence of Iran's regional rival Saudi Arabia into Afghanistan.

Iran's position in Afghanistan, opposing the Taliban, supporting Karzai, and favoring aggressive drug-eradication efforts, was far closer to America's than was the posture of Pakistan. Holbrooke thought he saw enough common interest between Washington and Tehran to bring Iran on board with a diplomatic process to end the war—as had been the case in Bonn in 2001.

For my part, I advised Holbrooke in 2009 that it was important to engage Iran on Afghanistan because if Iran came to see America's growing military presence there as a threat, then Tehran might start viewing the Taliban less as a foe than as a potential ally. That would strengthen the insurgency and put us in a difficult spot. We should not assume that Iranian hostility to the Taliban could never soften; nor, I said, should we assume that the Taliban's dislike of Iran was so great that it would withstand any amount of increasing U.S. military pressure. Taliban cadres pressed hard enough might well reach out for Iranian help in their fight with America.

A year later, I learned from an Iranian diplomat that the big question being debated in Iranian ruling circles was: Who is the bigger threat, America or the Taliban? The answer was increasingly America. "The

Taliban we can handle, but American presence in the region is a long-run strategic headache." Iran, he said, had started working with the Taliban and influencing Karzai to undermine America's plans for Afghanistan.

In late May 2009, there was a conference on Afghanistan at The Hague. During one of the breaks, while all the delegates were milling around a coffee table, Holbrooke walked over to Iranian deputy foreign minister Mehdi Akhoundzadeh, extended his hand, and said hello. Then, without missing a beat, Holbrooke started talking about an Asia Society exhibition he had seen that featured artworks from the era of the Safavid Persian monarchy (or at least that is what he told me later). The startled Iranian envoy was too dumbstruck to say anything. He grinned and nodded, and was very happy when the fifteen-minute courtship was over. The next day the press went wild with the story. It was thought that, as promised, the Obama administration had started its engagement of Iran, and Afghanistan was the vehicle.

Little did anyone know that Holbrooke did this on his own, hoping to break the ice with Iran and to press both Washington and Tehran on Afghanistan issues by taking the first step for both. But neither side appreciated his guerrilla tactic; Washington in particular was resistant. The White House was allergic to the idea of talking to Iran about Afghanistan. Holbrooke was hopeful that the White House would give diplomacy a chance and believed that it would come around to backing his effort to explore all channels and avenues. But he was wrong. He tried time and again to persuade the administration otherwise, but with the exception of Secretary Clinton, who thought that America was big enough to "walk and chew gum" (that is, talk to Iran about Afghanistan while being tough on them on the nuclear issue), no one else was supportive.

On the other side, there were plenty of signals that Iran was willing to engage the United States on Afghanistan—approaches by diplomats and intermediaries. It was our routine that every time there was an opening, Holbrooke and I would write a memo on why it mattered to engage

Iran on Afghanistan. We would reiterate the point that Iran alone among Afghanistan's neighbors could serve as a counterweight to Pakistan, and engaging Iran was at the very least an insurance policy to make it less likely that they would work actively to undermine us, and that there was an upside if Tehran decided to reinforce common objectives with Karzai. If there were side benefits to be reaped in terms of managing the nuclear issue, then so much the better, though that was not the main goal. We would brief Clinton on the memo's contents and then with her approval would send it on to the White House. Holbrooke would then follow up the next time he went to the White House, usually by visiting his old friend Tom Donilon, who served as deputy to the national security adviser at the time before taking over that portfolio himself. Every time, Holbrooke would return dejected. I would ask him what had happened. "Tom says: 'We have a different theory of the case,'" he would tell me. The White House did not want to talk to Iran on Afghanistan, and Holbrooke's entreaties fell on deaf ears, and he never got to make his case to the full National Security Council or the president.

Clinton, too, made the case for engaging Iran on Afghanistan at the White House, and did speak directly to the president about the matter. She did not see talking to Iran on Afghanistan as a goodwill signal or a trust-building exercise—although it could have served that purpose. Instead, she simply maintained that it was reasonable to think that given Iran's geostrategic location and ties to Afghanistan, it ought to be a part of the solution, if only so that it did not become part of the problem. The president seemed to agree,[9] but then he let White House staffers decide, and they scuttled the idea.

The White House argued that talking to Iran about anything other than their willingness to abandon their nuclear program would show weakness. The Iranians might try hard to be helpful in Afghanistan only as more cover for obduracy on the nuclear issue (Iranian nuclear obduracy, as we now well know, happened anyway). By the spring of 2012, U.S. policy on Iran had failed, and relations were on the edge of a cliff. Not talking to Iran on Afghanistan had made no difference. In fact, had there been progress in that arena things might not have gone quite as badly as they did—but we will never know. Engaging Iran on Afghanistan would likely have been good for both Afghanistan policy and Iran policy. Failure to engage showed a lack of imagination in managing both those challenges.

The heart of the Afghanistan matter, of course, remained reconciliation talks between Karzai and the Taliban. This was where all the Venn diagrams had to intersect, the only agreement that could end the fighting. It was also the necessary cover for U.S.-Taliban talks. As the two military forces on the ground, they did all the fighting, and they had to find their way to a cease-fire.

In 2009, talking to the Taliban was taboo. The Bush administration had not even countenanced Karzai talking to them—no one should talk to the enemy. The Obama administration was more open-minded; it did not slap Karzai down when he hinted in public that he was talking to the Taliban. Karzai took advantage of this change in attitude and boldly touted reconciliation as a serious option for ending the war, which complicated his already difficult relations with the U.S. military. Karzai claimed that he was in regular contact with Taliban commanders and imagined a grand bargain that would bring true peace to Afghanistan. When, in August 2010, Pakistani intelligence arrested senior Taliban commander Mullah Baradar, Karzai was quick to claim that Baradar (a fellow tribesman of the president's) was being punished by Pakistan for talking to Karzai.

Several American allies, too, were busy with Taliban engagement. By mid-2010, it looked as if everybody was talking to the Taliban except us. There was not a week when we did not hear about some contact or meeting with Taliban officials or front men, or receive scintillating messages offering help with release of captured U.S. personnel or proposing a trust-building exercise that expressed the Taliban's readiness to talk. Britain, Germany, Norway, Saudi Arabia, and even Egypt all reported similar contacts with various Taliban emissaries. It was hard to separate the wheat from the chaff, especially since opposition to talks by the U.S. military and the CIA made it difficult to verify which claims were true.

Around this time, in fall 2009, Holbrooke and I had a meeting with

Egypt's foreign minister. Egypt's intelligence chief, General Abu Sulei-man (who later became vice president when Mubarak fell), was also in the room. At one point he turned to Holbrooke and said, "The Tali-ban visited us in Cairo." Holbrooke said, "Really, who came? Do you remember?" Abu Suleiman reached into his bag, pulled out a piece of paper, held it before his face, and read three names. The last one made us all pause. It was Tayeb Agha, a relative of the Taliban chief, Mulla Omar, as well as his secretary and spokesman, whom we knew to be actively probing talks with the United States on the Taliban's behalf. We knew Tayeb Agha to be a player, but we did not know then that he would become America's main Taliban interlocutor in first secret and later for-mal talks that began in 2011 (and were made public in February 2012).

Holbrooke took note of all these reports, gauged which ones were serious, and assessed what could be gleaned from them in order to move us closer to the talks. Some in SRAP were frustrated that everyone was talking to the Taliban except America—we were being marginalized, losing out, they would argue. But Holbrooke would say calmly, "Don't worry, nothing matters until we are at the table. It is good that others socialize the idea and clear the underbrush; our time will come." As part of his routine reporting, he would tell the White House of every account of talks with the Taliban to get them used to the idea.

One report in particular proved game changing.[10] In February 2010 at the Munich Security Conference, Holbrooke's German counterpart, Bernd Mutzelberg, told Holbrooke that he had met with Tayeb Agha twice in Dubai, and that the channel to Mulla Omar and the Quetta Shura was real. In their last meeting Tayeb Agha had told Mutzelberg he wanted to talk directly to America. Holbrooke lost no time in tak-ing Mutzelberg to National Security Adviser Jim Jones and his Afghan affairs deputy, General Doug Lute, who were also in Munich. The White House team listened but was not ready to grab at the opportunity.

Back home, Holbrooke went into overdrive, lobbying hard with the White House to bite on the offer, test Tayeb Agha, and see whether there was anything to what the Germans had stumbled on. Despite Pentagon and CIA objections and White House reservations—but with Secretary Clinton's aggressive backing—Holbrooke got his way. Secret meetings with Tayeb Agha started, first in Munich, then every so often in Doha.[11]

Holbrooke never participated and did not live to see them gain momentum, culminating in the Taliban establishing an office in Qatar and formally declaring their readiness for talks with America in February 2012—two years after the Munich meeting. Getting the White House to the table with the Taliban, finally getting diplomacy into the mix in AfPak strategy, had been Holbrooke's greatest challenge, and he had finally succeeded. It will be his great legacy.

However, the Obama administration's approach to reconciliation is not exactly what Holbrooke had in mind for a diplomatic end to the war. Holbrooke thought that we had the best chance of getting what we wanted, and what would be good for Afghanistan and the region, if we negotiated with the Taliban while our leverage was at its strongest—when we had the maximum number of troops on the ground in Afghanistan, and when it was believed that we were going to stay in full force. He had not favored the Afghan surge, but he believed that once the troops were there, the president should have used the show of force to get to a diplomatic solution.

But that did not happen. The president failed to launch diplomacy and then announced the troop withdrawal, in effect snatching away the leverage that would be needed if diplomacy was to have a chance of success. "If you are leaving, why would the Taliban make a deal with you? How would you make the deal stick? The Taliban will talk to you, but just to get you out faster." That comment from an Arab diplomat was repeated across the region.

But it was exactly after announcing its departure that the administration warmed up to the idea of reconciliation. The idea was not that success in talking to the Taliban would clear the way for a noncatastrophic departure from Afghanistan. It was that since we were leaving anyway, we might as well try our hand at a political settlement on our way out the door. The outcome of talks with the Taliban had no bearing on the course of the war. The war would wind down with or without a peace deal. Reconciliation was an afterthought, a piece of cover to make our sudden withdrawal look more promising than it was.

Facts on the ground punched a hole in the perception of victory. As we went from "fight and talk" to "talk while leaving" the prospect of a good outcome began to grow dimmer. The Taliban did not think that we were winning, they thought that *they* were winning. Talks were not about arranging their surrender, but about hastening our departure.[12] They could sit at the table and drag out talks. They did not have to compromise on governance when they could just promise to pave the way for our departure. There would be a sense of progress, with the Taliban agreeing to consider a particular offer and then making a minor concession, but all along our forces on the ground would be shrinking—and as they shrank, the balance of power would be shifting in the Taliban's direction. All they had to do was show some patience, keep their powder dry and their numbers intact, and they would inherit Afghanistan. In the end, there will be talks and small agreements, but not the kind of settlement that would anchor broader regional peace and stability.

Concerns about human rights, women's rights, and education were all shelved. None was seen as a matter of vital American interest, and now they had turned into noble causes that were too costly and difficult to support—and definitely not worth fighting an insurgency over. I remember the day in August 2010 when *Time* magazine put on its cover a gruesome picture of a young Afghan woman named Aisha, a bride in a marriage arranged when she was twelve, whose nose had been cut off as punishment for fleeing her abusive in-laws. The caption under it read: "What Happens if We Leave Afghanistan."[13]

We in SRAP thought the sky would fall. There would be indignation and protest at the highest level in the State Department and White House, and a reiteration of our duty to protect fundamental rights in Afghanistan. But there was nothing—deafening silence. We had shed the moral obligation that we assumed as our mantle in Afghanistan. Now in private meetings you could hear whispers of "Even if Afghanistan returns to civil war after we leave, we don't care, it will not be our business." Washington's mantra was no longer "Afghan good war" but "Afghan good enough."

The White House seemed to see an actual benefit in not doing too much. It was happy with its narrative of modest success in Afghanistan and gradual withdrawal—building Afghan security forces to take over from departing American troops. Pursuing a potentially durable final settlement was politically risky, and even if it worked it would yield no greater domestic dividends than would muddling through until the departure date arrived. The goal was to spare the president the risks that necessarily come with playing the leadership role that America claims to play in this region.

The problem is that what might appear sensible in the context of domestic politics (and that proposition may yet be tested if a broken Afghanistan begins to export horrors again) does not make for sensible foreign policy; definitely not if the goal is to be taken seriously around the world. The region was looking for sage strategy and follow-through. It got neither. The confusion over the rise and fall of COIN was compounded by vacillation over reconciliation.

In addition to its poor timing, the White House's vision of reconciliation was so narrowly conceived that it was virtually guaranteed to fail. Unlike what Holbrooke had had in mind, this reconciliation would be a limited, so-called Afghan-led process, but in effect involve negotiations between America and the Taliban.[14] If it ever got off the ground it could have only the narrow purview of producing an agreement over the terms of American departure.

There would be no effort to include other regional actors in the talks—America promised to keep everyone informed of what happened in the talks and, of course, expected that they would accept the outcome. So Pakistan was asked to deliver the Taliban to the talks (i.e., allow them to travel outside Pakistan to meet American and Afghan negotiators) but not to expect a role in shaping them, nor a seat at the table.

Afghanistan's two most important neighbors were shut out of talks about the Afghan endgame. Since the Taliban's fall in the wake of 9/11, one or the other of these two pivotal neighbors had been at America's side. In Bonn in 2001, Iran had been a key player in the talks and backed America's Afghanistan strategy. In 2009 and 2010, America kept Pakistan positively engaged. Now America was trying to go it alone. Worse, America was trying to fix Afghanistan while actually escalating tensions with both Iran and Pakistan, as if peace could somehow be made to take hold in Afghanistan when the country's immediate neighborhood was roiled by acute instability. A chaotic Afghanistan in a stable region was hard enough to handle; a chaotic Afghanistan in an *un*stable region, and with its two most important neighbors in conflict with America, seems nearly impossible.

Against this backdrop President Obama decided to write his own narrative of the war's end. He used the grand occasion of the NATO summit in his hometown of Chicago to say, come hell or high water, American troops will leave Afghanistan by 2014. They will do so because the (wobbly) Afghan security force of around 230,000 (down from the original 400,000 number) that we are training is taking over the security of the country (which will cost us about $4 billion a year), and also because a partnership treaty we have signed with Karzai will ensure stability and continuity in that country after we leave.

But if we leave Afghanistan to a shaky security force and an erratic president, how will we ensure that the state we built will not buckle before the Taliban break up and disintegrate? Afghanistan has none of what Iraq had when we left in December 2011. Iraq had close to a million men in its security forces. It also has oil revenue as well as the requisite education system and social infrastructure to build and maintain a force of that size—and even so Iraq is still teetering on the verge of chaos.

Can we be sure that Karzai will not toss aside the Afghan constitution to stay in power beyond 2014? Will resulting protests and civil conflict add to the still-raging insurgency to make real the Afghanistan of our worst nightmares? Most important, if we leave will we have any influence? Not likely.

We have not won this war on the battlefield nor have we ended it at the negotiating table. We are just washing our hands of it, hoping there will be a decent interval of calm—a reasonable distance between our departure and the catastrophe to follow so we will not be blamed for it. We may hope that the Afghan army we are building will hold out longer than the one the Soviet Union built, but even that may not come to pass. Very likely, the Taliban will win Afghanistan again, and this long and costly war will have been for naught. Our standing will suffer and our security will again be at risk.

And then there is Pakistan to consider.

WHO LOST PAKISTAN?

President Asif Ali Zardari is an enigmatic figure. He inherited the leadership of Pakistan's largest political party after his wife, Benazir Bhutto, was killed in a vicious bomb attack blamed on Pakistan's homegrown branch of the Taliban. Pakistanis don't like Zardari much. They think he is a hustler, and the memory of his corruption in the 1990s when his wife was prime minister has forever been chiseled into the country's collective memory. But he should not be dismissed so easily. He is a survivor and a shrewd operator. General Pervez Musharraf, Pakistan's military ruler between 1999 and 2008, jailed Zardari on corruption charges and sent his wife into exile. The two made a comeback in 2007 after Musharraf's rule started to unravel. The years in jail were a trial by fire that turned Zardari into a formidable politician, cunning and ambitious enough to climb his way up to the presidency.

One evening in June 2009, soon after I joined Holbrooke's team, we called on Zardari at the presidential palace in Islamabad. Holbrooke had brought along journalists on the trip to show them firsthand how important Pakistan was to the Afghan war. Zardari was eager to play his part. As if he had read Holbrooke's mind, he lost no time in subjecting the note-taking reporters to a long and meandering rigmarole liberally seasoned with an idea that could be paraphrased as "Pakistan deserves more of Uncle Sam's cash—a *lot* more!"

"Pakistan is like AIG," he said to drive his point home. "Too big to fail." What he meant was that his country was "too strategic," "too dangerous," or, as Republican presidential hopeful Michele Bachmann would later put it, "too nuclear," to fail. "You gave AIG one hundred billion dollars; you should give Pakistan the same," said Zardari. Then he waxed lyrical about all the dangers that Pakistan faced and in turn would pose for the West were it to fail. Surely, he indicated, all this was self-evident to Washington.

Holbrooke smiled through these conversations. He agreed that Pakistan was too important to ignore and that, whether we liked it or not, the United States had an abiding interest in its stability. But he thought Zardari's attitude betrayed a disturbing dependence on America, and even worse, a sense of entitlement in spite of failure. Holbrooke didn't like the image of Pakistan holding a gun to its own head as it shook down America for aid. We should help Pakistan, but Pakistan too should pull itself up by its bootstraps, getting its political house in order and attending to development.

That said, Holbrooke agreed with Zardari that Pakistan was more important than Washington seemed to realize at that moment. Not only in the long run because it was a nuclear-armed country of 180 million, infested with extremists and teetering on the verge of collapse, but more immediately because it mattered to the outcome in Afghanistan. We could not afford for Pakistan to fail, and that meant we could not leave Pakistan to its own fate. We had to improve ties with Pakistan—however difficult that might turn out to be.

Over the next two years, Holbrooke pressed for a strategy of engaging Pakistan. He thought engagement would get the most out of not only Zardari but also the generals who wielded real power in the country, and help promote stability there, too, which also matters (or should matter) to America. The White House tolerated Holbrooke's approach for a while, but in the end decided that a policy of coercion and confrontation would better achieve our goals in Pakistan. That approach failed. The more America and Pakistan drifted apart, the less America got from Pakistan, and the less influence we now have in shaping the future of a dangerous and troublesome country that is only growing more so.[1]

When it comes to Pakistan, the country where the SEALs found and killed Osama bin Laden in May 2011, the mood in America has turned dark. High officials and average Americans alike are understandably wary of the place. But perhaps more important still, they are tired of trying to change its perverse ways. Political scientist Stephen Krasner captured this mood well when he wrote in the January/February 2012 issue of *Foreign Affairs* that after decades of efforts to buy Pakistan's cooperation with generous U.S. aid, plenty of public praise, and outsized amounts of face time for its leaders, the country still supports extremist organizations. These groups, as then–Joint Chiefs chairman Admiral Mike Mullen told the U.S. Senate Armed Services Committee on September 22, 2011, "serving as proxies for the government of Pakistan are attacking Afghan troops and civilians as well as U.S. soldiers." Mullen called the Haqqani network—a particularly vicious and brutish outfit that is an autonomous part of the Taliban—"in many ways, a strategic arm of Pakistan's Inter-Services Intelligence Agency." When he first became America's top military officer, Admiral Mullen had called Pakistan "a steadfast and historic ally."[2] Now he was expressing a different sentiment, the one that the *Atlantic* magazine captured in a cover story titled "The Ally from Hell."[3]

Such observations, Krasner argued, should lead us to treat Pakistan much the same way we treat Iran and North Korea—as a hostile power. Rather than assist, praise, and coddle Pakistan, we should think of how to contain it.[4] We can fight terrorism without Pakistan's help, the argument goes, since stepped-up drone attacks will do the job. And indeed, there is a growing sense that we are well on our way to confrontation with Pakistan.

However, what these critics don't say is how drones can get the job done if we lose access to the timely, ground-level intelligence that currently provides drones with their targets, or what happens if Pakistan decides to start shooting down these low- and slow-flying pilotless planes. Drones are labor-intensive. They don't need pilots, true, but they do require small armies of analysts and spies, including locals who are willing and able to attach homing chips to the people, vehicles, and buildings that drones are supposed to hit. For every one person on the ground that a jet-fighter mission needs, a drone mission needs ten. Pakistani authorities may not be able to stop U.S. drones from overflying their territory (though they can shoot them down), but they can cut the chain of intelligence gathering, analysis, and chip planting that makes drones effective. They can blind the drones and render them useless.

For decades, America bought Pakistan's cooperation through aid sweetened with public shows of friendship and support. In the ten years after 9/11, America poured $20 billion in civilian and military aid into the relationship. During its first two years in office, the Obama administration increased the flow of support and raised Pakistan's profile as a vital ally even further. In return, we got intelligence cooperation—more agents, listening posts, and even visas for the deep-cover CIA operatives who found bin Laden. We got improved relations between Kabul and Islamabad, which, although not as warm as we would have liked, were nonetheless warm enough to help our counterinsurgency efforts. We got more distance between Pakistan and Iran. And we finally persuaded Islamabad to go to war (however reluctantly) against the Taliban on Pakistan's own soil. Had the Pakistani military not taken on those Taliban forces, the fighting in Afghanistan certainly would have been worse. At least a measure of the battlefield success that the U.S. military has achieved in the Afghan theater—the success that has allowed President Obama to order troops home—can be ascribed to Pakistani cooperation.

There is plenty in Pakistani behavior to anger America too. Many observers think that Pakistan's regional interests are so far removed from those of the United States that no degree of aid and friendship can bridge the gap, making a collapse in the relationship inevitable all along. American ambassador to Pakistan Anne Patterson captured this sentiment best in a September 23, 2009, cable: "Money alone will not solve the problem of al-Qaeda or the Taliban operating in Pakistan. A grand bargain that promises development or military assistance in exchange for severing ties will be insufficient to wean Pakistan from policies that reflect accurately its most deep-seated fears. The Pakistani establishment, as we saw in 1998, with the nuclear test, does not view assistance—even sizable assistance to their own entities—as a trade-off for national security."[5]

Indeed, Pakistan has long been a "frenemy." But in dealing with frenemies, the question is always whether it makes more sense—in view of one's own interests and circumstances—to stress the friend part or the enemy part. And one should also be ready to ask whether a frenemy relationship can be moved—ever so slowly—toward the "friend" column.

The critical turning point in America's relations with Pakistan was the annus horribilis of 2011. That was the year in which a series of unfortunate events, mishandled by both sides, put relations in a deep freeze. It was also the moment when America decided to experiment with a whole new way of managing Pakistan, as an adversary rather than a friend, substituting pressure for engagement.

The twisted course of the year of horrors began with lethal gunplay on a traffic-packed Lahore thoroughfare. On January 27, 2011, an alleged undercover CIA agent named Raymond A. Davis shot and killed two Pakistani men on a motorbike, men he thought were going to rob him or, worse, abduct him. Pakistan put him in jail until the United States paid $2.4 million in compensation to the men's families and the CIA agreed to revise the rules by which it was operating in Pakistan.[6] By the time Davis was released on March 16, ties between Islamabad and Washington were severely strained, and it did not help that the very next day a massive drone strike hit a tribal gathering at Datta Khel in North Waziristan. Taliban commanders and fighters were killed, but also dozens of civilians. Then, at the beginning of May, helicopter-borne U.S. commandos flew from Afghanistan into Pakistan under conditions of utmost secrecy on a mission, launched and executed with no warning to Pakistan, to capture or kill bin Laden. They found him at a compound in the city of Abbottabad located in shockingly close proximity to the Pakistan Military Academy and the homes of numerous retired officers. The coup de grace came in November when American forces chasing Taliban fighters killed twenty-four Pakistani border guards in a botched firefight. Relations between the two countries went into deep freeze, and a real rupture, for the first time since Pakistan's creation in 1947, became a distinct possibility.

Mistrust was thus already profound when Admiral Mullen spoke to the Senate in September, accusing Pakistan outright of involvement in attacks on U.S. targets in Afghanistan.

Ever since Pakistan was created out of portions of British India in 1947, America's relations with the country have traveled a winding and rocky road. There have been periods of intense friendship followed by long bouts of neglect and even alienation.[7] Over time, the two sides have developed an unhealthy distrust of each other. Americans fear and resent Pakistan, and Pakistanis think American friendship is fickle and transient. Americans think Pakistan promised not to build nuclear weapons, and then went ahead and built them. Then it promised not to test more warheads, and broke that promise, too. That Pakistan deliberately cultivates Islamic extremism as the cornerstone of its regional policy has done little to assuage concerns over its nuclear arsenal. Nowadays it is quite clear that America's favor lies with Pakistan's neighbor and nemesis, India, and at times it seems as if Pakistan is reacting to that uncomfortable fact by embodying all the anti-American anger and angst that have washed over the Muslim world in the past few decades.

The relationship has been in a new and critical phase since 9/11. Experts well knew that Pakistan had been complicit in the creation of the Taliban and turned a blind eye to its support for al-Qaeda. But the Bush administration decided that conflict with Pakistan was not a good choice, and that buying Pakistan's cooperation would be the better option. Pakistan's military ruler quickly embraced the idea and aligned his country—for public consumption, at least—with the United States.

A cozy relationship soon took shape. Bush liked General Musharraf, who loved to talk a "moderate Muslim" game, and frequently complimented him as a staunch ally in the battle against terror as well as a reformer who would bring "enlightened and liberal Islam" to Pakistan. Evidence of Pakistani double-dealing was ignored as the emphasis was placed on the positive: the periodic nabbing of a terrorist (Khalid Sheikh Mohammed, the 9/11 mastermind, was captured with Pakistani help in Karachi in March 2003), Musharraf's tough antiterror rhetoric, and his promise of changing Pakistan into a forward-looking democracy. Posing as a hero of counterterrorism required a degree of chutzpah bordering on performance art, and Musharraf proved a master at it.

Somewhere along the line, to my shock, it became clear that the Bush administration had started to believe the act. One day in 2006 I was giving a talk on the latest developments in Pakistan to a group of U.S. government analysts whose job was to keep up with, and make sense of, what was happening on the ground so they could inform their higher-ups and provide options for possible action. As we were walking out, a young Pakistan watcher asked me what I thought of "Jinnah's Islam." General Musharraf had coined the phrase—a reference to Pakistan's founding father, the Shia-with-a-secular-spin Mohammed Ali Jinnah (1876–1948)—as a way of advertising his promise to reform Islam in Pakistan and imbue it with liberal values. Taking Islam back from extremists and making it something more like what the country's liberal founder, a London-trained lawyer, would have liked seemed an attractive idea for a country in the grip of extremism.

The answer was easy. I said I thought the whole thing was a shameless autocrat's cynical and transparent manipulation. The analyst, barely able to hide a smile, said, "Well, our customers [government lingo for members of Congress and senior administration officials] are very interested to know how we can support it." I said, "Surely you're kidding." How could we possibly put any stock in the idea of a whiskey-chugging general posing as an Islamic Martin Luther? "The Pakistanis already hate us because they think we're sinister," I went on. "Now they're going to think we're stupid, too." The analyst laughed and said, "You have no idea how much of this [our customers] lap up. We have to write a report."

No, Musharraf was not the ally that Bush and his lieutenants made him out to be.[8] The relationship was a magician's act. It all rested on misdirection, with more than a dash of suspended disbelief. While the general was cozying up to the Bush administration, extremists were thrusting their roots deeper into Pakistani soil—Osama bin Laden in particular (who could have waved at General Musharraf as he jogged right by bin Laden's house on a visit to Abbottabad) was getting comfortable in his new hideout in an army garrison town, protected by five military checkpoints. Also on Musharraf's watch, the Taliban started rebuilding their forces in Pakistan in preparation for an all-out war against American troops and the Afghan government.

Musharraf helped Washington pretend—and even believe—that what was happening in Pakistan was not happening. The country we touted as a determined wayfarer on the shining path to moderation and democracy was sinking deeper into the morass of extremism and had put its shoulder to wrecking what we were building in Afghanistan. Cynics called the two-faced strategy Pakistan's "double game." But the delusion of the Taliban being crushed with the aid of their straight-shooting partner Pakistan served a purpose, letting the Bush administration turn its gaze from Afghanistan and Pakistan and focus instead on the war in Iraq.

General Musharraf would later explain his motivation in cozying up to the United States by claiming that after 9/11 America had threatened to send Pakistan back to the Stone Age if it did not change course.[9] Several U.S. policy makers had supposedly impressed that point on Musharraf's intelligence chief, General Ahmad Mahmoud, who had by chance been in Washington on September 11. When Mahmoud, the godfather of the Taliban and the mastermind behind the 1999 coup that put Musharraf in power, reported back to his boss, he minced no words. So Musharraf summoned the army's nine corps commanders—in effect his cabinet—and told them that Pakistan was in trouble. Pakistan was no Syria, he said, part of a larger Arab world that would defend it from America's wrath. Pakistan was alone, facing a hostile India as always, and now inviting the enmity of the international community. To protect strategic assets such as its nuclear weapons program and its influence in Kashmir and Afghanistan, Pakistan would need to go along—or at least it would need to *act* like it was going along—with American demands. It would have to execute a kind of temporary tactical stand-down by helping America in Afghanistan, by dialing down the jihad against India in Kashmir, and by agreeing to fight al-Qaeda. The rewards would include not just billions of dollars in international aid, but also American support for military rule and an end to the international isolation that Musharraf's coup had triggered. And, of course, America would eventually leave Afghanistan, after which there would be ample time and opportunity to rebuild what would have to be temporarily given up. There were dissenters, but by and large the top brass accepted Musharraf's game plan.

Average Pakistanis were not impressed with the "Bush-Mush" love affair. The relationship had no roots in the two countries, and not only did it not benefit average Pakistanis, it actually hurt them by sustaining the military dictatorship and funding its jihadi auxiliaries.

The feel-good image of Musharraf's Pakistan—fighting extremism, blossoming culturally, and growing economically—was a mirage.

Musharraf was neither a reformer nor an ardent counterterrorism warrior. The economic boom that came on the heels of U.S. aid and the post-9/11 flight of Muslim capital from the West had turned to bust by the time his rule ended. By contrast, the extremism that he was ostensibly uprooting was instead blooming in dangerous parts of Pakistan, and was in full flower by the time he fell from power.

The Bush administration was oblivious to all this until near its own end. For much of Bush's time in office, from 2002 to 2008, Afghanistan had been stable, and American troops there saw their mission as keeping order and cleaning up the remnants of the insurgency while the new Afghan state took form. Washington was certainly concerned with what al-Qaeda was doing in Pakistan, but it did not see the Taliban through the lens of Pakistan, and hence did not treat Islamabad as integral to the solution in Afghanistan. It is arguable that for much of its time in office, the Bush administration did not even think that it had to come up with a solution to Afghanistan. The mission had been accomplished. The Taliban had been chased out of Kabul and out of the country altogether while Afghanistan's George Washington, Hamid Karzai, was building a city on a hill. Any evidence that Pakistan was not on board with America's plans for Afghanistan Washington either dismissed as coming from Afghans looking for convenient excuses for their own failings,[10] or blamed on so-called rogue elements of the ISI, which, with our support, Musharraf would eventually bring to heel. Then a particularly gruesome bombing attack on the Indian embassy in Kabul in July 2008 was traced back to the ISI. That, and undeniable evidence of a Taliban surge in southern Afghanistan, blew a big hole in Washington's happy Pakistan narrative.

What the Bush administration had failed to fully appreciate was that Musharraf was far more willing to help with the fight against al-Qaeda than he was to raise a hand against the Taliban (and, to be fair, Washington was not really asking him to target the Taliban). Under Musharraf, Pakistan had made a merely tactical withdrawal from Afghanistan and was only waiting for the right time to go back. Afghanistan was simply too important to Pakistan's sense of its own security and to its strategic ambitions for it to stop meddling in its neighbor's affairs on America's say-so.

By 2009, Pakistani complicity in the Taliban resurgence was undeniable. Now Pakistan was the staple of every explanation given to President Obama for why violence in Afghanistan was on the rise and American troops were facing an energized insurgency. Many on the right, in Congress and in the media, still thought that all this was happening only because Musharraf had been forced out of office in 2008. As one high-level Bush administration official who had worked on Pakistan put it to me: "The only problem with Pakistan is that Musharraf is no longer there." In reality, Musharraf had been the architect of the Taliban revival. The Taliban surge of 2008 and 2009 would never have been possible without preparations, recruiting, training, and capability-building activities that the Taliban undertook in Pakistan or with Pakistani help and that went back several years—to the time when Musharraf was in charge.

The problem did not have much to do with Musharraf as an individual. It was structural. The fact was that Pakistan had strategic objectives in Afghanistan, and it was pursuing them with us there and despite its own budding partnership with us.

When the Iraq war began to wind down following the 2007 troop surge, drones and Special Forces were moved east, and American intelligence turned its attention to Afghanistan and Pakistan. The closer we looked, the less we liked what we saw. The CIA got a proper gauge of its leaky partnership with Pakistan's ISI, seeing firsthand that its targets were adapting with uncanny speed to the agency's tracking methods. The most likely explanation was that the very ISI agents who were working alongside CIA operatives to hunt down terrorists and insurgents were also teaching these enemies how to avoid being killed or captured. Once, shortly after the CIA shared information with the ISI regarding an insurgent explosives factory, satellite images captured trucks pulling up to the factory to ferry its contents somewhere else.

There was ample evidence that Pakistan provided critical support to the Taliban, and worse yet, to its most vicious and lethal branch, the Haqqani network (which the United States formally designated as a Foreign Terrorist Organization in September 2012).[11] The *New York Times* reporter David Rohde, who was kidnapped and held hostage by the Haqqanis for seven months between 2008 and 2009, told Holbrooke's team at the State Department soon after his release from captivity that the clan operated out in the open and in view of Pakistani troops in the border town of Miramshah. On one occasion, a member of the Haqqani clan drove Rohde to a location for a video shoot. When they came across Pakistani troops on the way, the driver would simply pull down the scarf covering his face and they would be waved through. Rohde spent much of his captivity within walking distance of a Pakistan military garrison.[12] Indeed, and perhaps to underline the double nature of so much that goes on in Pakistan, the Pakistan Army also played a critical role in Rohde's liberation: after he and a companion escaped from the compound where they were being held, they managed to find an army scout who took them to the Frontier Corps base where they were airlifted to freedom.

As further evidence of Pakistan's less than good intentions, in 2010 the number of roadside bombs in Afghanistan grew to a shocking 14,661.[13] The nitrate used to build these devices came from Pakistan's fertilizer factories. America has pushed to get Pakistan to curb the trade in nitrates, but with scant success. Its conclusion was that there was plenty of double-dealing afoot in Pakistan.[14] But the problem was not to prove what Pakistan was up to—that was easy—but how to get Pakistan to transform its ways.

There is one constant in Pakistan: fear and envy of India. The rivalry with its larger neighbor has so consumed Pakistan that the country pretty much defines itself as the Muslim "anti-India." Thus it should come as no surprise that Pakistan would see Afghanistan only through the prism of the Indian challenge.

Except for the dozen years between the Soviet retreat and 9/11—a stretch of time when, for the most part, the Taliban were ruling in Kabul—Pakistan has had a rocky relationship with Afghanistan.[15] Afghans have never recognized their border with Pakistan—the famous Durand Line. The real border, think many leading Afghans as well as ordinary ones, should be the Indus River, far to the south and east of Sir Mortimer Durand's line, which divides the Pashtun northwest from the fertile plains of the Punjab. Pashtun nationalists have always claimed Pakistan's North-West Frontier Province (the NWFP, or, as it is now officially styled, Khyber Pakhtunkhwa) and the FATA, the notorious "agencies" along the Durand Line where al-Qaeda set up shop after 9/11, for Afghanistan. Some 40 percent of Afghans and 15 percent of Pakistanis are Pashtun. Given Pakistan's much larger population, this means that there are more Pashtuns in Pakistan than in Afghanistan. Pakistan lives in constant fear of a secession-minded, India-backed "Pashtundesh" (rhyming with Bangladesh, which in 1971 separated from Pakistan with India's help and humiliated Pakistan militarily in the bargain). Aggressive Pashtun nationalism to the north is a danger to Pakistan, especially when New Delhi is lending the irredentists a hand.

It is clearly better for Pakistan to have Pashtuns thinking of Islam and fighting to the north against Tajiks and Uzbeks in Afghanistan and Central Asia than to have Pashtuns dreaming of nationalism and looking south and east with visions of a homeland crafted in no small part out of Pakistani territory. Pakistan has thus forged deep ties to the Taliban since these "students" first appeared in Afghanistan in 1994 and proved effective in radicalizing young men and imposing local rule. With Pakistani help, they soon controlled large swaths of Afghanistan. The official story was that the peace they imposed on Afghanistan, which had been caught up in civil war since the Soviet departure, would help secure the building of roads and gas and oil pipelines that Pakistan needed in order to make itself a key conduit for trade between Central Asia and the Indian Ocean basin. The crucial reality was that the Taliban helped Pakistan face down India in the contest over Afghanistan.

It did not worry Pakistan that the Taliban were laying waste to Afghanistan, destroying the priceless giant Buddhas of Bamayan, closing schools, brutally punishing people for owning TV sets or having insufficiently long beards, nurturing a drug economy, and sheltering al-Qaeda. These "Islamic students" were serving a larger purpose by keeping Pashtuns busy and India out. At the height of the Taliban's power, Pakistani generals spoke confidently of the "strategic depth" that proxy control over Afghanistan gave Pakistan in the great game against India.

It is little wonder, then, that the generals seem to have so little real enthusiasm for shutting down the Taliban. Nor is it a mystery why Islamabad remains so suspicious of the independent Afghan state that America stood up after toppling the Taliban in late 2001 and early 2002. In the Indian-educated and pro-Delhi president Hamid Karzai, a Pashtun of the southern Durrani clan, the Pakistanis see the specter of Pashtun nationalism.

Countries can do dangerous things in pursuit of national interest, and in Pakistan's case, unsupervised generals were allowed to decide what the national interest was. By 9/11, Pakistan was deeply tied to the Taliban and jihadi fighters even as they and their al-Qaeda allies were about to bring down untold wrath from America. And, worse, backing the Taliban in Afghanistan inevitably meant more tolerance for extremism at home.[16] Pakistan could sustain its jihad in Afghanistan only by nurturing the infrastructure required for recruiting, indoctrinating, training, and managing jihadi fighters.[17] That meant cultivating radical madrassas and extremist parties, creating financial networks and training camps, carving out plenty of space to gather and swarm fighters on its borders, and maintaining close ties among jihadis and their ISI handlers. Years after 9/11, that infrastructure remains and is the bedrock of a persistent extremist menace in Pakistan.

Indeed, Pakistan was the first among Afghanistan's neighbors to suffer blowback from the fires that it had stoked in Afghanistan. By 2008, Pakistani versions of the Taliban had coalesced around Baitullah Mehsud's militia, Tehrik-I-Taliban Pakistan (TTP), and established emirates of terror in mountainous pockets of northwestern Pakistan. In 2009, the TTP led its confederation of Taliban look-alikes to take over territory in Pakistan proper, establishing draconian control amid the alpine scenery of the Swat Valley.[18] The government's effort to dislodge them from this perch sparked a brutal terror campaign against the government and people of Pakistan that in 2009 alone claimed the lives of 3,318 Pakistanis (up from 164 in 2003). On the tenth anniversary of 9/11, the tally of Pakistanis killed by terrorists and in suicide bombings over that decade stood at about 35,000.[19]

Was it not time for Pakistan to abandon its carelessness regarding extremism, understand the cost that the country was paying by playing with fire, and once and for all renounce extremism as a tool of foreign policy? We could now argue to Islamabad that the chickens had come home to roost; our problems in Afghanistan—extremism, the Taliban, suicide bombings, and instability—were now their problems, too. But in fact the explosion of extremist violence, though it made Pakistan's leaders more vulnerable, also made them more impervious to pressure. In the peculiar calculus of Pakistan, the more the military was threatened by a Frankenstein's monster that it had helped create, the less leverage we seemed to have to argue for serious change—especially since the Pakistani people appeared intent on blaming America rather than their own government for the violence and instability.

Pakistanis did not blame their terrible predicament on their own reckless investment in extremism, but rather on American counterterrorism efforts stirring the hornets' nest of terrorism in their backyard.[20] Musharraf was willing to go along with this. But the more Pakistanis came to blame America for the terror in their streets, the less impressed they were with the rewards that Musharraf had negotiated as recompense for their cooperation. Pakistan got $20.7 billion in assistance from the United States in the decade after 9/11. Pakistanis did the math and decided America was in the red. Zardari's AIG analogy reflects the deep sense of injustice that Pakistanis felt over what they regarded as their disproportionate sacrifices in the war on terror. Meanwhile, the U.S. Congress and the U.S. media complained about all the "free" money "given away" to Pakistanis who did little in return. Together, those perspectives reveal the gulf of misunderstanding dividing the two countries.

The Obama administration came to office with eyes wide open. America had finally fully understood that controlling Afghanistan was a fundamental Pakistani strategic objective, and that the Taliban were Pakistan's weapon of choice for realizing that goal. To solve the Afghan perplex, America had to first deal with the Pakistani complex. The question now was how.

The Bush administration had treated Afghanistan and Pakistan as if they were on two different continents. At the White House, Afghanistan and Iraq were managed out of the same office while Pakistan was bundled with India and the rest of South Asia. The Obama administration changed that. Afghanistan and Pakistan belonged together: they were in fact one policy area—AfPak—managed first by SRAP at the State

Department and, after Holbrooke died, by General Lute at the White House.

Pakistanis and Afghans did not like the shorthand, mostly because they don't like each other. But seeing Afghanistan and Pakistan through a single policy lens made sense. Richard Holbrooke had coined the AfPak term even before he was tapped to run the policy area. This was not just an effort to save five syllables. It was an attempt to drive home awareness of the reality that there is a single theater of war straddling an ill-defined border.[21]

Holbrooke became more convinced of this imperative after he started working on the problem. The problem with Afghanistan was Pakistan, and without a solution to Afghanistan, Pakistan would explode into an even bigger problem than al-Qaeda and the Taliban combined. If the Pakistani state was brought to its knees—which in 2009 was a serious worry in Washington, especially after TTP extremists in the Swat Valley started pushing toward Islamabad—then Afghanistan would be unsalvageable; and if Afghanistan collapsed into chaos and extremism, then Pakistan would be imperiled. America would have to pour in ten times more resources to protect that much bigger—and nuclear—country. That was how Holbrooke explained "AfPak" to anybody who asked.

The wisdom of the argument was clear, but the war was being fought in Afghanistan; that was where our troops were risking life and limb, so that is where our focus remained and where we spent our money. We proceeded to look for victory on the battlefield. Obama was convinced that is where we would find it when he sent 17,000 more troops to Afghanistan shortly after taking office.

But he was putting the cart before the horse. The key to ending the war was to change Pakistan. Pakistan was the sanctuary the Taliban insurgency used as a launching pad and as a place to escape American retaliation. We knew by then that Pakistan allowed it and we knew why. It was Pakistan's strategic calculus that we had to change, not troop numbers in Afghanistan.

That was Holbrooke's argument. More troops in Afghanistan would be useful if they could put pressure on Pakistan, sending Islamabad a signal that we were determined, and that it would be futile to persist in supporting an insurgency in an effort to control Afghanistan. Conversely, Holbrooke felt that it would not be wise to dispatch more soldiers simply to duke it out toe to toe with the Taliban. But to convince Pakistan that we meant business, we had to first prove that we were going to stay. The Pakistanis never believed that American intervention was more than just a bump in the road, and they did not have to wait long to be proven right. Holbrooke thought that we had a shot at changing Pakistan's strategic calculus, or at least at convincing them that they did not need the Taliban to realize some of their strategic objectives. They could work with us and the Karzai government. It was a long shot, and it had to begin with putting much more effort into fixing our relations with Pakistan. Even if we did not convince Pakistan of the wisdom of change, keeping them engaged around this discussion might pay us the dividend of more time and space to change things in Afghanistan. Unfortunately, not keeping them engaged is what they had come to expect.

Pakistan's double-dealing was in part a symptom of its bitterness over having been abandoned and then treated as a rogue state after a previous Afghan war, against the Soviets, had been won and the Soviets driven out in 1989. Pakistan was also deeply insecure about India's meteoric rise and growing strategic value to the West. Pakistanis were playing things very close to the vest. We had to get them to open up. Could we convince them that our plans for Afghanistan would address their strategic interests in the country? If we could, perhaps in time they might reassess their strategic interests in a way that was more favorable to ours.

Holbrooke argued that we had important interests in Afghanistan but vital interests in Pakistan, and that we had far more opportunity to realize our strategic goals in Pakistan than in Afghanistan. If we did that, it would be better for us and for the world. We will live to regret our insouciance, he warned, and the consequent loss of an opportunity to set things on the right track. If we don't set Pakistan on a different course, he would say, in twenty years the place will be a vast 300-million-person Gaza: out of energy, out of water, radical, and nuclear-armed to boot. It reminded me of what a senior CIA official once told me: "We will be concerned with Pakistan for a long time . . . my grandchildren will be waking up in the middle of the night worried about Pakistan." It was easy to convince people in Washington that Pakistan was a looming disaster. It was harder to convince them we should do something about it.

Holbrooke understood that the White House, the Pentagon, and the CIA wanted Pakistan to cut ties with the Taliban and do more to fight terrorism. But that would never happen without at least some semblance of a normal relationship between the two countries. Holbrooke favored an iceberg metaphor: "There is an above-water part to the relationship," he would say, "and a below-water part." The part below the water was the intelligence and security cooperation that we craved, while the part above water was the aid and assistance that we gave Pakistan. This is where the iceberg metaphor broke down. With countries, unlike floating chunks of ice, making the above-water part bigger will make the whole situation more stable—at least that is what Holbrooke was arguing. In 2011, after he was gone, it simply sank to the bottom.

Already in 2009, half the American diplomatic mission in Pakistan worked on intelligence and counterterrorism rather than diplomacy or development. Our consulate in Peshawar was basically bricks shielding antennas. And it paid big dividends. The CIA collected critical intelligence in Pakistan that made possible drone strikes on al-Qaeda targets and on more than one occasion prevented a terror strike in the West. The Obama administration began carrying out drone strikes in Pakistan on an industrial scale, decimating al-Qaeda's command-and-control structure and crippling the organization.[22] Even with all the Pakistani double-dealing and foot dragging going on, there was still cooperation between the CIA and the ISI on al-Qaeda, and everything the administration claimed by way of success against al-Qaeda depended on it.[23]

But hunting terrorists was not popular in Pakistan, and drone strikes in particular angered Pakistanis. In public the authorities denied making any deal with the United States, but it was obvious to citizens that the drones flew with their knowledge and even cooperation. Pakistanis thought the drones were daily violating their country's sovereignty, showing it to be feeble and defenseless. There were wild rumors about collateral damage, civilians dying unnecessarily as drones targeted suspected terrorists. It did not matter that drones killed many terrorists, including TTP chieftain Baitullah Mehsud, the notorious jihadi who had claimed responsibility for scores of bombing attacks on civilians and was believed to have killed the popular former prime minister Benazir Bhutto in December 2007. The anger would only get worse as the number of drone attacks grew through 2009 and beyond.

The "don't ask, don't tell" policy around drones suited Pakistani leaders but had a corrosive effect on U.S.-Pakistan relations. We knew that the drone issue was a problem on TV talk shows and in Pakistan's big cities, but our hands were tied. There was a case to be made for the program—in the places where the drone strikes were actually happening, up in the FATA, they were less of a provocation. There the locals knew exactly where the missiles were landing and on whom, and the locals had no love for many of those being targeted. But drones were a deeply classified topic in the U.S. government. You could not talk about them in public, much less discuss who they were hitting and with what results. Embassy staffers took to calling drones "Voldemorts" after the villain in the Harry Potter series, Lord Voldemort, "he who must not be named."

By 2012, drones had become a potent political issue in Pakistan. The populist politician and former cricket star Imran Khan built a powerful political movement in part around protesting drone strikes, which he argued were responsible for growing extremist violence inside Pakistan. Drones then had two sets of targets: "high-value" ones, meaning known al-Qaeda leaders, and "signature targets," which meant concentrations of suspected bad guys—or what some in the Pentagon called MAMs (for "military-aged males"). Most of the controversy revolved around whether drone strikes on MAMs were really eliminating terrorists or killing civilians and producing anti-American fervor. Pakistani intelligence was able to exploit the controversy—when drones started targeting Taliban fighters in 2011, the ISI started fueling anti-drone opposition in a bid to force the United States to agree to a more limited target list.

At this time Pakistan asked repeatedly for joint ownership of the drone program, which meant we would work together on gathering intelligence (previously intelligence was gathered by the CIA and then selectively shared with Pakistan) and operating the drones. They also asked if we would sell them drones; Pakistanis would not object if drones killing terrorists had Pakistani markings on them. They also suggested we let them hit the targets given to drones with their F-16 fighter jets.

The CIA's answer every time was no. We will not sell Pakistan drones, jointly operate them, or let them use their planes to hit the same targets. The program would remain "American." And as such it would invite anti-Americanism.

We knew from early 2009 that the drone problem meant the intelligence relationship with Pakistan was headed for trouble. During my early days working with Holbrooke, when we were crafting a new Pakistan policy, one of Holbrooke's deputies asked him, "If we are going to seriously engage shouldn't we make some changes to the drone policy, perhaps back off a bit?" Holbrooke replied, "Don't even go there. Nothing is going to change." We had to build ties despite the drag the drone program had on building normal relations with Pakistan.

Holbrooke believed all along that by showing Pakistan a road map to a deeper relationship with America you could distract attention from the intelligence relationship. The key to winning over Pakistan was simply giving Pakistan more (much more) aid for longer (far longer), in order to change the dynamic of the relationship through economic engagement. If Pakistani leaders had a good story to tell their people, the CIA's job would become easier, and in time Pakistan would become vested in a different relationship with America. Average Pakistanis had to see a benefit in having a relationship with America, and in 2009 they didn't. It is easy to be angry at America if you think you don't get anything from the relationship other than drone strikes and retaliations for them in the form of devastating suicide bombings.

To counter that narrative, Holbrooke started by calling together the newly created Friends of Democratic Pakistan in an international gathering in Tokyo to help Pakistan rebuild its economy. He got $5 billion in pledges to assist Pakistan. "That is a respectable IPO," Holbrooke would brag, hoping that the opening would garner even more by way of capital investment in Pakistan's future.

Holbrooke thought that we should give Pakistan much more aid, and not just the military kind. We should do our best to be seen giving it, and to make sure that it improved the lives of everyday Pakistanis in meaningful ways. Holbrooke had gleaned these insights from talking to Pakistanis high and low. Pakistan's finance minister (and later foreign minister) Hina Rabbani Khar gave Holbrooke a tutorial on U.S. aid to

Pakistan. They met on the veranda of the magnificent Chirağan Palace Hotel in Istanbul, a former home to Ottoman sultans that was the venue for an international conference on Pakistan. Khar said to Holbrooke:

> Richard, let me tell you a few things about your aid: First, no one in Pakistan sees what you spend it on. People can point to the Chinese bridge; they cannot identify a single thing your aid has done. Second, most of the money never gets to Pakistan; it is spent in Washington. Of every dollar you say you give to Pakistan, maybe ten cents makes it to Pakistan. Finally, you never ask us what we need and what you should give aid to. So your aid does nothing for your image and does not serve your goals with Pakistan. If you want to have an impact, you have to fix that.

And that became Holbrooke's objective. American aid could make a difference if it was visible and effective. Only then would Pakistanis think that there was value to a relationship with America.

If we wanted to change Pakistan, Holbrooke thought, we had to think in terms of a Marshall Plan. After a journalist asked him whether the $5 billion in aid was not too much for Pakistan, Holbrooke answered, "Pakistan needs $50 billion, not $5 billion." The White House did not want to hear that—it meant a fight with Congress and spending political capital to convince the American people. Above all else, it required an audacious foreign policy gambit for which the Obama administration was simply not ready.

Yet in reality we were spending much more than that on Afghanistan. For every dollar we gave Pakistan in aid, we spent twenty on Afghanistan. That money did not go very far; it was like pouring water into sand. We would have been doing ourselves a big favor if we had reversed that ratio. It seems we had no problem spending money, just not on things that would actually bring about change and serve our interests. Even General Petraeus understood this. I recall him saying at a Pakistan meeting: "You get what you pay for. We have not paid much for much of anything in Pakistan."

In the end, we settled for far more modest assistance to Pakistan. The Kerry-Lugar-Berman legislation of 2009 earmarked $7.5 billion in aid to Pakistan over a five-year period—the first long-term all-civilian aid package. It was no Marshall Plan, and Congress could still refuse to fund the authorization, but it made a dent in suspicious Pakistani attitudes.

Holbrooke also believed we needed more aggressive diplomacy: America had to talk to Pakistan, frequently and not just about security issues that concern us, but also about a host of economic and social issues that they cared about. The more often American leaders met their Pakistani counterparts and the more diverse the set of issues they addressed, the more broad-based the relationship would become. And if Pakistanis saw something tangible coming out of these meetings they would warm up to closer ties with the United States. Holbrooke knew from the many hours he had spent with Pakistani leaders, academics, and journalists that they wanted to see a long-term relationship with the United States—a commitment to friendship that was not limited to the duration of our engagement in Afghanistan. It was critical for us not to peddle a so-called transactional relationship but to show interest in something more strategic.

Holbrooke convinced Secretary of State Hillary Clinton that America had to offer a strategic partnership to Pakistan, built around a Strategic Dialogue—a type of bilateral forum that America holds with a number of countries, including China and India. America would talk to Pakistan about security issues but also discuss water, energy, and social and economic issues. Holbrooke thought that Clinton was the perfect American leader to lead this effort—she had a history with Pakistan (she had traveled there as both First Lady and senator) and was well liked by Pakistanis. Clinton was also America's chief diplomat, and who better to engage in diplomacy with Pakistan than the chief?

Clinton was not ready to cut Pakistan any slack on their support for the Taliban or terrorism, but she was serious about engaging Pakistan's leaders and showing them a path out of their foreign policy quandary. She believed pressure should be combined with engagement and assistance.

In one of her first meetings with Pakistan's military and intelligence chiefs she asked them point blank to tell her what their vision was for Pakistan: "Would Pakistan become like North Korea? I am just curious, I would like to hear where you see your country going." The generals were at a loss for words. So were a group of senior journalists when, during a 2009 interview in Lahore, she pushed back against their incessant criticism of U.S. policy, saying: "I can't believe that there isn't anybody in the Pakistani government who knows where bin Laden is." She was tough. But she was just as serious about engaging Pakistanis on issues that mattered to them.

Clinton was hugely successful in capturing the attention of Pakistanis high and low. Her willingness to invest time in the relationship and engage the country's media, civil society, youth, and businessmen provided a palpable new dynamism in the troubled relationship. But the White House was not all that taken by the diplomatic effort, and would not shore it up when the actions of the military and CIA undermined it.

America's relations with Pakistan between 2009 and 2011 ran on two tracks. On the first track, the CIA and the Pentagon were leaning hard on Pakistan to give us more help that we could use against al-Qaeda and the Taliban. The CIA had one goal: protect America from another al-Qaeda attack. Pakistan remained a big worry in that regard, especially after the failed May 1, 2010, SUV-bomb plot to attack New York City's Times Square was traced back to the country. The bomber, Faisal Shahzad, was a Pakistan-born U.S. citizen who had received terror training in the FATA and had been arrested at JFK Airport while sitting on a flight bound for Islamabad. The Pentagon, for its part, had a war to win and wanted Pakistan's help to finish off the Taliban. On the other track, the State Department was slowly repairing America's damaged relations with Pakistan.

But the two tracks were not complementary. The CIA and the Pentagon decided on America's goals vis-à-vis Pakistan. These were predictably narrow in scope and all terrorism focused. The CIA and the Pentagon benefited from the positive climate that the State Department was fostering, but their constant pressure on Islamabad always threatened to break up the relationship. Whether meeting Pakistanis face-to-face or debating policy in Washington, they set a pugilistic tone for America's talks with Pakistan, but then bore no responsibility for the outcome. I remember Holbrooke shaking his head and saying, "Watch them [the CIA] ruin this relationship. And when it is ruined, they are going to say 'We told you, you can't work with Pakistan!' We never learn."

Holbrooke knew that in these circumstances, anyone advocating diplomacy would have to fight to be heard inside the White House. He tried to reach out to Obama, but his efforts were to no avail. Obama remained above the fray. The president seemed to sense that no one would fault him for taking a "tough guy" approach to Pakistan. If the approach failed (as indeed it did), the nefarious, double-dealing Pakistanis would get the blame (as indeed they did).

After Abbottabad, Washington was in no mood to soft-pedal what it saw as Pakistani duplicity. Pressure started to build on Pakistan. Gone were promises of aid and assistance, strategic partnership, and deep and long-lasting ties. The Pentagon and the CIA now came clean to say they did not want relations with Pakistan, just Pakistan's cooperation. The administration threatened to cut aid and shamed and embarrassed Pakistan through public criticisms and media leaks. Some of the leaks retold familiar tales of Pakistan being reluctant to cooperate in fighting terrorism or undermining the American pursuit of al-Qaeda outright; others revealed dark truths about how Pakistani intelligence had manipulated public opinion and even gone so far as to silence journalists permanently.

Pakistan's top brass understood this line of attack to be directed at weakening them and driving a wedge between the military and the Pakistani public. Perhaps, the generals thought, it was even meant to rally the media and pro-democracy forces that had brought down Musharraf to the idea of challenging the military's grip on power once again—essentially promoting regime change. Kayani and his fellow corps commanders thought that, having sensed weakness in the wake of the humiliating bin Laden raid, America was going for the military's jugular. Once close, the Pakistani and U.S. militaries were now in a clearly adversarial relationship.

The charges that Admiral Mullen made in his September 2011 Senate testimony sent a clear message: We're taking off the kid gloves when dealing with Pakistan.[24] It is time to treat it like any enemy and find ways to contain its most dangerous forms of waywardness.[25] It was common for White House meetings on Pakistan to turn into litanies of complaints as senior officials competed for colorful adjectives to capture how back-stabbing and distrustful they thought Pakistani leaders to be. The most frequently stated sentiment was "We have had it with these guys."

But a policy of containment has a high price. It means that U.S. troops will have to stay in Afghanistan less to fight the Taliban than to keep an eye on Pakistan. That would be nothing short of failure in our regional strategy. In the end, all we will have achieved is to entrench American military presence in the region.

After Holbrooke died, the White House kept Clinton and the State Department at bay over AfPak policy. But their attention to Pakistan was intermittent; the country bobbed onto the White House radar screen every time there was a crisis, but otherwise the relationship was left to founder.

The public campaign against Pakistan proved self-defeating. Openly shamed, the generals turned defensive. Accustomed to thinking of themselves as both the shield and cement of the nation, they feared that America had made it a matter of settled purpose to undo them, so they banished any thought of cooperation and curled up like khaki-clad hedgehogs.

As I have noted, Osama bin Laden was hiding in Abbottabad in circumstances that make it difficult not to accuse Pakistan's military of sheltering him;[26] but we would not have found him and many other militants who were targets of drone attacks in Pakistan were it not for stepped-up Pakistani cooperation on intelligence collection and for their letting CIA operatives into Pakistan.[27] Pakistanis did not want to issue as many visas to potential CIA operatives as they did, but given the upward trajectory of U.S.-Pakistan relations in 2009 and 2010, they felt compelled to do it.

I lost count of how many times Holbrooke told Pakistani officials, "How could you deny our people visas when we are doing so well in our Strategic Dialogue?" It worked every time. I am sure the Pakistani military later rued the degree of cooperation it extended, but Holbrooke was right: You get more out of Pakistan if there is a positive trajectory to the relationship. Pakistan wasn't giving us all we wanted, but we were getting something, and even if it was not optimal, it was not trivial either. When we replaced promises of partnership and assistance with raw pressure, we found that the little bit of cooperation we were taking for granted soon went away.

After the relationship fell apart in 2011, many in the administration and the media put the blame on Pakistan. They said it was Pakistan that decided to blow up the relationship, beginning with the way it reacted to the Raymond Davis affair. But the reason Pakistan acted as it did was because our policy of complementing pressure with engagement and aid had been successful in getting out of them more than they had been willing to give. It was a mistake on the part of the administration to respond to Pakistan's reaction by abandoning a policy that was working. We should have doubled down on what had worked.

In July 2011, National Security Adviser Tom Donilon asked Senator Kerry to talk to General Kayani and see if he would put U.S.-Pakistan relations back on track. The senator and the army chief agreed to a secret meeting in Abu Dhabi, and the two men met for nineteen hours over two days. It was the most substantive and thoroughgoing conversation America had had with Pakistan in some time. Kayani and Kerry worked together to put Kayani's thoughts into a white paper for Obama, which Kerry brought back with him to Washington.

Kayani thought the two-day exercise would get the White House engaged in a meaningful strategic discussion that could clear the air, repair the relationship, and chart a course forward. It was an effort on both sides to dial back the relationship to its more productive phase in 2009–2011. Kerry was carrying on where Holbrooke had left off.

The nineteen-hour meeting and the white paper did not elicit an immediate response from Washington. But three months later, in October, Tom Donilon, Marc Grossman, and the White House's AfPak point man, General Lute, went back to Abu Dhabi to meet Kayani. Relations had not improved, and Donilon wanted to smooth things over with Pakistan. Kayani in turn was hoping to hear a response to his paper and more on America's vision for the region—what was the strategy?

The follow-up meeting was much shorter, and soon it became clear Donilon had one agenda: reading Pakistan the riot act for its support of the Haqqani network. Donilon made no reference to Kayani's paper or the road map he and Kerry had explored. Instead he presented Kayani with a laundry list of Pakistani misdeeds, backed with intelligence evidence. Pakistan was advised to close up shop in Afghanistan, abandon its strategic goals, and liquidate the Taliban or else. All we cared about was mop-up operations in Afghanistan, and we expected Pakistan to cooperate.

In his colorful blow-by-blow account of the meeting between Donilon and Kayani (which shocked Kayani when it appeared in print—he declined a follow-up meeting with senior White House officials), David Sanger of the *New York Times* muses that all Kayani did in the five-and-a-half-hour meeting was to blow the "refined smoke of his Dunhills" into the faces of his American interlocutors.[28] But that was perhaps because the general was flummoxed by the fact that the Kerry mission had come to naught. And he could have been thinking as well, "If you are leaving Afghanistan, then I may need the Haqqani network even more. And you are forgetting that you need my roads to get out."

In the months that followed, Washington's pressure-only policy threw relations into a downward spiral that put us at great risk. America quickly learned that Pakistan could be even less cooperative, and to our surprise, we could not live with that. A policy of worsening relations to improve them—getting more out of Pakistan by giving less—was a nonstarter. Pakistan did not reward coercion with cooperation. On the contrary, Islamabad started shutting down supply routes, cut back intelligence cooperation, and finally in March 2012 demanded a "reset" in relations with Washington, beginning with a shutdown of the U.S. drone program (although that did not happen). The headaches this meant for our effort in landlocked Afghanistan were obvious. If Pakistan cooperated less, then the president's claims of success to date and his hope to wind up the war by 2014 would both be in jeopardy. When Obama declared that the situation in Afghanistan had improved enough for American troops to start heading home, he was assuming that Pakistan would continue the level of cooperation it had given America during his first two years in office. Otherwise, violence might spike and put U.S. troop-withdrawal plans in doubt.

The nadir of relations was finally reached with the Salala incident. On November 26, 2011, U.S. forces were serving as backup to the Afghan army in hot pursuit of Taliban fighters near the Pakistani border posts in Salala on the Afghanistan-Pakistan frontier. At some point in the firefight Pakistani soldiers joined in and started shooting at American and Afghan troops. American helicopters and fighter jets responded, pounding the Pakistani posts and killing twenty-four Pakistani soldiers.

An American investigation revealed that Pakistani soldiers knowingly shot at American troops. Pakistan claimed that American troops had not followed proper procedure and had failed to notify them that Afghan ground troops with U.S. fire support were in the area. Thus when suspected Taliban forces in the area started taking fire from Afghan and NATO forces, Pakistani soldiers responded thinking the Taliban or Afghan soldiers were shooting at them. At that point, American firepower punished them mercilessly for hours—Pakistanis claim that even after American commanders learned they were shooting at Pakistanis, they did not stop.

The use of firepower sent a powerful signal that U.S.-led NATO forces operating on the Afghanistan-Pakistan frontier could be a direct military threat to Pakistan. The Pakistanis took the episode to mean, in effect, "This is how it's going be from now on. We will come at you backing Afghan forces."

It was the last straw. The Pakistani public was incensed, and the one-sided firefight once again left the Pakistan military feeling humiliated by what looked like another American violation of their sovereignty. Pakistan demanded a formal apology. None was forthcoming. The attitude in the Pentagon was that the Pakistanis got what they deserved for supporting Taliban fighters, and they had better be prepared for more of the same. For his part, Obama worried that offering an apology would give his Republican opponents an excuse to accuse him of "apologizing for America" and to a country that the administration itself had painted as hostile to American interests. The White House made a decision: no apology. To make that crystal clear one senior official told Pakistan's ambassador, "We will never apologize; it will never happen. Get over it."

Still, to cool tempers America had to suspend drone strikes for a good two months. The unfortunate bottom line was that a show of force along the Durand Line had led to less rather than more terrorist fighting, and Washington was worried that the lull in drone strikes was giving al-Qaeda dangerous room to regroup.[29] So shortly after New Year's 2012, a bevy of worried American officials got on the phone with their Pakistani counterparts. The calls were menacing and the message was simple: "The United States reserved the right to attack anyone who it determined posed a direct threat to U.S. national security anywhere in the world."[30] This was the administration's counterterrorism "red line" and it meant that America was done with the drone cease-fire and wanted Pakistan to permit new attacks. In the past, Pakistanis would have grumbled but acceded to American requests. This time they refused to back down. The drones resumed flying over Pakistan and shooting missiles at targets, but Pakistan now was openly opposed to the program and getting closer to enforcing their objection.

I remember meeting high-ranking members of the administration right after those calls. Everyone asked, as if it had been a topic of discussion in the Situation Room, "What is our leverage with Pakistan?" I did not need to think hard to answer that one. "None," I responded. We had worked hard at not having much leverage. We had cut back our aid and all but ended the programs that were meant to build bilateral ties, and we had taken off the table the promise of a long-term strategic relationship. We had assumed that threats and pressure would do what aid and diplomacy had achieved in the past. America's strategy with Pakistan was not "three cups of tea," but "three bangs on the table." The Pakistani view was that you cannot threaten to take away a relationship that is not there—and threats of military action against Pakistan were just not credible, not when we were barely keeping our head above water in Afghanistan and, what's more, had declared loud and clear that we were on our way out.

In return, I asked those who wondered about our leverage, "What do you think is Pakistan's leverage on us?" Several levers came to my mind: We relied on Pakistan to supply our troops in Afghanistan with everything from fuel to drinking water; we needed Pakistan's cooperation to gather the intelligence necessary to make drone strikes effective; and above all we needed Pakistan to make our Afghanistan strategy work. Given these dependencies, we had done ourselves a disservice by taking an ax to the relationship. Bullying wasn't going to pay.

With no apology forthcoming the situation got tenser. Pakistan closed its border to trucks carrying supplies for American troops in Afghanistan, threatened to openly break with America on intelligence cooperation, and shunned international conferences on the future of Afghanistan. The relationship was in tatters.

With the Pakistan border closed, the U.S. military was paying an additional $100 million a month to supply its troops in Afghanistan (by May 2012 the total cost was close to $700 million). Without Pakistani roads, the U.S. military would not be able to get its heavy equipment out of Afghanistan on time or on budget once the time came to leave. If Pakistan remained off-limits, the United States would have to rethink its entire exit strategy from Afghanistan. Another arrow in Pakistan's quiver was that it could also close its airspace to U.S. planes flying between the Persian Gulf and Afghanistan. The next escalation in this conflict would put the United States, not Pakistan, in the pincer.

Clinton all along thought we should say "Sorry" and move on. Now, as months had passed, Clinton told the White House that enough was enough; she was taking charge. She gave a simple direction to her top deputy at the State Department, Tom Nides: "I want you to fix this." Nides flew to Islamabad to negotiate with General Kayani a tepid U.S. apology in exchange for Pakistan opening the border—and hence preventing the relationship from going over the cliff.

The White House acquiesced to Clinton salvaging the relationship. Not only had their Pakistan policy failed, but Obama also realized that Putin was the main beneficiary of Pakistan's spat with Washington. The alternatives to Pakistan's supply routes were Central Asian and Russian land and air routes, which gave Putin leverage. Obama decided he preferred apologizing to Pakistan to depending on Putin. It was a critical realization for the White House that the real menace to America comes not from states like Pakistan but powers like Russia. But the relationship is not out of the woods yet. Pakistan is still intent on protecting its ties to the Haqqani network and the Taliban—looking past America to protecting its position in the future Afghanistan. The relationship may still give way to more confrontation.

Seldom has the loss of one statesman proved as consequential as the death of Richard Holbrooke. Without his wisdom and experience, America's Pakistan policy went off the rails and there will be long-run costs. What happens to Pakistan will always matter to America for several reasons, not least among them the presence of nuclear weapons. We should want more and not less influence in Pakistan, and Pakistan's stability is not the only factor. There is also the matter of China.

When the Obama administration came to power, there was a genuine sense that Pakistan was on the edge of national collapse. That is much less the case today. But as our relations with the country soured, the business community and affluent middle classes started to write off America. The anger at American hubris became much easier to afford as burgeoning trade with China started to make up for reduced business with America. Fewer American businesses deal with Pakistan, but hotels in Islamabad or Lahore are filled with Chinese businessmen carrying on a brisk trade in commodities, manufacturing, and even software services.

The Chinese option buffers Pakistan from U.S. pressure, but in the long run it will also chart a different future for Pakistan. Beijing is unhappy over America's strategic partnership with India, and especially dislikes the jewel in that partnership's crown: the civilian nuclear deal struck by George W. Bush that will upgrade India's nuclear capabilities. There is even more consternation in Beijing at the idea of a U.S.-Indian effort to contain and countervail China's growing influence in Asia and the Indian Ocean region.

In this great-power rivalry, Pakistan is a strategic asset to China— a thorn in India's side, a useful balancer that occupies many of India's military and diplomatic resources and distracts India from focusing on China. By effectively conceding Pakistan to China, we have set ourselves back in the far more important rivalry with Beijing.

And Pakistan is not out of the woods. American pressure of late has in particular targeted the Pakistani military. We have always drawn a distinction between the civilian government and the military in Pakistan. There have been times when civilian politicians irked us and we saw our salvation in the military. It used to be that we relied on the military to get things done and keep the place going. We faulted the generals' authoritarian tendencies, but it had become the custom in Washington to pinch our nostrils with one hand and bless the soldiers' political meddling with the other. Otherwise Pakistan would surely sink under rising tides of corruption, misrule, and violent conflict. We did not like the military's rattling of sabers at India, but thought that the men in khaki alone could safeguard the country's nuclear arsenal, keep jihadis at bay, and help the West against the threat of extremism. The Pakistani military created problems and seemed to be the only solution to them at the same time. It was nice work if you could get it.

Humiliating and weakening a military that is choking democracy is not a bad thing. That is the only way to change the balance of power in favor of civilians and give democracy a chance. But Pakistan is not Spain or Argentina. The combination of ethnic tensions, extremist revolt, a sagging economy, and political gridlock with a war next door and no real institutional alternatives means that weakening Pakistan's military could mean opening the door to the unknown. It is possible to envisage the gradual growth of democracy as the military's control over politics fades—Turkey has seen a process of this sort unfold over the past two decades. But that delicate transition needs stability, time, and positive U.S. involvement. None of these are at hand in Pakistan. Whatever its shortcomings, the military remains the one functioning institution in Pakistan—the skeleton that keeps its state upright. One may well ask whether in the haste to get "deliverables" on short-run "asks" Washington was now jumping from the frying pan into the fire, jeopardizing Pakistan to America's own detriment. America's pressure strategy is just as likely to produce the Pakistan of our worst nightmares as it is to bend the country's will to our counterterrorism demands. A Pakistan that bends is likely to be a weaker and more vulnerable state, a larger, more dangerous South Asian Yemen.

Much eludes America in its singular focus on drones and the Taliban.

Pakistan is a democracy with a vibrant civil society, a rambunctious free press, an independent judiciary, and a sizable middle class and private sector that are eroding the military's grip on power, deepening democracy, and pushing for economic ties with India. But to get to a better place Pakistan needs stability and support—which, again, are not on the American agenda right now.

There is also much to worry about in Pakistan. The country suffers from severe electricity shortages. It is now common for large urban centers like Lahore to go without electricity for as long as sixteen hours. Factories shut down, workers are sent home, and in sweltering summer heat tempers flare in the form of protests, riots, and street clashes. What is happening with electricity today will happen with water tomorrow. The hopelessly outdated irrigation system leaks water to no end, and rapid population growth is straining the water supply—which is bound to dwindle as the glaciers melt away.

Urban violence involving criminal gangs and ethnic mafias is on the rise—Karachi's constant gun battles, assassinations, and street violence bring to mind drug turf battles in Colombia and Mexico, but mixed with ethnic clashes of the sort seen once in Bosnia or Northern Ireland.

Entire populations want out. The Baluch are engaged in a war of liberation, and a bevy of other ethnic groups want recognition, special treatment, and, when possible, their own provinces. The military has kept separatism in check, but for how long and at what price?

The gap between the rich and poor is widening, not just in terms of wealth but also education, health, and access to social services. Pakistan's massive middle class is as large as 30 million people—a mid-sized country in its own right—surrounded by five times as many poor slum dwellers and peasants. There is not enough economic growth to improve the lives of those at the bottom rung of the ladder, and even many in the middle class may lose their footing and slide down into economic trouble.

Some think economic pressure of this sort could produce a "Pakistan Spring." But Pakistan had its spring in 2008 when its lawyers, media, students, and civil society joined hands to send General Musharraf packing. If there is another big nationwide protest movement, it is likely to be anti-drone and anti-American—the Pakistani equivalent of the Arab demand for dignity seems to be directed at Washington.

From the 1950s, when Pakistan had been counted as an important part of the so-called Northern Tier—allies upon whom America could rely to contain Soviet influence in West Asia—the U.S. and Pakistani militaries enjoyed close ties. The Pentagon thought of Pakistan's military as an important asset in a troubled region. The Afghan war against the invading Russians brought the two militaries even closer together. After that war, the State Department thought of putting Pakistan on its list of state terror sponsors and of sanctioning it for A. Q. Khan's nuclear program. But the Pentagon intervened, arranging for Pakistani troops to lend a hand with UN peacekeeping in Somalia, where Pakistan's Frontier Force Regiment lost twenty-four men in a battle against local clan militias in June 1993 and helped rescue U.S. troops in the Black Hawk Down incident in Mogadishu that October. State Department plans to spank Islamabad were shelved. During Musharraf's presidency, it was again the Pentagon that lobbied the president hard to view Pakistan in the best light, as a staunch ally in the war on terror.

In the past two years, that pillar of U.S.-Pakistan relations has come crashing down. The Pakistani military has started to view America not as an ally but as a threat. In March 2012, America put a bounty on the head of the Punjabi terrorist Hafiz Saeed, who masterminded the Mumbai attacks that killed 164 people over four days in late November 2008. It was high time that America pressured Pakistan to stop supporting anti-Indian terrorists, but America chose to do this long after the attack on Mumbai and as another signal of getting tough with Pakistan. In Islamabad, this was seen as a significant expansion of America's war on terror into Pakistan proper. The United States and Pakistan had their disagreements, but Pakistan's military had never before seen America as a country to be on guard against. Did the U.S. military now think a war with Pakistan might be in the offing? Pakistan was not ruling it out.

Nothing symbolized this dismal turn of events better than Admiral Mullen's testimony. Mullen had been friendly with General Kayani. Their personal rapport had symbolized the close historical ties between the Pentagon and the GHQ (Pakistan's military headquarters in Rawalpindi). The personal friendship was over, and so were the strategic ties between the two militaries.

In time we will ask, "Who lost Pakistan?" We will also have to ask why. Holbrooke understood that Pakistan would change its foreign policy only if something more than America's immediate counter-terrorism needs bound us together. But after the U.S.-Pakistan Strategic Dialogue finally got going, Holbrooke passed away and, following the first crisis of 2011, Washington quickly froze the talks. Holbrooke's successor, Marc Grossman, told an incredulous Pakistani press that America was looking for a "transactional relationship." We have no common interests, he told his Pakistani counterparts, just common objectives. The Pakistanis read that as code for "American objectives, which Pakistan is expected to fulfill."

Pakistan was always going to be a hard case, a difficult problem. My point is that we made it harder than it had to be. We failed when it came to strategic vision and imagination, and we failed in our commitment to diplomacy. We further destabilized the world's so-called most dangerous place—in effect compounding our own headaches. We have less influence in Pakistan in 2012 after a year of confrontation than we had in 2011 after two years of friendship. We acted as if we could walk away from Pakistan—which of course we cannot and will not do, and they knew it all along. Ours was not just an empty bluff, it was worse than that—it was folly we believed in and crafted our policy on, and all Pakistan had to do was wait for reality to set in.

We could have managed Pakistan better. We did not have to break the relationship and put Pakistan's stability at risk. That course of action has not gotten us any further than the more prudent course of greater engagement—in fact, it's gotten us a lot less. We have not realized our immediate security goals there and have put our long-run strategic interests in jeopardy. Pakistan is a failure of American policy, a failure of the sort that comes from the president handing foreign policy over to the Pentagon and the intelligence agencies.

IRAN

Between War and Containment

Looking back at how President Lyndon B. Johnson's administration decided to "Americanize" the Vietnam War by using air power against the North Vietnamese, Johnson's national security adviser McGeorge Bundy reflected on what had surprised him most about that war. "The endurance of the enemy," he concluded. His belief in the persuasive power of coercion had blinded him to the possibility that the North Vietnamese could withstand the full brunt of American military power. This failure of imagination, widespread throughout Johnson's team, was singularly responsible for the calamity that followed.[1] The road to foreign policy disasters is paved with false assumptions that, when repeated enough in America's closed-circuit foreign policy discussions, can take on the quality of self-evident truths.

His worst mistakes, thought Bundy long after the last U.S. helicopter had left Saigon, were never asking what the North Vietnamese would absolutely refuse to give up and failing "to examine what could be done to make the best of a bad business while not escalating."[2] War in the end had not been the best option, and not exploring other possibilities had proved America's undoing.

Decades after Vietnam, the George W. Bush administration repeated these mistakes in Iraq. There, too, a set of false assumptions, intelligence blunders, and overblown claims about Iraq's nuclear and chemical-weapons capabilities led us into a futile and costly war. In Iraq, we discovered that we could create giants out of straw men and become prisoners of scary images we drew ourselves. This sort of bogeyman foreign policy has not served us well—we will still be counting the cost of the Iraq war long into the future.

McGeorge Bundy's ruminations were popular reading at the White House in early 2009. Everyone, President Obama included, seemed to be studying this cautionary tale in order to avert a similar disaster in Afghanistan.[3] But Bundy's warning was just as relevant to the fog of another conflict, the one with the other American bugbear, Iran. That was apparently lost on the administration.

America's approach to Iran's nuclear challenge over the past decade has reprised too much of what led up to our two recent ill-fated wars. Exaggerated descriptions of the threat, false assumptions, and overly narrow reasoning have been resounding through the foreign policy punditry's echo chamber.

It is taken for granted that Iran's nuclear program is a national and global security concern—especially in light of that country's fairly advanced missile-delivery system—and an existential threat to Israel, an unacceptable strategic game changer that will destabilize the Middle East by eventually placing nuclear material in the hands of terrorists or leading to a regional nuclear arms race and more broadly endangering world peace by fueling nuclear proliferation. In short, Iranian nukes are a red line that must not be crossed. America will "not countenance" Iran getting nuclear weapons, said President Obama as he insisted that an American policy of pressure and coercion would ensure that that would not be the case.[4] Bending Iran's will thus became a key test of U.S. power and effectiveness, in American minds as well as those of friends and foes alike. This approach came with a large downside risk, however, for it committed America to a path of increasing pressure, backed by military threats, to realize what was from the outset an improbable goal.

Those who thought that perhaps the Iranian nuclear threat was not all it was made out to be, or who assumed that Iran could be talked out of its nuclear program, were viewed as no different from the "doves" of 1965, those who "labored under the weakened argument predicated on the 'fancifully hopeful' expectation that there existed a negotiated diplomatic settlement that could end the war in Vietnam and achieve a grand compromise with communist power."[5] As one veteran diplomat told me, "all this chest-beating on Iran" feels like Vietnam. "There is only one line of argument; anyone suggesting something different is dismissed as a 'wimp.' "

But unlike Johnson, Obama was not looking for war. In fact, he assumed that the Iran problem could be managed without resort to military action. When war talk rose in Washington in the spring of 2012, Obama pushed back, challenging his Republican critics and making the case to the American people that the nation did not need war at this time. That was a bold and deft maneuver.[6]

Yet Obama's own assumptions about resolving the crisis, which favored all manner of pressure short of war, were flawed from the outset. His administration succumbed to exaggerated Israeli and Arab fears of Iran and exaggerated promises of Arab support for American action against Iran. He did not pursue rigorous diplomacy and chose to rely on pressure alone, and so inevitably led America back to where it had been in 1965—on the slippery slope to war. The only alternative left would be to accept a nuclear Iran and adopt a strategy of containment to deal with it—which Obama promised he would not do. Over the course of his presidency, Obama's position on Iran steadily moved to the right, its assumptions and strategy hardly distinguishable from those of the Bush White House. By 2012, Obama was compelled to run from a huge boulder he himself had started rolling downhill—trying to rescue American foreign policy from the path to confrontation upon which he had set it.

The United States and Iran have been at loggerheads since an Islamic revolution toppled the pro-American Pahlavi monarchy in 1979. Many contentious issues and a plethora of clashes and recriminations have divided the onetime allies, but the plain truth is that anti-Americanism is embedded in the ideological fabric of the Islamic Republic. Iran is the last bastion of a sort of anti-imperialist Third Worldism that was once ubiquitous outside the West; its dictatorship sees power and glory in resistance, sheathing old-line anti-West nationalism in a thin veneer of Islamic extremism.

For much of the past three decades, America has largely ignored Iran. A hostile stalemate has reigned, with both sides happy to eschew formal ties and meaningful relations. Despite Iran's truculent stance—menacing its neighbors and posturing against the international order—Washington has contemplated neither engagement nor military action. Washington has contained Iran when necessary, otherwise leaving it to stew in its own resentments as U.S. policy makers wait for the day when the rash Shia theocracy, burdened by a raft of internal inconsistencies, crumbles in the face of popular discontent.

But Iran has always been hard to ignore. Its geostrategic location, vast oil and gas reserves, and significant influence on public opinion in the Muslim world, and especially the Shia part of it, all conspire against America being able to act as though the Islamic Republic does not exist. And if that were not enough, Iran has been a menace to its neighbors and a disrupter (along with its Syrian, Lebanese, and Palestinian allies) of Middle Eastern stability. Iran has continuously dabbled in terrorism. Its elite military intelligence unit, the Revolutionary Guards' Quds Brigade, enjoys an almost mythic reputation as the dark force behind all manner of rebellions and extremist attacks across the region. In Iraq, it waged a brazen campaign of violence against American forces, a veritable war, in General Petraeus's estimation.[7] Tehran has also—much to Washington's as well as its Arab neighbors' quiet annoyance—encouraged Palestinians to continue pushing back against Israel and refusing to make peace. Beyond encouragement, Iran has given radical Palestinian factions substantial material support.

Iran's rulers seem bent on maintaining their regime's revolutionary vigor. To that end, they are wedded to anti-Americanism. In a region where angst about the long historical decline of the once-glorious Muslim civilization cuts deep, defiance of the West and vows to reverse the writ of history have a certain appeal. And herein lies the big difference between Iran and its economically successful and diplomatically astute Muslim neighbor, Turkey. Turkey looks to a robust GDP to satiate its longing for international influence, Iran to anti-Westernism backed by nuclear capability. The ruling Turkish party grew out of a similar yearning to make political Islam ascendant but now sees power and glory in joining, and doing well in, the world order and the global economy.

Iran has decided to make its mark in a region that sets great store by muscular shows of power through a strategy of defying America and challenging Israel. For generations now, toughness against Israel has been the mark of power in the Middle East. There is deep sympathy for Palestinians across the Muslim world, but its relative intensity from country to country tells of a different dynamic at play: The Palestinian drama has become something of a gladiator game for reigning and aspiring regional players, one in which Iran has done exceedingly well. But with Islamism (seasoned with anti-Americanism) washing over the Arab world, the returns on anti-Israeli posturing will likely diminish.

It seems as if Iran will not or cannot get past the 1979 revolution. It is determined to keep alive the reign of rigid ideology the world thought had died when jubilant Germans tore down the Berlin Wall. Iran basks in the image of the outsider challenging the status quo, the inconvenient spoiler that keeps the region on the edge. In the parlance of international relations "realism," Iran is the epitome of an "insurgent" regional power arranged against the "status quo" forces in its vicinity.

In 2003, when America was getting ready to topple an Arab nationalist dictatorship in Iraq, there were those who thought that the battle for liberal values in the region would be won only when the theocracy in Iran was laid low as well. After all, it was in Iran that Islamic fundamentalism first rose to challenge the West; that challenge would end only when the Islamic Republic ended too. The disastrous Iraq war tempered enthusiasm for carrying the fight to Iran. But Iran's leaders fully understand that their country is a trough in the otherwise ever-flattening world of growing democratic expectations, global trade, and liberal international institutions. Iran's leaders know in their bones that their system of government and view of the world are anomalies in a global order that reflects the American imagination far more than it does their own. The world cannot, in the long run, tolerate troughs. A confrontation is inevitable. As Henry Kissinger put it, Iran will have to decide "whether it is a nation or a cause."[8]

But Iran refuses to decide. One reason Iran covets nuclear capability is that it will allow it to retain this in-between position. A nuclear shield will mean neither war nor peace. America will never go to war with a nuclear Iran to remove this last remnant of yesteryear's ideological defiance and disruptive revolutionary activism. In turn, Iran will not have to make peace with America, compromise on its ideology, and come in from the cold to avert war or isolation.

In the last decade U.S.-Iran relations have gone from a high point of cooperation on the war in Afghanistan to today's low point of incessant talk of incipient war. In late 2001, Iranian diplomats and even some in the Revolutionary Guards made the case for cooperating with the United States in toppling the Taliban and bringing a new political order to Afghanistan. Supreme Leader Khamenei conceded, and Iran offered air bases, search-and-rescue missions for downed American pilots, help in tracking and killing al-Qaeda leaders, and assistance in building ties with the anti-Taliban Northern Alliance.[9] As we have seen, Iran was also an important reason for the success of the Bonn Conference that was convened in 2001 to decide Afghanistan's future. When the dickering over who would get what ministry in the new Afghan government hit a dead end, it was Iran's ambassador to the UN, Javad Zarif, who saved the day, persuading Yunus Qanuni, the head of the Afghan delegation, to compromise.[10]

Still, even then Khamenei told his diplomats and military commanders that they should approach cooperation with the United States with eyes wide open. A stable Afghanistan no longer under Taliban rule would be good for Iran, but they should not see cooperation with the United States as a stepping-stone to better relations. "America will not embrace a cooperative Iran with open arms," he warned them. "America is also not ready to talk to Iran about regional security issues because that would mean recognizing Iran's role in the region. In short, America is not ready to accept and live with the Iranian revolution."[11] Khamenei should have added that the Iranian revolution was not ready or willing to live with American influence in the Middle East either. Iran's continued support for terrorism and constant challenging of U.S.-backed policies across the region could not be read any other way.

So the close cooperation in toppling the Taliban and putting Karzai in its place proved to be of no great consequence. Shortly thereafter, the Bush administration let it be known what it really thought of Iran by including it in its exclusive "Axis of Evil." And just in case there was a misunderstanding and the Axis of Evil designation was not Washington's final word, in 2003 Iran offered comprehensive negotiations on all outstanding issues between the two countries, only to be decisively rejected. Iran even put in writing that it was prepared to discuss an end to its support for radical Palestinian groups, having Hezbollah lay down its weapons, signing on to Saudi Arabia's 2002 plan for a comprehensive peace between Israel and the Arab states, cooperating in fighting al-Qaeda and building a new state in Iraq, and finally, signing the Additional Protocol to the Nuclear Non-Proliferation Treaty.

Iran may have hoped that the momentum Bonn had created for improved relations would continue, or perhaps Iran was frightened by America's determination to bring about regime change through force of arms in neighboring Iraq. Either way, Tehran seemed to be doing something that it had never done before—reach out to America with the offer of a breakthrough in relations.

The Supreme Leader gave his blessing to this ambitious offer, but with a caveat. Khamenei told Iran's reformist president Mohammad Khatami, "I am not going to object to your plan, but mark my words: America will not agree to this offer. They will see it as a sign of our weakness."[12] He was right. The Bush administration saw no value in the offer, never replied to it, and admonished the Swiss government for even bringing it to Washington.

Administration hawks calculated that Iran was weak and vulnerable. Why throw it a lifeline by talking to it? But they misjudged the situation. As Iraq turned into a quagmire, the balance of power shifted; Iran grew stronger and, rebuffed by America, took its offer off the table.

Iraq did not turn out as America had expected. Quick victory proved to be a mirage, and America found itself facing an insurgency and escalating violence bordering on full-fledged civil war. And Iran had a hand in that, supporting radical Shia factions who resorted to violence to end the American presence in Iraq. Meanwhile, Washington's expectation that regime change in Iraq would undo clerical rule in Iran proved untrue. With its economic and political influence spreading in Baghdad and across the Iraqi south, Iran actually looked to be the winner in the Iraq war.[13] That provided another opening for talks.

Senior Iraqi Shia leader Abdul Aziz Hakim, who had close ties with Khamenei, made common cause with influential Iranian conservative leader Ali Larijani for the purpose of getting Tehran to talk to the United States about Iraq. Khamenei agreed, and the Iranians approached Iraq's president Jalal Talabani to carry a message to the Americans in Baghdad. He came back from a trip to Iran with the news that Tehran "was ready for an understanding with America from Afghanistan to Lebanon. They are ready for discussions in order to reach results that please both sides."[14] But the talks never happened. By one account, the United States scuttled the meeting shortly before it was supposed to take place because Iran was sending Larijani and Revolutionary Guard commander Yahya Rahim-Safavi—the United States was then angry over Iran's deadly support for Shia militias, but also Washington did not want to deal with Iran seriously and at the highest level. In the end, American and Iranian ambassadors met in Baghdad but never got beyond reading aloud charge sheets in which each side lamented the other's bad behavior.

Iran has since become a growing headache for American policy makers. At issue is Iran's ever-expanding nuclear program, which first came into public view in 2003. Washington might have turned down two offers to negotiate a grand bargain, but it would certainly like to see an end to the nuclear program. Iran, however, sees no value in giving up the program without resolving all outstanding issues between the two countries. As former Revolutionary Guard commander Mohsen Rezaie has put it, "Either talks resolve all outstanding issues between the U.S. and Iran or there is no point in talking at all." Iranian leaders have come to believe that what the United States wants is not just an end to their nuclear program, but an end to their regime. There is plenty of truth in that.

With mutual suspicion so high, it should not be surprising that Iran's nuclear program has unfolded like a game of cat and mouse. As Muhammad Javad Larijani, a senior adviser to Khamenei, put it, "America will never let Iran into the nuclear club through the front door, so we will have to jump over the wall."[15] And that is pretty much what Iran has been doing: confounding diplomats and inspectors while building its program inside hidden sites, spread around the country and fortified to withstand military strikes.

Iran has all along claimed that it does not want nuclear weapons. Khamenei is on record saying in 1995 that "from an intellectual, ideological and *fiqhi* (religious law) perspective, the Islamic Republic of Iran considers the possession of nuclear weapons as a big sin and it believes that stockpiling such weapons is futile, harmful and dangerous."[16]

Iran says that its nuclear program is intended for peaceful purposes. It wants nuclear power, the regime insists, in order to address its growing electricity needs. That is why the Shah first invested in a civilian Iranian nuclear program in the 1970s—he wanted Iran to be the world's fifth-largest economy by the turn of the millennium. It was he who created nuclear research facilities in Iran's universities, built the Tehran Research Reactor, and started the construction of Iran's only nuclear power plant in the southern city of Bushehr on the Persian Gulf. He also ordered another two dozen reactors from Canada and France and sent dozens of students to study nuclear physics at places like MIT in the United States or Imperial College in England. Many of these foreign-trained students now run Iran's nuclear program.

Iran's rulers have similarly told their populace that by mastering nuclear technology, Iran can leap to the head of the development pack. The atom, they claim, can do for Iran what software has done for India. Ali Larijani told a 2007 gathering I attended in Dubai that the key technologies for emerging economies are 1) nanotechnology, 2) biotechnology, and 3) nuclear technology. Iran, he went on, has settled on number three to win its future. By denying Iran nuclear technology, argue the country's leaders, the West wants to keep Iran backward and subservient.[17] Going nuclear is a matter of claiming equal rights to progress—an issue of what Iranians routinely call "international technology democracy."

There is an overlay of Third Worldist rhetoric in the way Iranian leaders talk about their nuclear program and the U.S. opposition to it. An Indian diplomat told me, "there is a spirit of Bandung [the Indonesian city where the non-aligned movement of Third World countries was born in 1955] at play in Iran's conversation . . . they tell us 'today it is us, tomorrow it will be you.' "

This line of argument plays well on the street in Iran, but there are also clear strategic reasons why Iran wants nuclear technology and perhaps the potential to build a nuclear arsenal. The Shah thought Iran would need nuclear know-how—just short of an arsenal—in order to emerge as a great power and assert hegemony over its neighborhood. Iran's rulers today may rail against the Shah, but they have bought into his ambitions lock, stock, and barrel. The theocracy's current vision of grandeur, of a nuclear Persia reigning unimpeded from the Volga to the Tigris, with the Persian Gulf as an Iranian lake, is, ironically, the Shah's vision.[18] Nuclear capability then, as now, was a passport into the global elite. The main difference between the Shah and the ayatollahs who toppled him is that the Shah was a lot better at the game of pushing toward this ambition. He skillfully used the Cold War to persuade the West to recognize Iran's strategically supreme position in the Persian Gulf, and to give him all the nuclear technology and expertise he could buy with Iran's considerable oil wealth.

Iran's desire for a nuclear deterrent today has much to do with how it sees its security needs in the region. In Iran's immediate neighborhood the main strategic threat comes from the U.S. military presence, which is far stronger than Iran's and prevents it from asserting its hegemonic ambitions. Tehran wants the United States out of the Persian Gulf so that Iranian power can run unimpeded and make the Persian Gulf states (which currently rely on American military power) fall into line.

A senior German journalist told me that at the end of a 1974 interview with the Shah, he mentioned to the monarch that he was headed for Abu Dhabi. "When the plane gets to the other side of the Persian Gulf," the Shah told him, "I want you to look out the window. You will see clear black circles visible in the golden desert sand. A thin black line juts out of each circle, connecting it to the next circle further inland. The chain stretches for miles. These are the remnants of the ancient Iranian irrigation system [*qanat*]. For as far as those circles and lines go is Iranian territory."

The Shah did not intend to literally invade Abu Dhabi the way Saddam invaded Kuwait in 1990 (although Iran did take over three strategic islands in the Persian Gulf from the UAE in 1974). But he did mean that Iran sees the Persian Gulf as its natural zone of influence stretching back millennia. That fundamental nationalist attitude is embedded in the Islamic Republic's view of the region. The clerical regime does not speak the language of imperial Persian glories, but it believes in them nevertheless. Iran thinks of the Persian Gulf as its "near abroad," and in the same way that Russia, China, and India (which for decades blamed America for enabling Pakistan to resist Indian hegemony) resent America's shielding of their smaller neighbors, Iran sees the U.S. presence in the Persian Gulf as hindering its great-power ambitions. It is for this reason that Iran peppers its statements on resolving the nuclear crisis with demands for talks about "regional security"; it is code for Iran's role in the Persian Gulf.

Nuclear capability combined with the U.S. departure from the Persian Gulf will enable Iran to realize foreign policy ambitions going back at least to 1971, when Britain's departure from the Gulf first allowed Iran to imagine the area as its zone of influence.

Iran also has broader ambitions to spread its influence over the whole Middle East. Before the Islamic revolution, Iran saw the Arab world as hostile territory. There may have been alliances of convenience with Egypt, Jordan, or Saudi Arabia, but Iranians were outsiders to a fiercely nationalist Arab world. The Shah saw no point in trying to gain regional leadership.

But Khomeini thought Iranians could lead Arabs if it was in the name of Islam. Since 1979, the Islamic Republic has spent blood and ample treasure to make its influence felt all the way to the shores of the Mediterranean. Yet Iran's Shia faith separates it from the dominant Sunni creed that reigns supreme in the Arab world, where Shias are an often despised and even hated minority. The more Iran pushed for Islamic unity, the more the Arabs resisted by mobilizing Sunni sectarianism.[19]

Iran had to settle for influence over pockets of Shiism in the Arab world, in Bahrain, Iraq, Lebanon, and Syria. Where the Shias could wield power—via Hezbollah in Lebanon, in conjunction with the Alawites (who stand close to Shiism and Iran) in Syria, and within the government of post-Saddam Iraq—Iran could realize its goal.

Iran achieved its greatest success with Sunnis by harping on the "secular" Islamic cause: Israel and the Palestinians. Khomeini's strategy had always been that Iran had to be more Arab than the Arabs, and that meant straining every nerve to stand tall against Israel. Iran could and should lead the Arabs against Israel, thought Khomeini and his successors, for success there would win Arab hearts and minds and convince Arabs of the value of Iranian leadership. The strategy was at its most successful when Iran's Holocaust-denying President Ahmadinejad attained rock-star status on the Arab street with his rhetorical attacks on Israel. He lost no opportunity to call for the Jewish state's demise and back the forces of Arab rejectionism.

But Arab favor proved fickle. When a rebellion against Syria's Assad regime erupted into a thinly disguised sectarian knife fight in 2011, the Arab world stopped lauding Iran for opposing Israel and took up denouncing the Persian Shia outsiders for foisting a minority Alawite regime on Syria's mostly Sunni populace.

Part of the problem feeding this regional wavering toward Iran is that its political ambitions lack economic legs. Iran does not have the checkbook power of Qatar or Saudi Arabia, or the commercial muscle of Turkey. Islamic unity and anti-Israeli posturing go only so far. They cannot build the kind of interdependencies that bind countries and amount to real and long-running influence. The catch is that the more Iran tries to win influence in the Arab world, especially by baiting Israel, the more it invites international isolation and thereby undermines its economy.

Nuclear capability is in many ways a solution to these problems. It pushes back against American intervention and reinforces Iranian claims to be fighting the real battle against Israel. Nuclear capability, Tehran calculates, will cow the Arabs and compensate for Iran's economic weakness.

The Islamic Republic first dusted off the Shah's nuclear program when it was worried that Saddam Hussein was going to resume his war against Iran, possibly with chemical weapons. The West would not stand in his way; only a credible deterrence could dissuade Saddam from carrying out such savagery.[20] Saddam is gone, but the strategic threat facing Iran remains. According to the Stockholm International Peace Research Institute, in 2011 Iran spent $8 billion (2 percent of GDP) on military purchases. In the same year, Saudi Arabia spent more than six times that sum ($43 billion, or 11.2 percent of GDP); the United Arab Emirates spent almost twice as much ($15.7 billion, or 7.3 percent of GDP), and Israel spent 1.5 times as much ($13 billion, or 6.3 percent of GDP). Nor is the disparity merely one of dollar amounts; Iran's regional rivals have weaponry that is technically superior and more advanced.

International sanctions—which began right after the 1979 revolution—

have cost the Iranian military access to the latest technology. Iran's air force, for instance, is hopelessly outdated. It relies heavily on old F-14 Tomcats (the plane made famous by the 1986 Tom Cruise movie *Top Gun*) and F-4 Phantoms that the Shah bought from the United States decades ago. Iran will not be able to close the yawning technology gap anytime soon. And the lesson of the two Gulf wars is clear: Middle Eastern militaries are no match for what the United States and other Western militaries can bring to a fight.

Nuclear capability is a convenient shortcut—the poor man's path to strategic parity. Iran has learned the lesson of the Cold War. The Soviet Union had many more tanks and soldiers on its side of Europe, but that mattered little. America's nuclear arsenal created a balance of power that kept the Red Army out of Western Europe.

The nuclear program is also at the heart of the Iranian regime's survival strategy. The atom seems as if it can make any dictatorship untouchable (though it did not save the Soviet Union), and that notion has clearly been swirling around in the minds of Iran's rulers as they have pressed ahead with the nuclear program despite international objections over the past decade.[21] It was common wisdom in Iran in 2003 that the big difference between North Korea and Iraq was that Kim Jong-il had nuclear arms and Saddam did not. And let us not forget that it was after the failed Bay of Pigs attempt at regime change that Fidel Castro invited the Soviet Union to station nuclear missiles on Cuban soil. Nor was American handling of India and Pakistan when those two countries went nuclear much of a discouragement. After decades of objecting to Indian nuclear weapons, the Bush administration reversed course and signed a civilian nuclear deal with India, proving that with time all will be forgotten and that once-illicit nuclear programs could become accepted and legitimate. Meanwhile, Pakistan's nuclear weapons have given the West an enormous stake in that troubled country's stability. Western governments may lament Pakistan's bad behavior, but they keep pouring billions into the bottomless pit of its economy as insurance against a collapse into mayhem and extremism. Iran draws from these cases the lesson that "forgiveness is much easier to obtain than permission." Make nuclear Persia a fait accompli, and the world will accommodate the new reality.

Iranians have always been ambiguous about precisely what "going nuclear" will mean. The official line is that Iran wants only the nuclear know-how needed to satisfy domestic energy needs—a curious claim from a country sitting atop such a large chunk of the world's oil and natural gas reserves. Many among the country's leaders, however, want the Japan option—which was also what the Shah was after. This means developing the knowledge and infrastructure needed to make nuclear weapons, but stopping "one turn of the screw short." A smaller but growing segment of the ruling elite wants an actual nuclear arsenal. The harsher Western sanctions become, the more compelling becomes this last group's argument. The seventy-three-year-old Khamenei, however, has not been willing to go along with it. In 2012, as domestic pressure to build the bomb continued to intensify, he repeated his 1995 fatwa declaring nuclear weapons a "great sin."[22]

Efforts to put a stop to Iran's nuclear program began shortly after it first caught the attention of the West in 2003 with the discovery of a uranium-enrichment facility at Natanz in central Iran. The United States, France, Germany, and Britain joined forces to demand that Iran abandon enrichment altogether and sign the Additional Protocol of the Nuclear Non-Proliferation Treaty (NPT), which gives the nuclear watchdog agency, the IAEA, considerably greater ability to monitor a nuclear program.

The hardest and most exacting part of a nuclear program to master is uranium enrichment. Low enrichment levels will suffice to fuel nuclear power plants, but a bomb needs highly enriched uranium. Very little time and knowledge separate mastering enrichment from building a bomb. Iran claimed that its right to enrichment is protected under the NPT, and that it was merely trying to produce fuel for medical centers and experimental reactors. Those outdated reactors need 20 percent enriched fuel (more modern reactors can make do with lower enrichment levels), and once you get to the 20 percent threshold (the real hurdle in mastering enrichment) it's a breezy dash to 90 percent or more (bomb-grade enrichment). One idea was that the United States should sell Iran newer research reactors that would take away Iran's argument for 20 percent enrichment.[23] Before that could be agreed, however, Iran decided it wanted to produce fuel for nuclear power plants too. The United States and its European allies bristled at the idea, and tensions grew as Iran expanded its enrichment capacity.

From the outset, Washington declared a nuclear Iran to be unacceptable. Iran would use its nuclear capability to annihilate Israel, and short of that could provide a nuclear shield from behind which Hezbollah and Hamas could escalate their attacks on Israel. Similarly, a nuclear Iran would pose a newly alarming threat to its Arab neighbors, bullying them on regional issues or oil prices. Iran's nuclear capability could also breathe new life into Islamic fundamentalism, energizing an ideology that Washington hopes will end up in the trash bin of history. Finally, Iran's nuclear arsenal could spark proliferation throughout one of the world's most volatile regions—not a comforting prospect for the West or Israel, which would surely find itself the target at which many of the weapons would be pointed.

The immediate strategic threat to Israel would be less Iranian nuclear missiles than the boost that Hezbollah, Hamas, and other "asymmetric" foes of Israel would gain from being able to hide behind Iran's nuclear skirts. The record of Hezbollah's actions in Lebanon or Hamas's in Israel (not to mention Iraqi Shia so-called special groups responsible for violence in Iraq and radical Shia outfits in Pakistan or the Persian Gulf) makes this a serious threat. Some have even argued that instead of threatening war with Iran, America should have focused on knocking out the Assad regime in Syria. Without its Syrian outpost, Iran's asymmetric capabilities would collapse (because Iran would not be able to support Hezbollah as effectively without using Syrian territory) and leave any possible Persian nukes with nothing to shield.[24]

With so many arguments arrayed against Iran going nuclear, Washington made preventing Iran from doing so a top foreign policy objective. And to underscore its determination, it threatened Iran with military action. "All options are on the table" became the phrase meant to signal that America was ready to use air strikes against Iran's nuclear sites.[25]

But first America looked to the Europeans to negotiate an end to Iran's nuclear program. And to make Iran go along, economic sanctions would be key. This policy of imposing sanctions while keeping open the prospect of talks (dubbed the "dual-track" policy) was the brainchild of Secretary of State Condoleezza Rice and her deputy, Undersecretary Nicholas Burns. It had its origins in Washington's desire to patch things up with European governments still stewing over the Iraq war. Washington knew that the Europeans would ignore or even oppose its efforts on Iran unless they were kept on board and, indeed, in the forefront.

Yet Washington remained wary of talks and worried that without some form of pressure on Tehran they would go nowhere. In practice, Washington embraced European-led talks, but it remained focused on coercion, lobbying to include Russia and China, whose support at the UN would be critical if serious sanctions were ever to become a reality.

The dual-track approach gave Bush a punitive course of action short of war that could also placate other stakeholders in the dispute, such as Saudi Arabia, the Emirates, and Israel. They all wanted reassurance that the United States would not accept Iran going nuclear and would take tough action to stop that outcome. Sanctions were also conveniently both low-risk and low-cost. They could bite hard without sparking a shooting war. And Iran would bear all the pain, with America not needing to spend money or risk a single soldier's life.

The problem with sanctions is that they are just too convenient. They are what you do when you cannot or will not do anything else. They offer a good feeling that a crisis is being handled, but in reality they are blunt instruments with a questionable track record.[26] When they work, they hurt the economy and state institutions of the country they target—along with its civilian populace—but do they reshape the bad policy behaviors that cause them to be applied in the first place? Sanctions impoverished Iraq and cost the lives of vulnerable Iraqis (including tens of thousands of children), but Saddam Hussein stayed in power and remained a hazard. Indeed, it could be argued that sanctions boomeranged on the United States because the Iraq that U.S. forces conquered and were then responsible for putting back on its feet had been left such a basket case.

Sanctions are not likely to work in the case of Iran either. The reasons Iran craves nuclear status run too deep for it to be swayed by economic pressure. And indeed, there is reason to worry that U.S. pressure is only convincing Iran it needs nuclear deterrence in order to protect itself from that very pressure. When Bush was president, Iran's rulers were certain that regime change was the U.S. goal and reasoned that an Islamic Republic shorn of its nuclear program would be that much more vulnerable.

Iranians are not easy to negotiate with. This is a nation whose complex psyche is reflected in its art. Think of the dazzlingly detailed miniature paintings or the spectacularly ornate Persian carpets they have produced for centuries, and you can grasp that Iranians are patient and fantastically complicated. The Western expectation of quick, straightforward deal making has met with frustration when it comes to Iran. I remember a conversation in 2006 with Jack Straw, who was then Britain's foreign secretary, about his time talking to Iran. He said,

> People think North Koreans are difficult to negotiate with. Let me tell you, your countrymen [Iranians] are the most difficult people to negotiate with. Imagine buying a car. You negotiate for a whole month over the price and terms of the deal. You reach an agreement and go to pick up the car. You see it has no tires. "But the tires were not part of the discussion," the seller says. "We negotiated over the car." You have to start all over again, now wondering whether you have to worry about the metal rim, screws, or any other unknown part of the car. That should give you a sense of what talking to Iran looks like.

Diplomacy with Iran was always going to be long and hard. Iranians are hard bargainers, tenacious and unlikely to budge unless they are under pressure. Diplomacy with Iran will be like doing business with the North Vietnamese at the end of the Vietnam War—they too were dogged, difficult, and appeared likely to bend only under pressure. And yet in the end there was a road to a deal with the North Vietnamese—it just needed American persistence and a clearheaded strategy for managing the process.

The problem with the dual-track policy with Iran was that in practice it relied on a single track: economic pressure.[27] It failed because it deviated from the goal of using coercion to bring Iran to the negotiating table. The United States started to look to pressure to do the job on its own.[28] The Bush administration was never interested in diplomacy. It left it to Germany, France, and Britain to sit down with Iran for talks—but Washington would hold a veto over the outcome. Nor was Washington interested in resolving all outstanding issues, improving relations, and resolving the nuclear problem in that context. The Bush administration wanted Iran to surrender. The United States said that it would talk to Iran only if Iran first gave up its nuclear program—we would accept Iran running a civilian nuclear program provided all enrichment activities took place outside Iran. In other words, diplomacy will follow only after its intended result has already been achieved.

Initially there was hope that Europe could persuade Iran to change course. A visit to Tehran by three European foreign ministers in 2004 led to a two-month suspension of nuclear enrichment, which President Chirac thought was "exemplary of how problems can be resolved by European diplomacy."[29] But those early positive steps led nowhere.[30] Washington stuck to its position that Iran would have to abandon its nuclear program in its entirety—no enrichment activity whatsoever—before any further discussions could happen.

Inside Iran, hard-liners argued that the temporary suspension had been misconstrued as weakness and had only emboldened the United States to pressure Iran into total surrender. This view fit a prevalent narrative in Tehran that the West views any Iranian concession as weakness and therefore grows more aggressive.[31] Iran's rulers thought sanctions were intended to weaken Iran militarily and change the regime. The best response was to get tough and even belligerent—which escalated violence in Iraq. As Khamenei told his advisers, "The West is like a dog, if you back away it will lunge at you, but if you charge, then it will back away."[32] Little wonder, then, that more sanctions only made Iran more recalcitrant.

Iran's rulers thought that hard-charging Mahmoud Ahmadinejad would make the West back off when he took over the presidency from the more pliable reformist Mohammad Khatami in 2005. But Ahmadinejad's menacing rhetoric and shows of defiance only hardened U.S. attitudes in turn. What Khamenei did not know was that American policy makers also thought they would get a reaction from Tehran only if they were menacing to the point of threatening Khamenei's grip on power. "He moves only if you hold a gun to his head," a senior administration official told me.

Washington responded to Ahmadinejad's defiance by tightening the economic noose. Iran and the United States found themselves in an uneasy standoff, with American pressure only inviting greater Iranian obduracy.

Ironically, no Iranian leader more badly wanted a deal with the United States than did Ahmadinejad, and yet none failed more miserably in wooing America to the table. Ahmadinejad was following his own dual-track policy. He hoped his vitriol, denying the Holocaust, taunting Israel, and rallying resistance to America would make him too important to ignore—the adversary that America had to talk to. But his plan backfired. He made himself a pariah, the leader whom everyone was *determined* to ignore. Ahmadinejad broke the taboo against communicating directly with an American president, writing first to Bush, then to Obama to congratulate him on winning the 2008 election. Neither one responded. Above all, Ahmadinejad supported deal making over the nuclear issue, first in Geneva with the United States and its European allies in 2009, and then with Brazil and Turkey in 2010. Those deals failed to take hold and he got no credit for trying to get them through.

The Bush administration blamed the failure of its dual-track approach on Russia and China, which stood in the way of UN sanctions against Iran. But in reality the problem was that pressure was not tied to real diplomacy. Pressure had become an end in itself.

During the 2008 campaign, Obama promised to break this logjam, to engage Iran in earnest—a new approach based on mutual respect that could produce a diplomatic breakthrough. Iran would be a symbolic corrective to Bush's approach to addressing international crises, which was heavy on pressure and light on diplomacy. At first glance, it may look as if Obama did just that, or at least tried to. But look closer and it becomes hard to conclude that Obama's approach was much of a departure from Bush's. In fact, it was Bush's policy in a "new and improved" version.

Obama tweaked the dual-track approach. He tried his hand at diplomacy, but only to get to the sanctions track faster, and to make sanctions more effective. Engagement was a cover for a coercive campaign of sabotage, economic pressure, and cyberwarfare. It was Bush's policy with more teeth.

The most obvious indicators of continuity were the people Obama chose to run his Iran policy. Dennis Ross, a veteran diplomat who had the final say at the White House on all things related to Iran until December 2011, was a firm advocate of the dual-track policy. Iran interpreted his appointment to that job as an ominous sign that Obama was not serious about diplomacy. And Iranians were not the only ones who took notice. A senior adviser to Turkey's Prime Minister Erdoğan asked me why Obama had chosen him. Before I could answer he said, "We are disappointed. You judge a man [Obama] by his advisers."

Another clear signal was Obama's decision to keep Stuart Levy, Bush's undersecretary for terrorism and financial intelligence, at the Treasury Department. Levy had led a highly effective campaign to rally financial institutions across the globe to stop doing business with Iran.[33] This additional layer of sanctions augmented economic pressure on Iran. Levy continued to tighten the noose even as Obama was getting ready to reach out to Iran. As my Turkish friend put it: same people, same policy.

Where Bush had failed—and where Obama succeeded—was in the task of securing international support for sanctions. To that end Obama said that the United States was ready to talk to Iran (Bush had sent the Europeans to do the talking and then report back), and he sweetened the pot by adding that suspension of enrichment was no longer a precondition, but instead a desired outcome. But in practice it was the same old policy of pressure, pressure, and more pressure.

Israel, Saudi Arabia, and the Gulf emirates were unhappy with Obama's approach. They feared that Iran would use talks to weaken Western resolve while nuclear work went forward—"talk and enrich," so to speak. Israel's prime minister, Benjamin Netanyahu, wanted Obama to stick to the zero-enrichment precondition, set a strict deadline allowing at most a few months for diplomacy to work, and adopt stiff sanctions (even before talks got under way).

Saudi Arabia and the UAE, meanwhile, leaned heavily on Obama.

The first time Obama went to Saudi Arabia, in early June 2009, he expected to speak with King Abdullah about the Arab-Israeli issue, but instead had to listen to an hour-long monologue on Iran. The Saudi ruler famously advised America to "cut off the snake's head" with military strikes. Top UAE officials, according to one surprised European foreign minister I spoke to, went even further by suggesting that tactical nuclear weapons might be used to penetrate the Fordo site hidden deep inside a mountain outside the city of Qom. "The region would be set back," they reportedly said, "but in the long run it would be better for everybody." They clearly did not want the United States to talk to Iran. That would run the risk of a breakthrough that would have shifted the strategic balance in the region decisively in Iran's favor. That was why Arab leader after Arab leader warned Washington not to trust anything the Iranians might say. Egyptian president Hosni Mubarak told former senator George Mitchell that he was not opposed to the United States talking to Iran so long as "you do not believe a word they say."[34]

America's Arab allies would rather see a U.S.-Iran war than a U.S.-Iran rapprochement. The Persian Gulf states in particular are afraid of the latter. They also dislike the scenario of regime change in Tehran (too much uncertainty) and prefer a permanent U.S. commitment to defend them. As Defense Secretary Robert Gates put it after hearing another earful on Iran from King Abdullah, the Saudis were eager to "fight Iran to the last American."[35] So they kept doing their best to nudge America toward war.

Whatever the Arabs' discomfiture, however, Obama was determined to explore the possibility of an opening with Iran. Two months after his inauguration came the New Year, *Nowrouz*, a pre-Islamic Persian celebration that marks the start of spring and is considered an especially auspicious time for friendly visits, house cleaning, and new beginnings generally. Obama took to YouTube on March 20, 2009, with a prepared message in which he warmly and positively addressed himself directly to the Iranian people. More important still, he wrote two letters directly to Khamenei (while opting not to answer Ahmadinejad's letter congratulating him on becoming president). Khamenei's reply was hardly what Obama had hoped for; it listed Iranian grievances and lambasted American policies, not just toward Iran but toward the entire Muslim world. The significance, however, lay not in what Khamenei said but in his answering at all.

Whatever positive momentum might have come from this soon dissipated when Iranian politics took an unexpected turn later that same spring. Washington was hoping that the 2009 presidential race in Iran would produce a fresh face untainted by Holocaust denial or calls for Israel to be wiped off the map. This would be a figure whom an American president might engage without paying a huge cost at home (Obama's fear of a domestic backlash had been a major reason why he ignored Ahmadinejad's letter). But the elections produced a June surprise. When Ahmadinejad was announced as the landslide winner, millions of Iranians poured into the streets to protest, asking, "Where is my vote?" The regime was caught off guard. For a time, it looked as if the theocracy might actually fall.[36] But then, just as quickly, the tide turned. Sensing the immediacy of mortal danger, the regime lashed out at the protesters with massive brutality that checked their momentum and ensured its survival.

When the dust settled, everything had changed. Gone was any pretense that the ruling elite could claim popular support and legitimacy. Gone also was Ahmadinejad's cocky attitude. The emperor had no clothes; Iran's rulers were now every bit as vulnerable as any Third World dictator. In the rulers' eyes, engagement with the United States now seemed even more suspect. Better not to engage at all than to risk having any more weakness revealed under the pressure of dealings with Washington.

Washington understood that the moment for diplomacy had gone up in smoke amid the tumult on the streets of Tehran. "They are now going to get themselves into a hard place," remarked State's man on Iran policy, Dennis Ross, as we watched the violent crackdown on television. "It will be very difficult dealing with them."

It was also difficult for Obama to engage a government that was busy brutalizing its young people, whose brave and technologically savvy calls for freedom had captured hearts and minds around the world and shown that it was possible to imagine a better, post-Islamist future for the Middle East. Critics both right and left goaded the administration to help the Green Movement topple the Iranian theocracy. But Obama, in what would become his signature reaction to the Arab Spring, was cautious. Moreover, the U.S. government had been surprised by events. By the time Washington got its head around what was going on, the Islamic Republic had weathered the worst of the protests. Getting into a tussle with Iran's rulers over a protest movement that was losing steam would be pointless. Nuclear talks remained the main thing, and the Islamic Republic, like it or not, remained the interlocutor. Any additional sanctions that might be applied, moreover, should be held as cards for use in nuclear talks. America's priority was Iran's nuclear program, not democracy.

In October 2009, officials of the shaken but still-standing Islamic Republic finally sat down with American and European diplomats in Geneva to discuss the nuclear issue. There was hope that the much-anticipated meeting would produce a breakthrough around a new concept: "the swap." The idea had first been floated as a confidence-building measure. Iran was in need of nuclear fuel pads (built with uranium enriched to 20 percent) that the Tehran Research Reactor could use to produce medical isotopes.[37] Would Iran be willing not to further enrich its low-enriched uranium (enriched to no more than 3 to 5 percent) and instead send its stockpile to some third country in exchange for readymade fuel pads?

The White House saw the swap as a clever way of "resetting" Iran's nuclear program while talks went on (Iran would give up its enriched uranium and would have to start over to get back to the same stockpile).[38] But the swap would mean that the international community would be accepting Iran's right to enrich uranium to 3 to 5 percent, a concession to Iran.

In Geneva, the United States proposed a trade. The Iranians would ship 1.2 tons of low-enriched uranium (about 80 percent of their stockpile) to Russia for further enrichment and then to a third country (France was the likely candidate) for further processing into fuel pads. There were details to work out: Would Iran send all low-enriched uranium at once? And how long would it take to get it back as fuel pads?

But a deal would be a win-win. Iran's ability to build a bomb would ship out along with its low-enriched uranium stockpile—thereby creating more time for negotiations over intrusive inspections and the signing of the IAEA's Additional Protocol—yet Iran would get acknowledgment of its right to enrich as well as a nice stack of handy fuel pads. Trust would mount, and diplomacy would gain momentum.

Iranians were suspicious. They did not want France involved. French president Nicolas Sarkozy was advocating zero enrichment and was to the right of Obama on Iran. But in the end they decided to go with the deal—at least in Geneva; details to be settled later.[39] At one point, Iran's chief nuclear negotiator, Saeed Jalili, said that he had to make a call. He left the room, then came back and gave a tentative thumbs-up.[40] It is not clear if Khamenei was on board, but Ahmadinejad was clearly supportive. He wanted to be the one to open up to the United States—that would have helped his political position after the reelection debacle.

Back in Tehran, worry set in immediately that this could be a ruse to get Iran to give up its low-enriched uranium, after which the United States and Europe would renege on their part of the bargain and cost Iran a lot of uranium and enrichment time. Were they missing something? Did the United States have something up its sleeve? What if they signed on to this deal and that became the legal basis to constrain their nuclear activities beyond current NPT and IAEA mandates? And even if this was a good deal, Ahmadinejad's rivals hardly wanted him to get credit for the breakthrough. An unholy alliance of hard-liners and reformists came out against the swap idea. They said Iran could not trust America and its European allies and should not become dependent on Russia for its enrichment needs. Iran had spent billions mastering enrichment and should not give that up. Iran said that it would agree to the deal only if the swap happened simultaneously—the offer in Geneva was that Iran would receive fuel pads two years after it handed over its stockpile.

In other words, the Iranians were too suspicious to countenance a deal and too divided to make any decisions.[41] The naysayers claimed that they were defending Iran's sovereignty, keeping its options open, and preserving its leverage. Khamenei took their side, and killed the deal by saying publicly that its backers (Ahmadinejad and Jalili) were naive and misguided.

With the collapse of the Geneva swap deal, Obama reacted to criticism from allies and Congress by shifting back to sanctions. Iran tried to revive the swap deal not long after, but Washington no longer seemed interested. It was happy to use the narrative of failed talks in Geneva to get to sanctions faster.

The Treasury Department redoubled its efforts to sanction Iran's financial institutions as U.S. diplomacy focused further on getting the UN Security Council to pass sanctions against Iran. The White House wanted to show Iran that there was a cost to walking away from the table. Obama also wanted to stay ahead of Congress, which was preparing its own, stiffer sanctions bill, one sure to affect global trade and raise the ire of important allies.

Getting China and Russia to agree to UN sanctions was the main challenge.[42] During the Bush years, Beijing and Moscow had always fought sanctions. One Asian foreign minister told me, "Moscow and Beijing have an understanding: on North Korea, Russia hides behind China, and on Iran, China hides behind Russia." Both Russia and China value stability and will cooperate with the United States and push Iran to do enough to achieve that. But that should not be confused with agreement with U.S. policy or leadership. America has had to resort to threatening war and instability combined with generous payoffs in order to get Russia and China on its side.

When America talks to Russia about Iran, it is all about nuclear Iran's threat to peace. Russia does not appear to imagine that it may itself one day be a target of Iranian nuclear weapons. In fact, Russia seems less worried about Iran than about America. Russia and Iran have some common strategic interests, foremost among them keeping America out of the Caucasus and Central Asia. Iran is Russia's bridge into the Middle East—Moscow has far more strategic common ground with Iran than with Turkey, Egypt, or Saudi Arabia. This became clear when Russia found itself on Iran's side during the Syrian crisis, and King Abdullah hung up the telephone in anger on Russian president Dmitri Medvedev over Moscow's unflinching support for the Assad regime.

In the 1990s, Iran had provided Russia with badly needed foreign currency in exchange for its work on the Bushehr reactor. During the Bush years, Russia had supplied Iran with weapons and sophisticated military systems, and some in Iran even contemplated allowing Russian bases on Iranian soil as part of a strategic alliance against the West.

The Russia-Iran partnership predates the final collapse of the Soviet Union. Mikhail Gorbachev was still holding on to the idea of the communist union when Moscow and Tehran agreed that they should jointly manage the vast region that lies between them from the Black Sea to the Ural Mountains. Back in the nineteenth century, Russia had taken most of this region from Iran, and for most of the next century Iran worried that the USSR would take the rest of Iran as well. But with the Soviet Union faltering and revolutionary Iran obsessed with America, Tehran saw less reason to worry about Russia and so cooperated with Moscow in steering the Caucasus and Central Asia toward independence and away from American influence.[43]

None of this is to say that Iran and Russia lack disagreements, or that Iran has forgotten the abuse that it suffered at Russian hands.[44] Russians still challenge Iran over control of the Caspian Sea. And Russia views Iran as a rival seller in the natural gas market. In particular, Russia would like to keep Iranian gas out of Europe, which depends heavily on Russia for energy. When Russian strongman Vladimir Putin went to Tehran in 2011, he offered support against American pressure in exchange for Iran staying away from the proposed Western-backed pipelines to carry gas from east to west. Russia has encouraged Iran to sell its gas eastward, to the vast populations of a rapidly developing Asia, offering to finance a gas pipeline that would run from Iran to Pakistan for starters, but which could readily be extended to India and China.

But the most important fact for Moscow when it comes to Iran is that it is the goose that lays the golden egg. Washington is so obsessed with the Iranian threat that it forgets about Russia's own threat to the West, and so is ready to pay almost any price to secure Russian help. Russia sees its Iran posture as a valuable commodity that it can make America pay for dearly.

When Russia got on board with UN sanctions after the Geneva talks failed, Obama was elated. His administration portrayed Russian support as a singular victory, a proof that Obama's Iran policy was working, and a sign that Obama was better than George W. Bush at foreign policy. But in reality, this was less a victory for diplomacy than the result of a straight-up business deal—one in which the Russians took us to the cleaners. To get Russia to say yes to sanctions, Obama stopped talking about democracy and human rights in Russia (until 2012, when Russians took to the streets to protest Putin's ham-fisted victory at the polls), abandoned any thought of expanding NATO farther eastward, washed his hands of the missile-defense shield that had been planned for Europe (Moscow hated the shield), and betrayed tiny Georgia (which Russia had attacked in the lopsided war of 2008). While Georgia's president, Mikheil Saakashvili, was telling Holbrooke, "You sold us to the Russians," Obama was lifting sanctions against weapons sales by arms makers associated with the Russian military.[45] Even after all this, it took additional "concessions" (bribes would be a better word) from Germany, Israel, and Saudi Arabia to turn the Russians.

China was not happy with Iranian obduracy, fearing that it made war more likely.[46] Washington told Beijing that if it wanted to avoid instability it had better support economic pressure. But the real lever was Saudi oil, on which the Chinese depend more than they depend on Iranian oil. A combination of enticements in the form of long-term contracts at concessionary prices and threats of reductions in Saudi oil shipments got China to "yes" on sanctions as well.[47]

The Chinese have an enormous and vastly growing thirst for oil—8 million barrels per day currently, and expected to rise to 15 million barrels by 2015. Of course China would say yes to lucrative Saudi oil contracts. But it is unlikely that it will give up on its option on Iranian oil. Iran has vast proven oil reserves and, more important, none of them are controlled by American oil companies. China could build a global company on the back of Iranian oil. Since 2009, while supporting sanctions, publicly calling on Iran to cooperate on the nuclear issue, and warming up to Saudi Arabia, China has expanded its trade with Iran and welcomed Iranian manufacturers who wish to escape the effects of sanctions by moving production to China and shipping their finished goods back to Iran. Western sanctions led by the United States have pushed Iran further into China's bosom, and China is far from unhappy about that.

Here is the heart of the problem with our Iran policy: America got Russia and China on the hook for Iran, but at what cost? Is Iran, a country whose economy is not all that much bigger than that of Massachusetts, a larger threat to U.S. interests than China or Russia? Is Iran so severe a danger that America should subsidize China's economic rise by pushing the Saudis with all their oil right into China's lap (where Iran is already sitting)? Does it make sense that America spends blood and treasure to keep the Persian Gulf secure while China gets cheap oil—at our behest? Should we be worried more about Iran or a Russia armed to the teeth with nuclear weapons, beating its chest with nationalist bravado, and invading small neighbors? The price for Russian cooperation from here on will likely be facilitating Russian domination over energy supplies to Europe—abandoning support for pipelines taking Azerbaijani or Turkmen gas to Europe. For much of the Cold War we worked hard to keep Western Europe from becoming dependent on Russian energy; now we seem to be encouraging it, all to pressure Iran into submission.

When the dust settles, this is what we will have accomplished: Iran will be weaker than it is now—maybe its economy will shrink to the size of Cape Cod's—and instead of getting a single bomb in five years and a credible arsenal in perhaps twenty, they will get a bomb in ten and an arsenal in forty. But by then China and Russia will have gobbled up Central Asia, cornered Europe's energy markets, and planted themselves smack in the middle of the Middle East. They will have emerged as global giants challenging America's place in the world and perhaps the primacy of the U.S. dollar as the currency of international exchange. And once that happens, it will be all but impossible to reverse. We would then face global threats, threats on a scale we encountered during the Cold War, threats that dwarf whatever danger Iran can ever pose. Is it really smart to contain Iran's threat by subsidizing China's and Russia's rise to the top? Before we get things backward, perhaps we should ask if we should be thinking of Iran as a player that can help contain Russia and block China's encroachments into the Middle East.

Just when Obama was claiming that talking had had its turn and it was time to toughen sanctions, diplomacy found a new lease on life in the form of an unexpected Brazilian-Turkish initiative. Admittedly, Brazil and Turkey seemed an unlikely duo to take charge of one of the most delicate matters on the world agenda. They were not part of the P5+1 group (the permanent UN Security Council members plus Germany) that sat across the table from Iran in Geneva. That the Turks and Brazilians tried their hand at fixing a crisis that the global bigwigs could not resolve was a testament to the "rise of the rest": middle-ranking powers with fast-growing economies and a yearning to leave their mark on global politics.[48]

Turkey in particular was keen to step up as a regional problem solver and bolster its "street cred" as a local power and a bridge between east and west. Brazil had no clear stake in the Middle East, but it too thought a great power ought to be able to solve great problems, and not just in its own neighborhood. Also, Brazil once had a robust nuclear program and, thinking that it one day might want to go back to it, was not quite comfortable with the precedent the Iran crisis could set for handling future aspirants to nuclear status.[49]

Brazil's president, Luiz Inácio "Lula" da Silva, had hosted Ahmadinejad and Turkey's president, Abdullah Gül, and premier, Recep Tayyip Erdoğan, and Turkish foreign minister Ahmet Davutoğlu had visited Tehran on a number of occasions. Lula and Ahmadinejad were both populists, while Turkey wanted to sell Iran on a different view of Islam in the modern world—democratic, economically open, and engaged in globalization. Davutoğlu told me that he spoke to Khamenei about this vision and explained how Turkey and Iran could create an arc of Muslim power and prosperity stretching from the southeastern corner of Europe to the northwestern corner of South Asia. For Turkey, this could be a new EU. Khamenei listened but did not react. A diplomatic success on the nuclear issue would give Turkey credibility and remove obstacles to Iran's involvement in the global economy.

Both Turkey and Brazil had a vested interest in keeping UN and congressional sanctions at bay. In 2009, Brazil did $2 billion in trade with Iran, and it was hoping to increase that number significantly. Turkish companies, too, were doing brisk business in construction, food, consumer goods, tourism, telecommunications, and energy in Iran. Neither Brazil nor Turkey wanted these ties cut. A deal could make sanctions unnecessary.

Davutoğlu joined forces with Brazilian foreign minister Celso Amorim to revisit the swap deal with Iran. At first Washington was not happy with this meddling and tried to persuade Erdoğan and Lula to drop the idea. But later Obama wrote to Erdoğan supporting the Turkish and Brazilian effort as a worthy undertaking that might address the international community's concerns. He even suggested that Iranian low-enriched uranium might stay in "escrow" in Turkey until the higher-enriched fuel pads were in Iran's hands.[50] That showed a high degree of engagement with the Turkish-Brazilian effort and a willingness to compromise to help it succeed. This was an early example of "lead from behind" strategy, which would eventually become the hallmark of Obama foreign policy. Turkey took the letter as a green light to go full speed ahead on negotiations.

Within Iran, meanwhile, thinking about the swap idea had started to change. The reason was Ahmadinejad. From November 2009 to May 2010, he crisscrossed the country explaining the swap and why it would be good for Iran. As more Iranians heard his arguments, the high-level resistance that had killed the deal began to soften. That Iran ultimately signed a swap deal, with public support from parliament, was a victory at home for Ahmadinejad.[51]

Erdoğan and Lula went to Tehran in May 2010 and after two days of intense negotiations got a deal. The Tehran Declaration was the first time Iran actually signed something regarding the nuclear issue.[52] At the heart of the deal was a swap of 1,200 kilograms of low-enriched uranium for 120 kilograms of nuclear fuel enriched to about 20 percent.

Erdoğan and Lula thought they had pulled a rabbit out of a hat, but Washington dismissed the deal for handing Iran too much and getting too little in return. Although the goal of swapping 1,200 kilograms of low-enriched uranium was in Obama's letter, Washington now claimed that Iran had much more than that, and the swap of 1,200 kilograms would not be as effective in checking Iran's progress toward a bomb as the sanctions then being pressed in Geneva.

The reality was that Washington never expected Brazil and Turkey to get a deal in Tehran—Obama endorsed their effort expecting that they would fail and in doing so make the case for sanctions even stronger. Now the two upstart nations were undermining the case for sanctions. Washington had invested too much in corralling international support for sanctions—especially getting Russia and China on board—to change course now. Sanctions had become the goal, not the means to getting to a diplomatic resolution. Ironically, the Tehran Declaration had happened because the sanctions threat was so serious—Turkey and Brazil feared them as bad for business. This could have been touted as a kind of bank-shot win for the dual-track policy: even the *threat* of sanctions could have a positive real-world effect! Washington could have gone back to the negotiation table and used the threat of further sanctions to build on the Tehran Declaration and get the diplomatic track going for good.

Instead, Obama's administration signaled that it was not really interested in a diplomatic solution; it had wanted sanctions all along. It wanted diplomacy to be tried but then fail; it was not ready or willing to deal with success. The White House thought that sanctions were politically safer. Following up on the Brazil-Turkey opening would be risky and would require the investment of political capital—Israel, Europe, the U.S. Congress, and the Arab states could all be expected to raise complaints. Sanctions were easier. And they would play better at home.

Israel had never supported diplomacy and saw Brazilian and Turkish intervention as a dangerous distraction. One senior Turkish official told me that Israel's attack on a Turkish flotilla carrying aid to Palestinians in the Gaza Strip in May 2010 in violation of an Israeli naval blockade was a deliberate shot across Turkey's bow, a warning to Ankara not to meddle in the Iran affair. Turkey got the message, but the attack inflamed Turkish public opinion and soured Turkish-Israeli relations.

France too downplayed the Brazil-Turkey deal, arguing that the vote for sanctions at the UN should go forward. The Europeans in general were not happy with being upstaged by Brazil and Turkey. The two had accomplished far more in a few months than the European powers had in six years. They were only too happy to kill the deal.

Russia and China were also upset. The two had been rewarded handsomely for agreeing to sanctions and were unwilling to give all that up just because Brazil and Turkey had made a breakthrough. Moscow and Beijing also wanted to teach Tehran a lesson: Do not try to go around us. Russia and China were benefiting from sitting between Iran and America, selling their favors to both sides and profiting from the impasse. They were in no mood to see Brazil and Turkey kill their cash cow.

Russia in particular is sensitive to challenges to its great-power status. From Moscow, Turkey and Brazil's presumption of equal status in resolving a major international crisis looked like a challenge. Russia's vote for the sanctions resolution at the UN was also about putting Turkey and Brazil back in their place.

On the eve of the UN vote, Washington tried to persuade Turkey and Brazil to refrain from voting on the sanctions resolution in the Security Council, on which both were then sitting as elected, nonpermanent members. That was too much to ask of the two countries. If they abstained, Washington could claim that the international community was united behind the sanctions, but how could Brazil and Turkey abstain after they had shown a way around the sanctions? Obama called Erdoğan and asked him to avoid voting no. When UNSCR 1929 came up for a vote on June 9, 2010, however, both Brazil and Turkey voted no. But the vote passed anyway.

American policy was now solely one of sanctions. By bringing Russia and China on board, Obama had made Bush's policy a "success"—in the sense that it now enjoyed buy-in from Moscow and Beijing, not in the sense of it actually solving the nuclear impasse with Iran. Through the whole process, Obama had been very concerned with shielding his right flank so as not to open himself to right-wing criticism. It is not going too far to say that American foreign policy had become completely subservient to tactical domestic political considerations.

In the end, Obama's Iran policy failed. He pushed ahead with sanctions for the same reason Lyndon Johnson kept up the bombing of North Vietnam—neither could think of anything else to do (nor wanted to assume the risk of doing it). Obama's sanctions-heavy approach did not change Iranian behavior; instead it encouraged Iran to accelerate its race to nuclear capability. The secretary of defense, Robert Gates, said as much in a January 2010 memo to Obama: sanctions coupled with engagement (the dual-track policy) plus covert action would not work, and furthermore, "we were not going to go to war to keep Iran from becoming a nuclear weapons state."[53] What he was suggesting was that Obama might say no to containment now, but that is the only option his policy has left for the United States. Perhaps it is true after all that "only Nixon can go to China." A Democratic president may be too vulnerable to public opinion on national security issues to make tough decisions.

The administration did claim success on another front. By mid-2010, clandestine initiatives to penetrate and subvert Iran's nuclear program were up and running. A particularly nasty computer worm called Stuxnet had been delivered (some reports indicate with Israel's help) into the intranet that supported Iran's nuclear program. Stuxnet interfered with the mechanisms that control the highly synchronized spinning of thousands of centrifuges at extremely high speeds. That wreaked havoc in the system, and the damage to the centrifuge infrastructure significantly slowed Iran's enrichment schedule. In May 2009, Iran had 4,290 centrifuges. In August 2010, that number had dropped to 3,772 thanks to Stuxnet.[54]

Stuxnet in Iran was the equivalent of drones in Pakistan or Yemen—a new and covert way for America to deal with world problems.[55] Stuxnet was followed by a series of deadly attacks on nuclear scientists and administrators, believed to be either at the hands of the United States or Israel, or both. A massive bomb that exploded at a military base housing part of Iran's missile program was assumed to be part of the same campaign. Iran also believed that Israel was fomenting ethnic trouble in Iran—working with Azerbaijan to stir up Azeri nationalism in the northwest and backing Jundullah, a vicious extremist group in Iran's Baluchistan province that was spearheading a secessionist campaign of terror there.[56]

These brazen attacks, some argued, were pressuring Iran's rulers and slowing the nuclear program. That some of them were happening openly in Iranian cities was a powerful signal of American and Israeli determination and its ability to stop Iran's nuclear program. In Israel, a lively debate erupted as to whether sabotage was obviating the need for open war.[57] A former head of the Mossad, Meir Dagan, broke with Prime Minister Netanyahu, arguing the case for covert war (later he was joined by several other military and intelligence chiefs). On the other side, former premier Ehud Barak thought that sabotage could do only so much and that Iran would soon devise ways to guard against further damage.[58] Still, Russian and Chinese backing for UN sanctions (complemented by harsher financial restrictions Stuart Levy's team had put in place), combined with intriguing cloak-and-dagger operations against Iran's nuclear program, made for a good narrative going into an election year: the Iran problem was under control, Iran was under pressure and weakening, Obama had succeeded where Bush had failed.

In truth, Obama's version of the dual-track policy was also not successful.[59] It was not even "dual." It relied instead on one track, and that was pressure.[60] Its gains were short-lived and illusory. The United States had forgotten that the object of pressure was to jump-start diplomacy, which meant that doors had to be kept open even as the squeeze was applied.[61] Not surprisingly, when Iran next met with the United States and its allies, in January 2011 in Istanbul, the talks quickly failed. Sanctions and sabotage remained the "dual-track" approach of choice.

This led Iran to step up its own dual-track policy of applying pressure to get America to negotiate in earnest. The difference was that Iran would periodically put options on the table, opening doors to diplomacy that the United States could walk through. The Tehran Declaration was one such door; another was Russian foreign minister Sergey Lavrov's "step-by-step" plan. Lavrov informed his American counterparts of his plan during a visit to Washington in July 2011. He suggested that both Iran and the United States should agree to a road map according to which Iran would address every IAEA concern, but one at a time, and would receive a corresponding benefit (in the form of a particular sanction being lifted) for doing so. The plan called for a freeze on further sanctions while the process was working.[62] Iran accepted the plan but the United States did not.[63]

With his reelection year approaching, Obama did not want to try anything new. Plus, there was the fear that step-by-step could stall. As sanctions were lifted, Iran might feel less compelled to provide further concessions. Such a piecemeal process might go only so far and then collapse under the weight of its own success.

Obama wanted to stay with the sanctions-only policy for now, but the happy narrative of successful pressuring and sabotage was just one headline away from crashing. The crash came on October 11, 2011, when Attorney General Eric Holder and FBI Director Robert Mueller made public a foiled, allegedly Iranian-backed, assassination attempt against Saudi Arabia's ambassador to the United States, Adel al-Jubeir. The sensational plot involved Mexican drug cartels, DEA informants, and the audacious idea of blowing up a popular Washington restaurant (Café Milano in Georgetown) frequented by the ambassador. To many the plot looked too amateurish to be the work of the dreaded Iranian intelligence services.[64] But it mattered little what skeptics thought. The administration believed the plot was real, and if real, the plot of course undercut the administration's claim to have Iran under control. It was clear that far from being cowed, Iran was mounting its own pressure tactics to bend America's will.

Then in November came a sensational new IAEA report that raised alarm about the military aims of Iran's nuclear program. Skeptics argued that the report revealed little that was not known previously, but the Obama administration saw the report as a game changer and told the public of the grave danger that Iran's nuclear program posed. The bugbear grew.

Israel, Saudi Arabia, the UAE, and Congress all concluded that the administration's dual-track policy had failed. Israel (publicly) and the Persian Gulf states (privately) renewed their talk of the need for military action. Congress made its own Iran policy by passing stiff new sanctions, most notably targeting the country's oil income by sanctioning its central bank. The Europeans followed suit by announcing that they would stop buying Iranian oil. Caught off guard, the administration tried to get back out in front by endorsing the new sanctions, escalating its own rhetoric, and announcing unilateral sanctions such as making it difficult for oil tankers carrying Iranian oil to get necessary insurance to do business—which led Iran to sell more of its oil through Iraq and Dubai.

Up to this point, sanctions had been harsh but mainly affected Iran's trade (restricting what Iran could import). Now they were going after

Iran's income (limiting how much oil Iran could sell).[65] With the United States and Europe pushing other oil producers to step up production, and those producers building new pumping infrastructure and signing long-term contracts with Iran's former customers, Iran would find it hard to get back into the game even if it bowed to international pressure on its nuclear program.

But tightening the screws did not show a way out of the crisis. Sanctions had hurt Iran's economy, and the new tougher sanctions cut to the bone. Both inflation and unemployment spiked, and shortages ravaged the economy. The government postponed an estimated $60 billion in infrastructure projects. Yet Iran still had ways to keep its head above water.

Iran had large gold reserves and since 2008 had been taking a larger share of its oil revenue in currencies other than the dollar. Iran keeps these currencies in their countries of origin and uses them to finance its international trade locally. That is costly, but it allows oil- and trade-related transactions to dodge financial restrictions. When Dubai turned the screws on Iranian financial institutions in 2011, Iran shifted its financial transactions to China, Pakistan, and Turkey. Dubai banks no longer support personal Iranian accounts and dig deep into activities of Iranian companies before clearing their transactions. Chinese, Pakistani, and Turkish banks do none of this. A dozen Pakistani banks keep open credit lines that allow Iranian merchants to buy goods in Pakistan and ship them across the border for sale in Iran.

Nor was the oil embargo's impact as worrying to Iran as was commonly assumed. The global supply of oil is fairly tightly matched to demand. So if Europe, for instance, cuts off purchases of Iranian oil, Iran will still be able to find buyers in other parts of the world, at least for a while. And if Iran is cut out of the already tight oil markets altogether, that will impact oil prices and the prospects for global economic recovery.

By early 2012, China, Japan, South Korea, Sri Lanka, India, and Turkey had all cut some of their oil purchases from Iran but continued to buy Iranian oil. The Iranian analyst Bijan Khajehpour estimated that selling about 1.75 million barrels per day to these countries combined—along with sales of natural gas to Turkey—could earn Iran sums well in excess of what it needs to pay for its imports. Thirst for oil in all these countries is expected to grow as their economies continue to boom. Iran also sells oil through Iraq and Dubai—literally sending oil on trucks and boats to those destinations, which then reship it as local oil.

Iran is unhappy with the way in which it has to sell its oil but remains confident that global markets will continue to provide room for it. In the longer run, the surge in energy demand in China and India alone, Iran thinks, will make Iranian oil indispensable. What worries Iran is that due to its inability to secure investment and new technology to upgrade its oil industry its production capacity will not grow—and will likely decline—and so it will not be able to take full advantage of growing world demand.

The sudden tightening of sanctions, then, did not break Iran's economy, but they did severely affect the daily lives of Iranians. So it was not a surprise that Iran reacted angrily to this sudden turn of events. It decided that Obama was adding pressure on Iran to placate his domestic critics because he still saw sanctions as a cheap, low-risk way to look tough on Iran. If Iran did nothing, it could only expect more pressure and perhaps even open conflict. It was better to deter the United States now and disabuse Washington of the belief that it could forever hide behind sanctions. Iran threatened confrontation, closing the Strait of Hormuz, through which a fifth of the world's oil supply flows, carrying out terrorist attacks, and stopping the sale of oil to European countries well ahead of when the EU planned to stop buying Iranian oil—that would catch Europe (then in the thick of frantic efforts to save the euro) off guard and cause an energy crisis and higher oil prices. It now looked as if sanctions were no longer a substitute for war but could be a cause of it.

Lifting these crippling sanctions—and preventing more being added onto them—now became Iran's goal. To get rid of sanctions, Khamenei calculated that it would be necessary to act tough in front of the West—to meet threat with threat and pressure with pressure—and to attain nuclear capability faster (because then Iran would have more leverage to negotiate sanction removal). Iran knew from Iraq's experience that once sanctions are imposed, they tend to stay in place. Even if Iran conceded on the nuclear issue, the U.S. Congress would ask for concessions on terrorism, and then on other issues before sanctions were ever lifted. This is what worried Khamenei—"that the U.S. would not be satisfied until Iran gives up its religious beliefs, values, identity, independence."[66] The Europeans would not reverse their oil embargo either, not unless every European country voted to do so, which would be unlikely. And the tens of billions of dollars' worth of arms sold to Saudi Arabia and the UAE to bolster their defenses against Iran would not vanish from those countries' arsenals if and when Iran gave up its nuclear program.

By this reasoning Iran would get nothing for cooperating on the nuclear issue and would have a stronger bargaining position if it got past the point of no return. In yet another ironic twist, rather than halt Iran's nuclear program, the new sanctions actually gave Iran ample incentive to forge ahead with it.

Iranian leaders also understood that giving up on the program at a time when sanctions were weakening the state and robbing it of the means to buy political support at home would doom the regime. Look at Libya, they would say. Gaddafi gave up his nuclear program, and then when his people rose up he had no way to keep the United States and NATO from intervening to topple him. Back in 2004 when Gaddafi gave up his nuclear program in exchange for normalizing relations with the West, Khamenei had told his National Security Council that the Libyan leader was "an idiot" and that this was the end of him. With memories of the 2009 Green Movement still fresh, Iran's rulers felt they could expect a Libya scenario only if they relinquished their nuclear program and then their unhappy and hungry masses rose up in protest.

The Iranian state relies on an extensive patronage system to rule. The sanctions have raised doubts about the viability of patronage politics—there is not enough money to dole out to buy off the population. If support for the regime softens and dissident factions peel off, the door could open not only to compromise on the nuclear issue but to a transition to a more open regime. That would be a best-case scenario for the West.

The downside was steeper. Countries that have built nuclear weapons have all had to make a decision to do so. Iran has so far decided to gain nuclear capability, but by most intelligence accounts has not made the decision to build a bomb. Could pressure, meant to keep it from such a decision, instead backfire and end up driving it to that very end?

Obama still hoped that there was life in the dual-track policy. He hoped that punishing economic pressure would persuade Iran's leaders that to survive they had to stop and not take that last fatal step across the red line that would trip a war with America. To give the status quo a chance, he moved the red line back to Iran attaining a nuclear *weapon*. Since 2009, Washington had indicated that it was willing to tolerate some enrichment activity in Iran, but it had never formally rolled back its red line from enrichment to weaponization—Obama did just that.[67] But in doing so he also painted American foreign policy into a corner. If you draw a clear red line then you have to defend it or risk looking weak.

That provided an opening for the American Right, backed by Israeli prime minister Netanyahu, to force Obama's back to the wall on Iran. The policy was a failure, Iran was closer to a bomb, and short of war there was no other way to stop it. That compelled Obama to put Iran policy at the forefront of his foreign policy agenda and to further increase pressure on Iran.

Publicly the president pushed back against war. He told a gathering of the pro-Israel group AIPAC that he would not countenance containment of a nuclear Iran—containment was not an option—and if it became clear that Iran was about to build nuclear weapons America would go to war to prevent that. But for now, the president was confident that pressure (and he was adding much more of it with his policy under criticism at home) combined with talks (which he now aggressively pursued with Iran) would work.

Khamenei welcomed Obama's pushback against war, and it was then that he reissued his 1995 fatwa—in effect saying that Iran will not build a bomb, so Obama does not have to go to war. Khamenei also agreed to return to talks. This looked like a victory for dual-track—although the pressure was on the United States this time. Israeli goading and the American Right were opening the door for diplomacy.

But once again Obama was not willing to walk through the door. In Istanbul America suggested that if Iran suspended 20 percent enrichment of uranium and agreed to send out of the country its stockpile of 20 percent enriched uranium, and if it proved that Khamenei's fatwa would hold, then America would discuss sanctions relief and include recognition of Iran's right to enrichment (the key Iranian demand) in the discussion. Talks resumed in Baghdad and Moscow. In the Russian capital Iran offered to make the fatwa a UN document, but now the United States backed away from its Istanbul offer. Recognizing the right to enrichment and talk of sanctions relief were off the table. The United States was prepared to offer only aircraft spare parts (the Iranian aviation industry is in desperate need of parts for its aging aircraft) and a promise not to pursue further UN sanctions if Iran agreed to what was asked of it—that is, we would not consider relaxing or even temporarily suspending any international sanctions, nor consider a moratorium on unilateral U.S. financial sanctions. In a lower-level meeting of technical experts after the Moscow talks, Iran offered to set aside its demand for recognition of its right to enrichment (its key demand all along) and asked what it could expect in sanction relief (and Iran wanted substantial relief) if it complied with U.S. demands that it cap enrichment at 5 percent and give up its stockpile of 20 percent enriched uranium. The answer, again, was aircraft spare parts. The sum total of three major rounds of diplomatic negotiations was that America would give some bits and bobs of old aircraft in exchange for Iran's nuclear program.

Ironically, economic sanctions had done what they were supposed to do—bring Iran to the table. But now it took a deal to end the crisis, and the White House wavered. A deal would be difficult to sell at home or to Israel, whereas sanctions played well domestically. As one senior State Department official put it to me, "any deal that is acceptable to Iran is unacceptable to Israel, and any deal acceptable to Israel is unacceptable to Iran. It is hopeless, no point in trying."

For the second time (the first was the Turkey-Brazil deal) the administration came to the edge of a diplomatic breakthrough and then walked away. Obama hoped that the status quo would hold until a new regime took over in Tehran. In effect, the United States now sought to resolve the nuclear issue not by taking away Iran's nuclear program, but, as a number of administration officials told me, by changing the regime that would oversee it. It was something like the peaceful coexistence we had with the Soviet Union; we lived with them until they were gone. Iran would go nuclear, but hopefully it would not matter to the United States and Israel when it did.

This long view is based on the assumption that sanctions have made Iran weak and vulnerable. By fall of 2012 there was plenty of evidence to support that impression. The Iranian economy was contracting, and dissent was on the rise. It took baton-wielding riot police and plenty of tear gas to break up street demonstrations when the rial collapsed in early October to a mere fifth of its value in 2011. That narrative certainly suits the administration—they can claim their strategy has been a success. Sanctions *have* weakened Iran, but that does not mean that Iran sees itself as weak or America's hand as particularly strong. Washington may believe that Iraq and Afghanistan have nothing to do with Iran, but Iran sees the unraveling of American military efforts there—not to mention growing instability across the Middle East—as a vulnerability for America and a boon for itself. It makes our military threat hollow and exposes us to many strategic vulnerabilities.

Washington also concluded that Iran was the big loser in the Arab Spring. America saw the crisis in Syria for the most part as a strategic loss for Iran (which it was). But that closed the door to talking to Iran on Syria, which could have led to an early resolution of the crisis. Failing to do so put regional stability at risk.

And, again, the view from Tehran is very different. Democracy in the Arab world proved fleeting, and at any rate it was not a bug likely to infect Iran—Iran's spring had already come and gone in 2009. What came out of the Arab Spring would hurt America more than Iran: Islamic fundamentalism and, even worse, Salafism were on the rise, threatening regional stability and pro-Western regimes that have protected it. The Arab Spring was a cauldron of instability, and that would affect American interests more than Iranian ones—even Syria, Iran thought, could prove more calamitous to America's allies in the region than to Iran. The value of the Arab Spring to Iran is that it will ensnare America in conflicts and distractions; Iran is not as weak as America thinks, because America is not as strong as it thinks. As one astute Middle East observer put it to me, "America is standing with its back to a tsunami. It does not see what is coming at it."

In the short run, Iranians may see benefit in such a status quo. Khamenei's ruling that nuclear weapons are a "great sin" still stands, and keeps Iran on the safe side of the new U.S. red line. But if the sanctions are going to lead to regime change, will Iran's rulers abide them over the long term? Surely getting to "one turn of the screw short" on a bomb—or many bombs—will give the Islamic Republic more leverage as it strives to push back against sanctions and win itself more breathing space?

Iran's strategy could be to build up its centrifuge cascades and its stockpile of 20 percent enriched uranium while perfecting its missile technology.[68] Then it could be as little as two to four months away from a whole arsenal of nuclear weapons. That could make Iran far more dangerous and formidable than racing to build a single bomb today.

The Obama administration claims that it put aside Bush's dream of regime change in Iran. But the unspoken goal, if not the immediate consequence, of America's stepped-up sanctions remains regime change. Some in the Obama administration thought hard-hitting sanctions would keep Iran from building a bomb long enough for a new regime to take over. Others argued for regime change as a policy goal and the only way out of the impasse with Iran.[69] But regime change remains more a pious hope than a real prospect.

Regime change is also a strategy fraught with risk. It may have seemed realistic for the brief moment when the Green Movement had the Islamic Republic back on its heels, but as of 2011 that rebellion had been eviscerated. I remember a conversation that I had with senior White House officials on the eve of the March 2012 parliamentary elections in Iran. They were hearing intelligence assessments of potential street riots, paralysis, and a Persian Spring. None of it happened. There is plenty of dissent in Iran, but no organized opposition tied to the hopeful Green Movement.

Growing sanctions confused Iranians. Sanctions made their lives hard, but few saw them as justified. Sanctions were not put in place to punish the regime for its human rights violations or to support the cause of democracy. Instead, they were there to turn the Islamic Republic away from what is actually a fairly popular goal. The Iranian public is not opposed to its country's nuclear program—indeed, by most accounts the public (much like Pakistanis or Indians) is more assertive than the government and would like Iran to actually have the bomb.

Isolation and sanctions are more likely to cause regime collapse than regime change. As mentioned earlier, the aggressive sanctions regime is undoing the patronage system that sustains the Iranian state. Without the money to keep the wheels greased, clerical rule could fall apart— more and more Iranians could take to the streets, with dangerous fissures opening up in the ruling ranks as elites struggle to respond. And the result may not be a halcyon transition to a friendlier regime, but a messy transition to something worse.

The collapse of the patronage system will wean Iranians from reliance on government, but as more and more are forced to fend for themselves, Iranian society could go the way of 1990s Iraq—a place where poor and radical conurbations such as Sadr City and Basra took the place of Iraq's once-urbane city culture. Economic pressure could cause social disarray, gradually turning parts of Iran into lawless bastions of crime and terror.

Our current policy will eventually turn Iran into a failed state. An Iran sliding into the failed-state column will make the nuclear problem worse, not better, and pose a new set of security challenges to the region and the United States.

The other more immediate result of our current policy is to amplify the talk of war. Israeli prime minister Netanyahu argued that further diplomacy was a waste of time, and that Iran's nuclear program would have to be stopped before it entered the "zone of immunity," meaning before most of the centrifuges moved under the mountain at Fordo. Israel takes Iran's nuclear threat seriously, but by harping on Iran's imminent threat, Netanyahu did a good job of jamming Obama into a corner— committing America to going to war to stop Iran from building nuclear weapons. He would continue this tactic throughout the summer and fall of 2012 to get Obama to commit to a clear red line with Iran.

The administration, too, did its part by trumpeting Israel's readiness to attack Iran. Every administration official who visited Israel came back saying Israel was ready to send its bombers on missions over Iran. The administration hoped this would scare Iranians into surrendering at the negotiations table—a good cop/bad cop diplomatic strategy. But in practice it made talk of war ubiquitous. It became commonplace for those on the inside and those reporting on the administration's thinking to see war around the corner, and the more hawkish voices in particular went further, suggesting it would be a clinical and effective step. The worst-case scenario for what Iran going nuclear would mean—Armageddon in the Middle East—was paired with the rosiest assessment of the effectiveness of an air campaign and its aftermath. "Iranians will not react, cannot react, and if they do it will be limited" was the argument. "They will cower into their hole, and then, weakened and subdued, with the program set back years, they will be a lesser threat."

The only ones who saw through the flimsiness of these arguments were the military. They knew war when they saw it. They knew it would not be easy or straightforward, predictable or cost free. One three-star army general told a private gathering of senior foreign policy hands, "The enemy gets to vote. You can't predict how Iran would react. In fact, they have every incentive to react. Not doing so will damage their standing at home and in the region, and surely they will not want America to get comfortable managing Iran as it did Saddam's Iraq. A war with Iran will be bigger than Iraq or Afghanistan combined. We should expect 15,000 American dead." The American military had learned the same lesson McGeorge Bundy had—there were some things Iran would never give up.

Many in the center and on the Left looked at the hash of Bush and Obama's policy and concluded it was time for the United States to accept the inevitable, that Iran would go nuclear, and that it would not in fact be Armageddon. America had dealt with such a threat before, and a combination of containment and deterrence would keep the Iranian threat at bay as it once had with threats from Stalin, Mao, and Kim Jong-il.[70] Iranians are unlikely to precipitate a nuclear war from which they have little to gain and everything to lose, nor give their nuclear material to terrorists—that is a worry we have with Pakistan, after all, and it has not led us to go to war there. And as for the argument that Iran's nuclear capability would lead to a nuclear frenzy in the region, that is a talking point with scant historical proof to back it up. After all, North Korea's nuclear bomb did not prompt Japan and South Korea to build nuclear bombs of their own. Nor did Bangladesh and Sri Lanka go nuclear to keep up with India and Pakistan. America has plenty of experience in managing exactly the kind of threat that a nuclear Iran would pose, and a far less impressive record bringing wars in the Middle East to successful conclusions.

However, while Iran crossing the nuclear threshold may fall short of Armageddon, it is nonetheless a failure for the United States, which has consistently said that this is unacceptable. If the dual-track policy collapses into either war or containment, it will be a defeat for Obama. Obama made the dual-track policy his own, fine-tuned it and gave it many more teeth, and then moved Bush's red line back from no enrichment to no nuclear weapon, and still that red line may be breached. On balance, the dual-track policy only gave Iran a reason to dig in deeper and clutch its nuclear ambitions tighter. The policy made Iran not less but more dangerous. It put America in the position of either contemplating war or losing face by letting Iran go nuclear. It would have been better to have seriously engaged Iran, slowed its march to nuclear capability earlier, and not risked war or a loss of face so late in the game.

The larger issue is that our policy will make Iran into a bigger threat than it is today. The result will be not to deny Iran nuclear capability but to create a North Korea smack in the middle of the Middle East. Sanctions will cause isolation, social and economic breakdown, and an increasingly hard-line regime protected by a nuclear shield. And if Iran turns into a failed state under the pressure of sanctions, a vast territory with no one in charge, a fragmented society and broken economy, it will become a monumental headache—a font of drugs and terror right in the middle of a strategically vital region.

The problem with North Korea is not that it is a nuclear state—its many conventional weapons alone and the proximity of so many of them to Seoul already make it highly dangerous—but that it is a dysfunctional and failing state, militaristic and radical, in a vital area of the world. Tightening the noose around Iran's neck is not changing its mind on going nuclear (it may in fact be convincing it to stick with its nuclear plan), but it is strengthening the hand of the Revolutionary Guards and other hard-liners. For some time now, the Obama administration has lamented the security forces' growing control over decision making in Tehran. But that is the consequence of saber rattling. Talk of war does not empower moderates and reformers.

Iran's economy is too big for the Revolutionary Guards to control by themselves. But a shrinking Iranian economy can become one that the Guards can control in toto. The private sector is being hit hardest by sanctions, leaving the Guards room to expand their reach and get their hands on the burgeoning black market that sanctions have created. How ironic if sanctions turn out to bolster the wealth and power of the Revolutionary Guards.

As noted above, sanctions have already begun driving Iranian manufacturing concerns to set up shop in China. There they use Iranian credit held in yuan to run their Chinese operations with Chinese labor. The final products are then exported back to Iran through Armenia, Dubai, Pakistan, Turkey, and especially Iraq. Businessmen and their partners in ruling circles continue to make money while jobs are disappearing in a country already struggling under massive unemployment. Unemployment spiked in 2011, which was also a record year for labor strikes and protests by disgruntled government workers.

The sanctions have not hurt the ruling elites or the well-to-do, but average Iranians are suffering, and Iran's social fabric is being torn. It is a singular failure of imagination and absence of strategic vision to pursue a policy the end result of which is to replicate the North Korean debacle in the Middle East, or to produce another Iraq.

In the coming decade, America is going to have its hands full dealing with the myriad problems that follow in the wake of the Arab Spring: wars, revolutions, failing economies, and rising Islamist extremism. The last thing we need is a radicalized, failing, and nuclear-armed Iran.

The weakening of Iran will open the Middle East to a surge of Sunni radicalism—combined with greater Chinese and Russian involvement—that will in the long run prove a far larger and knottier strategic problem for America than Iran currently poses or is ever likely to pose. Iran is clearly not an ally in our attempts to manage this tumultuous region, but it could play the role of a natural balancer to the forecast of Sunni extremism. We should not forget the value of balance-of-power politics. For this reason alone, we will likely look back at our Iran policy over the course of the past four years as a strategic blunder.

IRAQ

The Signal Democracy

On December 12, 2011, Iraq's prime minister, Nouri al-Maliki, met with President Obama at the White House. It was an important meeting. Iraq was no longer in the headlines, but a lot was still riding on what happened there. During the election campaign Obama had promised to end the war that George W. Bush had started, and now, on the eve of the next presidential campaign, Obama was ready to close the book on Iraq, announcing an end to U.S. military operations there and bringing home the rest of the troops (although many would be heading to Afghanistan).

During the meeting, Maliki told Obama he had evidence that his vice president, the prominent Sunni political leader Tariq al-Hashemi, and other key members of his Iraqi National Movement (known as al-Iraqiyya) were guilty of supporting terrorism. This was a serious accusation; if true, it meant that Iraq's fragile unity government was a farce and about to unravel. Maliki wanted to gauge Obama's reaction, to see whether America would prevent him from attacking Hashemi and his party, a move that was sure to scuttle the semblance of sectarian peace that America had brokered in 2007. Iraq would be stepping close to the edge of the precipice right when America was leaving.

Obama was in no mood to get sucked back into Iraq's problems. He told Maliki what he wanted to hear: the issue was an internal Iraqi affair. Maliki interpreted Obama's insouciance as a green light to go after Hashemi without worrying about consequences from America. Once the meeting was over Maliki told his entourage, "See! The Americans don't care."

Three days later, on December 15, Secretary of Defense Leon Panetta brought a formal end to the American military presence in Iraq at a ceremony in a fortified compound at Baghdad International Airport. That night, after the pomp was done and Panetta had flown out, Iraqi tanks surrounded the homes of Hashemi and two other Iraqiyya leaders in the government. On paper, the charge was terrorism, but in reality Maliki was exacting revenge. He was angry at Iraqiyya because it had garnered more votes and seats in the March 2010 elections than had Maliki's coalition. Maliki also believed (though this was not part of the charge sheet) that Iraqiyya was now in the pay of Saudi Arabia, working to undo the government.

To avoid arrest, Hashemi fled to Iraq's Kurdish region. Iraqi politics then plunged into crisis. Sunni provinces demanded greater autonomy from Baghdad. Al-Qaeda went on the offensive, killing hundreds in scores of bombing attacks in a campaign of terror that went on for months. Iraq was inching its way back to mayhem. This was not the denouement to a tragic war that Obama was looking for. The Americans' exit was not supposed to tear open old wounds and reignite the conflict. But that is exactly what events portended.

And that is not all. Iraq's slide into chaos, violence, and internecine conflict put its very existence as a nation in doubt. The process of disintegration that started in 2006 was poised to move to completion. America's troop surge in 2007 managed to slow its pace and perhaps even halt it for a time, but mistake after mistake in 2010 and then a hasty exit in 2011 removed all that was holding Iraq's demons at bay—the demons we had unleashed in 2003.

The Obama administration told Americans that our departure from Iraq showed that we were leaving behind a country strong enough to stand on its own feet. But what Iraqis and the rest of the Middle East understood was that we were leaving Iraq, like Afghanistan, to its own fate. We had broken Iraq, and for a while we cared to put it back together; now we did not care. Obama's shrug when Maliki told him about Hashemi meant that it was no longer America's responsibility to keep Iraq whole; we were going to let the Band-Aids holding its broken pieces together come off.

Iraq is important, and not just because it is an ancient, oil-rich country sitting in the heart of the Middle East. Post-Saddam Iraq matters because it is a signature American project whose outcome will be the measure of our reliability and the legacy of our power in the Middle East. For the better part of two decades we have tangled with Iraq, first beating back its regional ambitions, then squeezing away its power, and finally breaking it. We told the region and the world that we knew what we were doing: Iraq and the Middle East would be better off for our intervention. We would build a shining city on the hill, an example of democracy and prosperity that would help transform the whole region. Iraq would show that American power was still a force for good in the world, and would convince naysayers that we should use it more often to ensure global security and spread freedom and prosperity. What the promise of globalization had not achieved, American military muscle could: we would bulldoze the holdouts against the new world order created in the wake of the collapse of the Soviet Union.

But Iraq turned out badly. American power failed the dream. As Iraq shattered into violence, placing the rest of the Middle East dangerously close to a vortex of instability and sectarian conflict, the region lost trust in American power—that we knew how to exercise it, and that when we did we could salvage some good from it. And worse yet, the region learned that we had neither the patience nor perseverance to see through what we started. The speedy American troop withdrawal from Iraq in 2011 was a confirmation of all this. Americans may celebrate that there are no more of our soldiers fighting in Iraq, but this is an end that offers no closure. It will take a lot to repair the damage the war did; the distrust sown by our withdrawal will only add to the tally.

On the campaign trail, Obama had said that Iraq was a misguided enterprise, a needless and costly war of choice that had tarnished America's image. So it was not a surprise that the White House celebrated when the last convoy of American soldiers left Iraq for Kuwait on December 18, 2011. It was the fulfillment of a campaign promise, or, as Vice President Biden called it, "one of the great achievements of this administration." (He went on to promise "a stable government in Iraq that is actually moving toward a representative government.")[1] Less was more, in the administration's thinking. The withdrawal would make achieving our goals there more likely.

When Bush left office, Iraq did look as if it was on the rebound. General David Petraeus's COIN strategy and the surge of troops in 2007 had turned the fiasco of the war into something of a success story. When Obama came in, Iraq was enjoying relative calm. The insurgency had ended, al-Qaeda in Iraq was a thing of the past, and the fragile peace between Shias and Sunnis was holding.

But storm clouds loomed. Iraq's government was hopelessly corrupt and ineffective. We were in part responsible for that failure by first hastily dismantling the Iraqi state and then giving Iraq a constitution that confirmed sectarian divisions while requiring an overwhelming majority before a government could form—which could be achieved by promising control of large areas of government to prospective allies to milk as they saw fit. Even then, it took Iraqi politicians six months of squabbling after the March 2010 elections to form a government. At best, in 2009 when the Obama administration took office, Iraq was going sideways, unity and peace beyond its reach.

The problem, many think, is Maliki. Since taking office in 2006 he has proven, at various times and in various ways, both ineffectual and dictatorial. He hails from the smallest of the three major Shia political parties, al-Da'awa, and has had to rely on the support of a constellation of Shia, Sunni, and Kurdish political blocs to govern.

His on-and-off relations with the firebrand Shia cleric Muqtada al-Sadr worry many, but by and large U.S. authorities have found ways to work with him. Once or twice he has even managed to pleasantly surprise America with bold action. No one found fault with Maliki's leadership when he saddled up in the spring of 2008 to lead the nascent Iraqi army into Baghdad's Sadr City neighborhood and then the southern city of Basra in order to flush out and defeat the so-called Mahdi Army, Sadr's private force of Shia militiamen.

But all told, Maliki has not amounted to the kind of leader that Iraq needs.[2] He is a weak manager,[3] and his authoritarian style has even alienated his own Shia (and Kurdish) allies.[4] Maliki is deeply sectarian, still nursing anger born from the years of abuse that Shias suffered at the hands of the Sunni dictator Saddam Hussein. When Maliki first emerged on the scene, he openly embraced Shia chauvinism and talked of revenge against Sunnis—payback for decades of mistreatment. He has favored Shias not only in civilian posts but also in the highest ranks of the military and police. Iraq needed a leader who would promote reconciliation. What it got instead is one content to stoke the fires of sectarianism.

Obama thought it futile to invest any more time and effort in this failed project. There were not going to be any more gains—the picture was not going to get any rosier. Staying in Iraq in great numbers, boosting Maliki, and keeping in place his alliance with Sunnis were not going to pay any dividends.

The U.S. military wanted to stay longer; the generals worried about Iraq backsliding into open conflict. But they had been touting the victories won by the surge and singing the praises of the new Iraqi security forces. And Obama had the war in Afghanistan to think about. Thus—in a pattern that repeated itself with respect to the latter country—he took the military's rhetoric of success at face value and announced that the situation in Iraq was good enough to make an American withdrawal possible.

Iraq policy was handed over to the vice president; he would see to our exit. Biden knew Iraq well. He had followed developments there closely from his perch as chairman of the Senate Foreign Relations Committee. His prediction in 2006 (made jointly with veteran foreign policy thinker Leslie Gelb) that Iraq would not survive the combined centrifugal pull of Shia revival and Kurdish autonomy, and was bound to split up along ethnosectarian lines and that the United States should not stand in the way, had made quite a stir.[5] Now he would be seeing to a precipitous American withdrawal, which could make that forecast come true. He was not a fan of the COIN strategy (in Iraq or Afghanistan), and inside the White House he advocated leaving Iraq sooner rather than later.[6]

In October 2008, the Bush administration had bowed to Iraqi pressure and pledged to withdraw all U.S. troops by the end of 2011. Obama used that deadline as his goalpost too, accelerating the drawdown of troops as they handed over security to Iraqi forces. The schedule depended on Iraqi politics holding together and Iraqi forces keeping the peace on the streets for a decent enough interval to give the administration plausible deniability when things fell apart after the U.S. departure. It was touch and go for a while, especially when the March 2010 elections took so long to produce a government. But much to everyone's relief, the long months of haggling between politicians brought little sectarian violence and even less al-Qaeda activity.

Alas, the facade of stability barely masked the trouble brewing under the surface. The year 2010 proved a critical one for Iraq. The country's political scene was still fractious, and held together only thanks to a fragile power-sharing arrangement that required close American management. But the Obama administration had no time or energy for that. Instead it anxiously eyed the exits, with its one thought to get out. It stopped protecting the political process just when talk of American withdrawal turned the heat back up under the long-simmering power struggle that pitted the Shias, Sunnis, and Kurds against one another.

The end of the drawn-out government-formation scrum in December 2010 left Maliki in the premiership. Before long, he was embarking on an ambitious power grab. Washington ignored his increasing abuse of the constitution, his illegal push for more de-Baathification, and his browbeating of the judiciary, all of which gave Maliki grounds to believe that the United States would place no impediment in the way of his plan to build a Shia authoritarian regime. Rather than develop trust in one another, the Shia, Sunni, and Kurdish factions grew further apart, jealously guarding their political fiefdoms (the presidency for the Kurds, the premiership for the Shias, and the lesser offices of vice president and parliament speaker for the Sunnis). Maliki thought that the premiership would be his forever, a permanent perch from which he could reach out to dominate the presidency and whatever offices Sunnis might hold.

The 2010 elections and their aftermath were a telling exercise in deal making. The Iraqiyya party won 24.7 percent of the popular vote and 91 of the one-chamber parliament's 325 seats. This showing nosed out Maliki's al-Da'awa, which won 24.2 percent and 89 seats. The results should have given Iraqiyya's leader, ex-premier Ayad Allawi, a shot at putting together a government. But Maliki moved quickly to block Allawi. Among other things, Maliki persuaded U.S. officials that the Shia majority would reject Allawi—a nominal Shia and former Baathist who had served as interim premier in 2004 and 2005 and was now rebounding with the backing of Saudi Arabia—so decisively that any government formed by him would plunge the country back into sectarian combat.

Maliki came out on top and resumed the premiership in December 2010, backed by the United States.[7] That the incumbent could finish second and still keep his job signaled flaws in the system. Iraqis now thought that it was America and not Iraqis who picked the prime minister. Indeed, but there was another power broker in Iraq with the same agenda: Iran.

Iranian leaders were at first divided over who should become prime minister (and confident in their right to choose). General Qasem Soleimani, the commander of the Revolutionary Guards' Quds Brigade and the day-to-day superintendent of Iran's political and military involvement in Iraq, was frustrated with disagreements between Iraqi Shia leaders—and blamed these for their inability to quickly form a government. Soleimani (and also Syria's ruler Bashar al-Assad) favored another Shia politician, Adel Abdul-Mahdi, to take the job. But Maliki and his allies resisted. Muqtada al-Sadr in particular objected because Mahdi's party, the Islamic Supreme Council of Iraq (ISCI), was Sadr's main rival. Sadr and other pro-Maliki Shia politicians lobbied Iran's Supreme Leader. Eventually, in December 2010, Khamenei wrote a letter to all Iraqi Shia leaders exhorting them to agree on Maliki as the choice for the premiership.

Iran then leaned on Syria to stop its support for Mahdi. Iran and Syria, generally allies, had not been on the same page regarding Iraq since 2003. Iranians supported the Shia rise to power, whereas Syria had backed the insurgency in all its permutations, from al-Qaeda to the Baathist diehards. Damascus had turned on Maliki after he had called for a United Nations investigation into Syria's role in bombings in Iraq. Syria had bankrolled Maliki's Shia rival, Mahdi. But with Iranian pressure mounting, Syria cut a deal: in exchange for dumping Mahdi, Assad was promised a gas pipeline from Iran. Iran then asked Hezbollah to mediate between Assad and Maliki.

In the end, Iran actually implemented what also happened to be American policy. The irony was not lost on Iraqis, and the more suspicious among them thought they could discern the outlines of a sinister U.S.-Iranian conspiracy to turn Maliki into a permanent prime minister—a dictator.

While there was no conspiracy, American policy in Iraq at this point was not committed to promoting national unity (though Obama did make an effort to promote reconciliation by trying to secure the presidency for Allawi as a consolation prize),[8] nor to continuing with institution building, but to ensuring a state strong enough to permit U.S. withdrawal. It was easier to see Iraq in terms of balancing its divisions—Biden thought of it as resembling the Balkans—than to chart a path to greater political unity. Pursuing real unity would require keeping America's commitment to Iraq, and a leader other than Maliki.

Washington's priority was not building Iraqi democracy but creating a security state around a strong leader, authoritarian by default. (The same would be true of Afghanistan and Yemen down the road, revealing the pragmatic or realist heart of Obama's approach to the Middle East).[9] It made for a disconnect between America and the Iraqi political leaders with whom Washington claimed to be working. Most Iraqi leaders were concerned with preventing the return of a dictator (when the leading candidate for the role was Maliki), and felt wary of growing Iranian influence. The Obama White House had different priorities and was perturbed by neither Maliki's authoritarianism nor the growing Iranian influence that it facilitated.

Obama had turned Bush's Iraq policy on its head. America went into Iraq to build democracy, but left building an authoritarian state as an exit strategy. It is obvious now that—talk about democracy in his Cairo speech notwithstanding—Obama was not really committed to democracy in the Middle East. We did not know it then, but Iraq in 2009 and 2010 was a preview of how the Obama administration would react to the Arab Spring in 2011, and a window onto his thinking about the Middle East.

The White House, not understanding Maliki's debt to Iran, misread Maliki, thinking that having won the elections with American backing he would now serve as the Shia strongman to do Washington's bidding—notably to provide the security cover for the United States to leave and sign on to a new Status of Forces Agreement (SOFA) to replace the one that Bush had negotiated and that would expire in 2011. But anointing him prime minister did not endear America to Maliki. He still thought that U.S. authorities had conspired with Allawi and Iraqiyya to rig the voting (Hamid Karzai would claim similar feelings of U.S. persecution after the 2009 elections in Afghanistan). Maliki grew more stubborn and even less willing to compromise. He both resented the suggestion that America had picked him and saw the United States as a hurdle to further consolidation of his power.

The Pentagon, meanwhile, continued to worry about the consequences of a hasty exit. It thought that danger was still lurking in Iraq and that the country needed an American presence to maintain stability and forward momentum. There was Iranian influence to worry about, and a U.S. military footprint in the heart of Mesopotamia would be a strategic asset, giving America influence along a wide arc stretching from the Levant to the Persian Gulf.

The question was how many U.S. combat troops would be needed for this, and under what terms would they stay in Iraq. High on the White House's list of demands was that American soldiers would enjoy immunity from local prosecution—something that the Iraqi government would have to agree to in the new SOFA.

Washington thought that Maliki would deliver on the SOFA. But he didn't, and neither would anyone else. Why should they? Maliki was tiring of the U.S. presence, and his rivals still viewed it as something that had served him and his ambitions, not Iraqi democracy. Why strengthen Maliki by keeping America in Iraq? With America gone, Maliki might be weaker and riper for a takedown. Later, after the die was cast, Sunnis openly rued not having backed the SOFA; by then it had become clear that the U.S. departure would mean a Maliki power grab.

The White House's gambit of choosing the SOFA over strengthening democracy proved to be a lose–lose proposition. America did not get a new agreement, and Iraq ended up with an authoritarian strongman who would push the country to the edge of a cliff.

Negotiations over that new agreement started in earnest in June 2011. Washington offered to leave behind 10,000 combat troops. Iraqis across the political spectrum thought that number showed a lack of seriousness and commitment, and even in Washington the chairman of the Joint Chiefs, Admiral Mullen, told the president it would "constitute high risk."[10] It confirmed what Iraqi defense minister Qadir Obeidi had heard from the administration in Washington in the spring of 2009—that the United States wanted to be pretty much completely out of Iraq by December 2011. If Washington were serious, then it would commit 25,000 or more troops to Iraq, he felt. Even if Iraqis had been impressed with the offer of 10,000 troops, it still would have left the United States capable of playing only a marginal role in protecting Iraq's security, and with little influence in Iraqi politics. Such a low number meant the American troops would do no more than protect themselves. If you are not there, then you will not matter.

Giving American soldiers immunity from local prosecution was not popular either. Many Iraqis thought that U.S. troops, and the private security forces that locals associated with the U.S. presence, had perpetrated violence on the population with impunity, and they wanted no more of that. In addition, giving American troops immunity ran counter to Iraqi nationalist sensibilities; it was an infringement on sovereignty. The powerful Iranian-aligned politicians, too, were opposed to the American troop presence in Iraq—Tehran had objected to the original 2008 SOFA and did not want to see it renewed.

The political cost of giving Washington what it wanted was too high for Maliki and his allies, and they were already content with the United States leaving. Thus the low number of troops that the administration promised was the perfect cover: negotiations broke down in October 2011, and the administration declared that all U.S. troops would be out of Iraq by the end of the year. In effect, Washington confirmed what Iraqis suspected: America was not serious about Iraq, it was not committed to its security, and privately it was happy not to have to leave behind even the 10,000 troops that it had offered.

The administration responded to the collapse of its halfhearted negotiations by declaring victory. It had extricated the United States from Iraq, fulfilling President Obama's campaign pledge and freeing resources to attend to Afghanistan. But it was a Pyrrhic victory, a testament to American fickleness—a break-it-and-bolt legacy that will be tough to shake. The region got the message loud and clear that America was out of the game. The claim of Hassan Nasrallah, the leader of Hezbollah, that America had been defeated in Iraq gained traction on the

Arab street, and not just in anti-American corners of Damascus or South Beirut. After we packed up and left, our influence would wane, and we would not even care.[11]

The surge had hardly made Iraq whole, and our speedy departure threatened to break it apart again. Far from Biden's "great achievement," Iraq could prove to be one of the Obama administration's greater mistakes.

American troops had barely left when Iraqi politics imploded. Two days after the last U.S. convoy crossed into Kuwait, the four key Sunni provinces of Anbar, Diyala, Mosul, and Salahuddin—the Sunni heartland and a bastion of Iraqi nationalism—asked for federalism and regional autonomy.[12] This was followed by the major crisis that had been baked in the cake when Maliki left Washington thinking that he had gotten Obama's go-ahead to hound Iraqiyya on terrorism charges. Iraqiyya threatened to leave the government and then appealed to Kurdish leaders for support to counter Maliki's growing "dictatorship."[13]

Relations between Maliki and the Kurdish leader Masoud Barzani were already tense. Baghdad had put its foot down—unsuccessfully— by declaring that the Kurdish region could not conclude its own oil deals with foreign firms. Kurds had bought into the concept of a united Iraq, provided it would be democratic. But with America leaving and Maliki turning his back on democracy, the Kurds felt vulnerable—it would be only a matter of time before Maliki would try to impose tight control over them. It was hardly a surprise, then, that the fleeing vice president Hashemi found the red carpet rolled out for him in the Iraqi Kurdistan region, or that the Kurds came to his aid by launching sympathetic remonstrations against Baghdad's increasingly dictatorial ways. Barzani has since hosted Maliki's Shia critics as well, and raised the possibility of holding a referendum in which the voters of the Kurdish region would be asked if they want to separate from Iraq—unofficial referendums on the same question have yielded 90 percent support for separation.

As a rift opened between the Sunnis and Kurds, on the one hand, and the Shia government in Baghdad on the other, Turkey entered the fray. Since 2006, Turkey had built strong ties with the Kurdish region. Moreover, and more importantly, Turkey felt compelled by its ambitions regarding regional leadership to take up the Sunni cause. It was the logical step for a majority-Sunni power eager to take the Arab world under its wing. An angry Prime Minister Erdoğan summoned Maliki's national security adviser to Ankara and dressed him down for his treatment of Iraqi Sunnis. The Turkish premier then brushed aside the Interpol warrant for Hashemi's arrest and gave him shelter in Istanbul under the full protection of the Turkish police. In Turkey, Sunnis and Kurds had found a patron in their quest to move away from Baghdad's control.

The fight against Maliki strengthens Iran's hand—Maliki will seek Tehran's support, and so will his Shia rival Sadr. Sadr has also been talking to Barzani and Iraqiyya's leaders, lending impetus to their resistance to Maliki. America, meanwhile, is in no mood to be dragged into Iraq's political drama. It is willing to go along with a Barzani-Sadr plan to unseat Maliki so long as it does not create a mess—which means implicitly endorsing a greater role for Iran in Iraq.

With Turkish influence growing in the Kurdish north and Iranian influence in the Shia south, Iraqi unity is fading fast. Normal politics is over for now. Coalition building between various parties intent on shoring up the center is giving way to a kind of political "warlordism." Political bosses will divide the spoils to serve their constituencies. They have no vested interest in the state, other than to carve up its resources; they will forge tactical alliances and go to battle with competitors to maximize their share. Iraq's political warlords will bring down the state to get rid of Maliki, but some will also sell out to Maliki if he meets their price. But even if all the stars align for Maliki to fall, it will not be a restoration of democracy or normal politics, only the gradual demise of the state—the coming apart of Iraq.

America's quick exit now looks to have doomed Iraq's experiment with democracy, and in an ironic twist it is America's man in Iraq who is the aspiring dictator.

All this is happening at a dangerous time, coinciding with the destabilizing force of the Arab Spring. Iraq was meant to send a signal that democratic government was possible in a part of the world that had never seen one up close. Instead it is signaling that sectarianism is ascendant.

When Tunisians and Egyptians revolted against corruption and misrule, many expected that Iraqis, too, irrespective of sect or ethnicity, would take to the streets to demand accountability and good government. After all, they suffer more than any other Arab people from corruption and misrule. A few demonstrations similar to those in Tunis and Cairo raised hope for a proper reckoning, but in Iraq the Arab Spring did not have any wind in its sails.[14] Here things were not straightforward.

Iraqis too want dignity, good government, jobs, and an end to corruption, but their politics does not yet turn on these issues. The Bush administration had assumed that once it got rid of Saddam, Iraqis would focus on bread-and-butter issues and building a democracy. But Saddam's dictatorship had also kept in place minority rule, giving Sunni Arabs a disproportionate share of power and resources, brutally suppressing Kurds and Shias in the process. The U.S. invasion ended that imbalance. Kurds and especially Shias gained as their numbers decided distribution of power and resources. When a dictatorship that keeps in place an inequitable distribution of power among sects and ethnic groups bites the dust, the first upshot is a torturous—and in Iraq's case, violent—rebalancing act. In Iraq, Sunni resistance to the writ of the Americans who had shattered the Sunni-run state plunged the country into a bloody sectarian war. The Sunni insurgency fought both the U.S. occupation and the Shia ascendancy it facilitated. The insurgency wanted America gone so it could restore Sunni dominance over Iraq.

When the guns fell silent in Iraq in 2008, the assumption was that the Sunnis had finally given up. The American troop surge had convinced them that Baghdad was beyond their reach and Shia control of Iraq was a done deal. America hoped that some combination of Shia magnanimity and Sunni acquiescence would guarantee peace and stability for Iraq—and give U.S. troops a ticket out of the war. But sectarian truce did not mean sectarian peace or a final consensus on the fate of Iraq. The country moved on from the Saddam years but not too far, and the sectarian violence that followed the invasion inflicted fresh wounds and set off fresh cycles of revenge. Shias still fear Sunni rule, and Sunnis rue their loss of power and dream of climbing back to the top. Each has a different vision of the past and a different dream for the future. There are still scores to settle, decades of them.

Sectarianism is an old wound in the Middle East.[15] But the recent popular urge for democracy, national unity, and dignity has opened it up and made it sting afresh.[16] This is because many of the Arab governments that now face the wrath of protesters are guilty of both suppressing individual rights and concentrating power in the hands of minorities.

The problem goes back to the colonial period, when European administrators created state institutions designed to manipulate religious and ethnic diversity to their advantage. They handed minorities greater representation in colonial security forces and governments in order to give these minorities an intense stake in the colonial regime and, in effect, make them its gendarmes. This is what the French did with the despised (by the Sunnis) Alawite minority in Syria; what the British did with the Hashemites, Bedouins, and Circassians in Jordan; and what the Ottomans and later the British did with the Sunni Arabs in Iraq.

The Arab states that emerged from colonialism after the First World War and the end of the League of Nations mandates promised unity under the banner of Arab nationalism. But as they turned into cynical dictatorships, failing at war, economic development, and governance, they, too, entrenched sectarian biases. They were still the same states Europeans had built. This scarred Arab society so deeply that the impulse for unity was often no match for the deep divisions of tribe, sect, and ethnicity. Some also argue that the infatuation with Arab unity prevented Arab states from developing proper national institutions, which also made them vulnerable to the surge of tribal loyalties and identity politics.

These sectarian states survived for a long time, seeking to hide their deep divisions via tricks such as taking census surveys as seldom as possible. Their authoritarian governments resorted to force when they had to, but more often persuaded restless majorities and minorities to accept things as they were by relying on what the scholar of ethnic conflict David Laitin calls a "hegemonic common sense."[17] Arab nationalism served as that common sensibility. The promises of fulfilling a historic destiny and standing up to America and Israel were potent enough to push sectarian worries to the side.[18] But over time the pan-Arabist ideology lost its allure, and as its promise increasingly rang hollow, states built to keep in place minority overlordship grew vulnerable.

Iraq is a preview of what the Arab Spring may bring across the region. The loosening of the grip of stolid and brutal states over society brings to the surface competitions for power and resources centered on long-suppressed ethnic and sectarian divisions.[19] At its worst, conflict could turn into full-scale civil wars culminating in the redrawing of maps. (Already the example of South Sudan, born after decades of conflict over irreconcilable differences, is looming large in the region's imagination—just ask the Kurds.) The specter also looms of broader regional conflagrations as developments in various countries—often involving the same issues, sects, tribes, and ethnic groups in ways that cross borders—become linked together in a chain of conflict. We thought of the fall of dictatorships in Asia, Eastern Europe, and Latin America as a democracy wave; in the Middle East it will be a wave of tribal and sectarian conflict. It is only now, after the American invasion of Iraq and the Arab Spring, that the Middle East is finally throwing off the yoke of colonialism and—via the terrible means of fratricidal bloodletting—getting past its legacy.

So it is that with Gaddafi's brutal regime gone, Libya is gradually coming apart along tribal and regional lines. Likewise, Yemen is inching closer to civil war and a north-south division, and Syria is descending into a sectarian war between the Sunni majority and the minority Alawites and their allies.[20] But the struggle that matters most is the one between Sunnis and Shias. The war in Iraq first unleashed the destructive potential of their competition for power, but the issue was not settled there. The Arab Spring has allowed it to resurface. Today, Shias clamor for greater rights in Lebanon, Bahrain, and Saudi Arabia, while Sunnis are restless in Iraq and Syria.

In a certain sense, the Middle East is starting to look like South Asia. Politics in India, Pakistan, and Sri Lanka can be messy. They are more open and democratic than Middle Eastern politics, but South Asian societies feature communal and ethnic divisions that can sometimes erupt into violence. Sri Lanka is the most violent example, and India arguably has done the best job of holding its many separatist groups together. The Arab world, with the exception of Lebanon, was the "anti"–South Asia: authoritarian but stable and united culturally (everyone claims to be Arab first, then something else) and politically (anti-Americanism and opposition to Israel encounter no dissent). But that is no longer true. We are seeing personal and civic ties that bind sects and ethnicities together coming apart,[21] and political incentives putting a wedge between erstwhile friends and neighbors—and sometimes right through families.[22] Weak states do less to protect minorities and lack capacity to prevent outbreaks of violence.[23] When the state's ability to contain communal violence collapses, yesterday's unity can quickly give way to today's hatred and disorder. Regions find peace when states and nations there mirror one another.[24] In the Middle East, states do not mirror their nations, and until they do the region will be racked by conflict.

Iraqis like to claim that there was no sectarianism in their country before the U.S. tanks showed up. Shias had Sunni friends, there were mixed marriages, collaborations, and partnerships—although mostly among the urban middle classes. The historian Niall Ferguson reminds us that pluralism was an inverse guide to ethnic and communal violence during the First World War. Wherever there was more intermarriage there was also more ethnic and racial violence.[25] We saw this happen in Sarajevo as well. The Middle East is now where Europe was in 1914—gone is the unity and peace that held sectarian violence at bay.

Along the arc from Syria in the Levant to Bahrain in the Persian Gulf, Arab dictatorship has kept in place the dominance of one sect—often the one that is locally in the minority—over the other. The very first consequence of the weakening of those states will be a knife fight between the stubborn, desperate minority that has held power and the energized majority that now wants it. In short, Arab dictatorships from Syria to Bahrain are variations of Saddam Hussein's state, and the Arab Spring is doing to them what the American invasion accomplished in Iraq: transferring power from the minority to the majority.[26]

So far Shia protests in Bahrain have gone down under hails of lead and failed to repeat the outcome in Tunisia and Egypt. The Bahraini monarchy has defended its grip on power with ferocity, and with generous Saudi support.

But what the Arab Spring did not do for Bahraini Shias, it did do for the region's Sunnis. The regime changes in Tunisia, Egypt, and Libya all empowered the Muslim Brotherhood and, more worryingly still, Salafis. This puritanical sect subscribes to a narrow reading of Islam and loves to patrol its constricted boundaries with an avid hostility toward deviants. Shias come in for special contempt not merely as infidels who refuse the message, but as heretics and apostates who insist on garbling and perverting it. The type of Sunni Muslim fervor that the Arab Spring has unleashed will not stop with vicious assaults against religious "outsider" groups such as Egypt's ancient Coptic Christian minority. On the contrary, it will take aim at perceived enemies within the house of Islam itself and allow greater scope for conflict with Shias.

The uprising in Syria also upset the sectarian status quo. Assad's Syria was the mirror image of Saddam's Iraq. Iraq was a Shia-majority country in the clutches of a Sunni regime, whereas Syria is a Sunni-majority country ruled by Alawites, generally viewed as part of the Shia family. True, Bashar al-Assad had been no friend to Iraq's Shias. To protect Syria's facade of Arab unity for domestic consumption, Assad decried the American occupation while joining in with the regionwide sympathy for Iraq's Sunnis (all the while continuing to suppress Sunnis at home). As a result, he supported all manner of Baathist and jihadist outfits in the insurgency that killed and maimed thousands of Iraq's Shias and challenged their newfound hold on power. Still, his fall from power and Syria's passage into Sunni hands (the Muslim Brotherhood and Salafis are major forces among Syrian Sunnis) cannot help but energize the Sunnis just across the border in Iraq. The despair that led them to accept the outcome in Iraq in 2008 could be replaced by exuberance and a belief that this outcome may still be reversed.

A Sunni regime in Damascus—or controlling large parts of Syria bordering on Iraq—could do for Iraq's Sunnis what Iran did for its Shias. If you add to that the full force (and cash) of Saudi Arabia, Qatar, and the UAE—to say nothing of Turkey, Egypt, and the rest—the Arab world could be quite a lonely place for Iraq's Shias. It was for this reason that Maliki lobbied on behalf of Assad with everyone he met while in Washington in December 2011. He even told President Obama that if the region's Sunnis—backed by the Arab Gulf states—try to roll back gains made by Shias, "we will all become Hezbollah"—that is, turn radical and wage armed resistance.

Iraq's Sunnis may still hope to take back Baghdad, but failing that they could opt out of Iraq. A larger Sunni zone stretching from Anbar to northern Lebanon on the one side and the Turkish border on the other would be sandwiched between Shia southern Iraq and Shia and Alawite pockets to the north.

Iraq's Shias would be sitting in the midst of a hostile Sunni world. Turkey and Saudi Arabia would be supporting their Sunni rivals, with the Turks possibly applying additional pressure via the Iraqi Kurds. Iran would then be the Iraqi Shias' only friend. The Arab Spring may have weakened Iran's influence in Egypt and the Levant, but it has confirmed it in Iraq. The political and religious resurgence of Sunni Islam is pushing the region's Shias closer to Iran.

People in the Middle East talk of religious and national unity, and there are voices calling for bridge building. Egypt's new president has reached out to Iran and wants his country to bring Iran into the Middle East fold. But sectarianism is the rising tide. It is setting in train complex and interrelated developments that will change the strategic—and possibly the physical—map of the Middle East, deciding regional dynamics for years to come. The sectarian impulse will guide strategic decisions such as Turkey's support for Iraq's Sunnis and Saudi Arabia's mobilization against Iran. America has had nothing to do with this second wave of sectarianism—that was the fruit of the Arab Spring—but the hasty U.S. departure from Iraq paved the way for the tsunami to wash unimpeded over the region.

We cannot prevent all conflict in the Middle East, but we can hope to reduce its impact. A more gradual withdrawal from Iraq or an earlier push for political settlements in Bahrain and Syria would have kept the embers of sectarianism from erupting into raging flames. Left unchecked, strife in Iraq and Syria (and, before long, Bahrain) could combine to produce a belt of instability stretching from the Mediterranean to the Persian Gulf. That would threaten America's allies in Jordan and Saudi Arabia as well as jack up oil prices and hence threaten the global economy. There would be ethnic cleansing, floods of refugees, humanitarian disasters, and failing states with ungoverned territories that would provide opportunities for al-Qaeda. As Ayad Allawi has sagely and succinctly put it: "The invasion of Iraq in 2003 may indeed have been a war of choice. But losing Iraq in 2011 is a choice the United States and the world cannot afford to make."[27] Too late.

THE FADING PROMISE
OF THE ARAB SPRING

The general verdict on the Obama administration's Middle East policy is that "it has not done too badly." There are no blatant mistakes, bleeding gashes, or crippling crises. In fact, the argument goes, the president's hands-off policy has been good in that it has made the Arab Spring about Arabs—at the height of the protests there were no American flags burning in Cairo or Tunis, and plenty being waved in Tripoli.

This may be "good enough"—for today—but it provides precious little assurance about tomorrow. America's aim remains to shrink its footprint in the Middle East, and so its approach to unfolding events there has been wholly reactive. It may get a passing grade in managing changes of regime as old dictators fall, but it has largely failed at the real challenge, which is to help new governments in the region move toward democracy and reform their parlous, sclerotic economies. Removing a dictator is only the first step on the road to democracy; beyond that, America has been nowhere to be seen. The Obama administration has neither come up with a strategy for capitalizing on the opportunity that the Arab Spring presented nor adequately prepared for potential fallout in the form of regional rivalry, the explosion of sectarian tensions, and deep-rooted economic crises.

What *are* America's interests in the Middle East? How will we protect them as old regimes fall and new ones try to take shape? Can we influence outcomes? How should we prepare for the rise of Islamism, civil wars, state failures, reversals, and recrudescence of dictatorship? We need answers to these questions and a strategy for realizing the best, avoiding the worst, and protecting our interests in the process. America cannot and should not decide the fate of the Middle East, but it should be clear about its stakes in the region, and not shy away from efforts to at least nudge events in more favorable directions as a critical world region faces momentous choices. A "lean back and wait" posture toward unfolding events will not be enough—a series of reactions and tactical maneuvers do not amount to a strategy. A strategy requires having a clear view of our interests and of how to realize them by influencing as best we can the dynamics that are shaping the region.

President Obama's approach to the Middle East has been distant from the outset. He has wanted to improve America's image in the Muslim world and feels that the best way to do this is to end America's unpopular wars there. His modus operandi has been disengagement: end existing commitments, foremost among them Iraq and Afghanistan, and avoid new entanglements. His approach to the Arab-Israeli peace process typifies this. Obama's June 2009 Cairo speech impressed Muslims with its call on Israel to halt the building of settlements in the West Bank. In 2011, he made a similarly provocative call on Israel to agree to return to its 1967 borders (with mutually agreed swaps of territory with Palestinians). But the Muslim world was wrong to assume that these exhortations signaled a readiness on Obama's part to roll up his sleeves and help fix problems.[1] In fact, "nowhere in Obama's foreign policy has the gap been wider between promise and delivery," writes former American diplomat and observer of the Arab-Israeli scene Martin Indyk, "than in the [peace process]."[2]

Obama started with a new approach to the issue. He was fervent in his commitment to Israel. Yet he also recognized the corrosive effects that the simmering conflict was having on America's image and the region's stability, and was not shy about speaking out against the everyday indignities that Israeli occupation meant for Palestinians. Many Arabs and Muslims were elated and many Israelis incensed, but no one on either side of the divide should have become so excited. All were wildly overestimating Obama's willingness to get involved in moving the peace process along.

What Obama had in mind was to placate Arab opinion while laying down markers for Israel to abide by. This, he hoped, would by itself spur diplomatic engagement and ultimately a solution. What he did not have in mind was to pick a fight with Israel or commit to a greater U.S. role in facilitating a diplomatic breakthrough. He definitely did not think about a comprehensive diplomatic strategy that would have created the proper context and framework for compromises by both sides (halting new settlement construction could have been a part of that). Instead, he proceeded in an uncoordinated and unproductive fashion by laying undue stress on a single unrealistic demand in a way that stopped the entire process in its tracks. He was determined to extricate America from the Middle East and thought he could do so by talking tough but from the sidelines.

Dealing with Arab and Israeli leaders on the Palestinian issue must have been eye-opening for the president. Publicly Arab rulers pressed him on Palestine, but privately all they wanted to talk about was defanging Iran (the same is true of the Israelis). Obama may have thought that fear of Iran would create common ground between Israel and the Persian Gulf monarchies, enough for them to join hands to resolve the Palestinian issue. The Saudi ambassador to Washington may have fueled such expectations by telling Obama early on that King Abdullah was eager for him to visit Riyadh and would not let him leave empty-handed.[3] But the Saudi King was definitely not prepared to lend a hand to Israeli prime minister Benjamin Netanyahu. When Obama met Abdullah in Riyadh in June 2009, most of the hour-long meeting was taken up with a royal lecture on the Iranian threat. The Saudi king wanted America to fix the Iranian problem, not the Palestinian one, and he did not want any linkages between the two issues. In that, the king and Netanyahu were on the same page.

Whatever his personal views, the president quickly handed off the management of the Israel-Palestinian problem to his special envoy, former senator George Mitchell. But in effect, it was Obama's senior White House adviser, Dennis Ross, who decided the matter. Ross had a long history with the issue, going back to managing the 1991 Madrid Conference that convened shortly after the first Gulf War. He differed with Obama over how best to influence events. He warned against publicly parting ways with Israel, such as by taking a stand on settlements—"showing daylight between the United States and Israel would only encourage Arabs to sit back and wait . . . rather than step forward and engage with Israel."[4] Ross argued that Netanyahu had to work with a difficult domestic coalition, and that the more Obama built trust with the Israeli public—by backing away from publicly pressuring Israel—the more likely the Israeli government would be to cooperate.[5]

Whether or not this was an accurate reading of the situation, it meant that what Obama said turned out to be different from what his administration did. No deeds matched Obama's bold words. Israelis found little reason to budge, and the Palestinians found themselves worse off. It was hard enough getting Israel to move, and nearly impossible when the president's lack of follow-through allowed Israel to stand its ground. The Palestinian Authority's president, Mahmoud Abbas, told the *Daily Beast*'s Dan Ephron:

> It was Obama who suggested a full settlement freeze. OK, I accept. We both went up the tree. After that, he came down with a ladder and he removed the ladder and said to me, jump. Three times he did it.[6]

But Abbas could not jump, and remained stuck in the tree. "How can I be less Palestinian than the president of the United States?" was how he put it to anyone ready to hear his complaint. In other words, how could Abbas ask for less from Israel than Obama had? Abbas had to start from the marker that Obama laid down and face the Israeli intransigence that Obama prompted and was unwilling to deal with. His plaint captured the souring mood across the Arab world.[7]

Obama reacted to Israeli intransigence and Arab disappointment in much the same way he dealt with the thorny problems posed by Pakistan: he walked away. The White House periodically repeated its desire for a breakthrough in peace talks, especially when crisis loomed, such as the Palestinians' threat to ask for UN recognition of their statehood in September 2011. But for all intents and purposes, the president put the issue on the back burner. Obama did not want to get involved, and by the end of his second year in office, relations with Israel had come to focus solely on managing Iran's nuclear program.

The White House attitude toward the Arab-Israeli issue reflected the administration's broader desire to dial back U.S. involvement in the Middle East. But that goal was frustrated by the onset of the Arab Spring. America was folding its tent when, in December 2010, a young fruit seller in an obscure Tunisian town set himself on fire to protest the daily injustices that he, like so many of his countrymen, suffered at the hands of a dictatorship. Mohamed Bouazizi's story went viral on social media as he lay dying in a hospital, and just like that, the wheels of history turned. Obama understood what was happening in the Arab world; in his inaugural speech he had told "those who cling to power through corruption and deceit and the silencing of dissent" that they were "on the wrong side of history."[8] He would call the Tunisian uprising that Bouazizi's desperate act set off "an inspiration to all of us who believe that each individual man and woman has certain inalienable rights."[9] But Obama's rhetoric did not make up for a reluctant and sputtering response to fast-moving events.

In early 2011, the Middle East looked poised for democracy—you cannot think of a transformation with more significant strategic impact. The outcome would mean much to America, perhaps even a final satisfactory solution to all that in the Middle East had flummoxed us, threatened us, emptied our pockets, and cost our soldiers' blood. That may be wishful thinking, and there is plenty of evidence today that the Arab Spring will produce illiberal new regimes, hybrid governments blending surviving security forces with rising Islamic parties of various hues. There will be civil wars, broken states, sectarian persecutions, humanitarian crises, faltering economies, and new foreign policy challenges (ranging from warming of relations between Egypt and Iran to new issues to fight over with Russia and China)—nothing resembling a resounding march to democracy and economic prosperity, and no clear embrace of free institutions and norms.

But we did not know this for sure in the heady and hopeful days of early 2011, nor can we say now that the Arab Spring would have been such a disappointment had we engaged with the region quickly and forcefully to give change an economic direction, helping bloated public sectors to reform and integrate into the global economy. We could have had an impact on the outcome had we had a strategy other than washing our hands of the region, and had we shown willingness to exercise leadership. We might not have averted conflicts and humanitarian crises, but we would have had a significant impact in those countries that got through the initial change of leadership and, in the fog of victory, needed help, especially with their economies.

As the extraordinary events were unfolding, there was certitude of a sort in the White House. Obama remained intent upon leaving the Middle East, and he was not going to let himself be distracted from that mission by sudden eruptions of pro-democracy protests, teetering dictators, and looming civil wars. He did not know whether the Arab Spring would lead to ubiquitous democracy or a prolonged period of instability, but regardless, he was determined that America would not try to influence the outcome—not if that meant reversing course to get involved in the region.

Take the case of Egypt, the most important Arab country and the touchstone for change in the Arab world. When hundreds of thousands of Egyptians jammed Tahrir Square to demand that President Hosni Mubarak give up power, Obama took the bold step of supporting their demand for change—first cautiously encouraging reforms, but soon calling on Mubarak to step down immediately.[10] This was a new chapter for America in the Middle East, but not one that amounted to a new approach to the region. Mubarak was on his way out, to be sure. But by encouraging him to resign immediately Obama was not making a commitment to support democratization across the board in the Middle East. America remained closely allied with some of the region's most authoritarian regimes, and calling for Mubarak to leave soon muddied the waters with them—with Saudi Arabia in particular. Faced with that reality, the administration toned down its unbridled support for change. Rulers in Bahrain or Yemen would not be subject to the same White House demands to heed their people's call for democracy.

Egypt had little in the way of sound political institutions—no party system to speak of, a weak judiciary, and an infantile civil society. There was nothing on the far side of Mubarak but the likelihood of instability at best, and chaos at worst. America would have liked to see Egypt's Facebook generation—young, technologically savvy, and relatively liberal—inherit Egypt, but they had no organization to sustain their political drive or charismatic leader to guide them. In time, the Muslim Brotherhood (and the bevy of more radical voices to its right), with its much sharper and more numerous cadres, would make mincemeat of them. The administration could only hope that the Brotherhood would stay the course with democracy—that our enthusiasm for Mubarak to go would not come back to bite us.

I know it is difficult to argue for caution in the face of the overwhelming exuberance that bubbles to the surface when decades of dictatorship at last give way to rays of democratic hope. But having been a child of the 1979 Iranian revolution, I also know how misplaced and even catastrophic such exuberance can prove to be. It would be a useful exercise to read the Western media coverage of Iran between 1977 and 1979. You will not find much concern with theocracy there; any such talk was quickly drowned by giddy and often Pollyannaish expectations of democracy's imminent triumph. But Iran's democrats, as attractive as they may have been, lacked the capabilities of the clerics and the communists. The Pahlavi monarchy's swift demise caught the democrats unprepared (not that they and their fans in the Western press understood this) and gave the upper hand to the architects of a new dictatorship, who already had a plan and a mass movement in place.

The protests in Egypt captivated the world, but Egyptian liberal democrats are no more likely to win the future than were their Iranian counterparts back in 1979. The Shah's rapid collapse benefited not democracy but theocracy. Given the decades-long surge of the Muslim Brotherhood, there is a strong chance that the same will happen in Egypt.

Hillary Clinton understood the implications. She argued early on that Egypt needed a peaceful, orderly transition to a democratic future.[11] It was better for Egypt's liberals if Mubarak held on for a bit longer and left gradually—a steady transition was better than sudden collapse. That would give Egypt's liberals time to make up some of their organizational deficiencies vis-à-vis the Islamists—not to mention afford America time to figure out how best to assist the democratic cause. Egypt's youth, however, were impatient for freedom and not ready for talk of gradualism. Nor were the American media forgiving of anything short of an uncompromising call for Mubarak to be gone. That is what happened in the end, but with Mubarak's quick exit the grip on power of the military and the "deep state" remained intact, and it was the Islamist forces of Salafism and the Muslim Brotherhood that dominated the political scene. The administration had no choice but to bet on the Brotherhood doing the right thing, opting for a future different from the one that became Iran's lot when the Shah fell from power.

In February 2011, Secretary Clinton suggested that President Obama should send a special envoy to talk to Mubarak—to assess the situation firsthand and tell the Egyptian president that he needed to plan an orderly exit and a proper transition to democracy. Clinton recommended veteran diplomat Frank G. Wisner to go to Cairo. Wisner knew Egypt well. He had served as ambassador there between 1986 and 1991. He shared Clinton's view that after decades of dictatorship a credible transition to democracy would take time and that a gradual process would benefit liberal forces, whose institutional weakness was masked by their momentary show of strength on the street. Obama seemed to be on the same page and instructed Wisner to ask Mubarak to plan for a transition.

Wisner delivered Obama's message of both American support and the imperative of meaningful reform to Mubarak. Mubarak was not ready to leave but agreed not to use violence against the protesters. But protests only grew in intensity, and with Egypt on edge Obama changed course. Wisner was still on a plane back to Washington when the president called on Mubarak to step down immediately. The change came so quickly that it caught Wisner unawares. He had just got off the plane when he told an international conference in Munich that the United States viewed President Mubarak as indispensable to a transition to democracy (i.e., America needed Mubarak for just a bit longer—to get rid of Mubarak). The press focused on the "we need Mubarak" part of his comments and that caused a furor.

With crowds in Tahrir Square growing daily, Mubarak's position was tenuous to be sure, and the United States was right to look past the stolid dictatorship to embrace the spirit of change.[12] But the president, swept up by the enthusiasm of the moment and egged on by his young staffers, threw caution aside and made a hasty about-face. He reacted to Mubarak's remarks and maneuvers as if dealing with a campaign news cycle, where every statement had to be quickly countered to catch the next set of newspaper headlines. It was a policy style that reflected the influence of those White House advisers who rose from Obama's presidential campaign to dominate foreign policy decision making.[13] They saw the Arab Spring then as "an epochal change in line with their own views of themselves as a new generation."[14] They had little experience at foreign affairs; what they knew was the fast-paced world of political campaigns. They were dismissive of foreign policy veterans and described them in terms that conjured Donald Rumsfeld's infamous put-down of France and Germany for questioning the Iraq war. "Old Europe," he called them—yesteryear's powers destined for history's ash heap. Rumsfeld's wisecrack did not stand the test of time. Wisner and company, too, may yet have the final word on the Arab Spring.[15]

Obama's call for Mubarak to go would not be repeated with other dictators in the region in the months to come—not in Bahrain or Yemen, not even in Libya or Syria as quickly or with the same conviction—and America would in fact deepen its reliance on authoritarian monarchies in the Persian Gulf. Calling for Mubarak to go was an isolated event; it reflected neither an embrace of change across the Middle East nor a commitment to Egypt's transition to democracy.

Support for dictators has been the bane of American policy in the Middle East. Since Anwar Sadat signed a peace deal with Israel in 1978, America has poured $30 billion in aid into Egypt, with the lion's share going to the military. The rest, another $3 billion or so earmarked for civilian use, also went to the military—the Egyptian government got to decide which economic or social agencies had technical competence to take advantage of the money and all of them were military owned or contracted their work to organizations and companies backed by the military. America subsidized the growth of the military in the security sector but also throughout the economy.

We have confessed time and again that investing in dictatorship was not a good idea, but we could not identify alternative means for protecting our interests. In time, authoritarian rule proved unstable, producing the very problems we relied on it to contain—and when it started wobbling we were quick to let it keel over. The Mubarak regime was the poster child for this dead-end strategy. Mubarak's regime was a rock of stability, seemingly unmovable for three decades. Over those decades, Egypt grew poorer and weaker, but also more anti-American and Islamic—with a worrying penchant for extremism. In time, the mismatch between the scale and intensity of Egypt's problems (including massive unemployment and nonexistent job prospects among the country's bulging youth population) and the regime's weak capacity to do anything about them created a tinderbox situation.[16]

Mubarak grudgingly embraced reforms, but they only accentuated Egypt's problems and exposed its vulnerabilities.[17] An unjust, unfree, and corrupt regime is always at its weakest when it begins trying to improve. The fall of Mubarak brings to mind Alexis de Tocqueville's explanation of the ferment that led to the French Revolution:

> Only consummate statecraft can enable a King to save his throne when after a long spell of oppressive rule he sets to improving the lot of his subjects. Patiently endured so long as it seemed beyond redress, a grievance comes to appear intolerable once the possibility of removing it comes to men's minds . . . people may suffer less, but their sensibility is exacerbated.[18]

We should expect authoritarian regimes to go. They cannot survive without changing, and if they change they could fall even more quickly. In the long run it is better to wean ourselves of our dependence on authoritarians and to anchor our interests in democracy instead. But that is a gradual process—and for now America's policies seem to be divided on this issue. On the one hand, we cheered the downfall of dictators such as Ben Ali, Mubarak, and Gaddafi; on the other hand, we now rely even more heavily than before on our old authoritarian allies, the Persian Gulf monarchs.

The handling of Egypt revealed Obama's lack of any game plan for Egypt or the region. Tunisia had been transitioning fairly smoothly, so why would Egypt not do so as well? Why not, in other words, just go with the flow? Tunisia had managed a rapid and painless end to dictatorship—the Tunisian army had wisely refused to fire on citizens or meddle much in politics at all, and Ben Ali was allowed to flee to Saudi Arabia. The administration assumed that Egypt—a larger, poorer, tenser, and less Westernized place than Tunisia—would somehow produce a similarly neat and satisfying outcome. Comparisons then abounded in Washington between what was happening in Tahrir Square and the fall of the Berlin Wall in 1989. Obama's coterie was afraid that unless he pushed Mubarak out, Obama would be caught on the wrong side of history. But the problem was that the administration had no plans for how to manage the messy process of democracy building that was to follow when Obama called on Mubarak to leave. Nor did Obama ever intend to take ownership of the change as had George H. W. Bush with regard to post-communist Eastern Europe in 1989. The administration's enthusiasm for democracy remained largely a matter of rhetoric.

What sort of strategy are we following when we aggressively push for democracy in Egypt while we double down on support for the region's stubbornly antidemocratic yet none-too-stable royal regimes? If we think that the protesters in Tahrir Square were on the right side of history, then why cozy up to monarchies that will be washed away by it? If we don't think the region is in the throes of historic change, why embrace the Arab Spring at all? Our zigzagging policy is confusing and unconvincing.

The administration was happy when the Egyptian military accepted the results of the first parliamentary elections (held in stages from November 2011 to January 2012) and allowed the Muslim Brotherhood to take power.[19] The White House thought that letting the Brotherhood experiment with governance—even if there was a danger that it might impose Islamic rule on a quarter of the people in the Arab world—would be less damaging to American interests than suppressing the election result. Short-circuiting the voters' verdict, the administration feared, might lead to an even worse Egyptian reprise of the bloody, decade-long civil war that broke out in Algeria in 1991 after the generals there shut down an electoral process that the local Islamists were winning.[20]

The administration was also hoping that Egypt's Muslim Brothers would take a page from Turkey's experience and worry less about Islamist ideology than about improving governance and fixing the economy. American envoys met with Brotherhood members, and the White House even hosted a delegation from the group in April 2012 to discuss economic and political issues and future U.S.-Egyptian ties. "They all had PhDs from American universities, and said all the right things," according to one person who attended the meetings. "It was easy to feel optimistic, but who knows." Placing a bet that pragmatism would outweigh ideology was a gamble, but it was the right one at the time, and letting democracy take its course regardless of which political or religious force came out on top sounded like prudent policy. It put America on the right side of history and in tune with the public mood in Egypt and the Arab world. But it would not be long before doubt set in, first when Egypt's new Muslim Brother president, Mohammad Morsi, went to Tehran on a state visit in September 2012, and then, shortly after, when he dragged his feet condemning an anti-American mob attacking the American embassy.

But there was nothing approximating a strategy here. The laissez-faire method was not a reflection of any carefully thought-out approach to improving democratic prospects in the region. Instead, it was an expression of the attitude of detachment from the Middle East that pervaded the White House. It was the right policy for a president who did not want to get any more involved than he absolutely had to with the problems of Egypt and the Middle East. Any other approach would have meant coming up with a strategy and a plan for implementing it. The detachment would be clear when it came to grappling with economic reform, without which democracy would remain stillborn, and the political stasis that would follow, combined with economic stagnation, could hand over the future to anti-American religious extremists.

The collapse of Mubarak's regime was nothing short of an earthquake in Middle Eastern politics, a significant historical development with far-ranging regional implications—or so was the consensus high and low in Washington. Egypt was going the way of Poland, the Philippines, Brazil, or South Africa—a key regional power turning toward democracy and pulling the rest of the neighborhood along with it. The democratic wave had at last made landfall on Middle Eastern shores.

If the Arab Spring were to bear fruit, America would have to get involved diplomatically and, more importantly, economically. American engagement had been vital to the success of previous democracy waves in Asia, Eastern Europe, and Latin America.[21] In those places, America had led international efforts to anchor burgeoning democracies in the closest alliances with the West that could be managed (the promise of NATO and then EU membership had served as a useful magnet for Eastern Europe). We influenced political discussions and helped with the work of writing constitutions, forming parties, holding elections, and stabilizing young democratic governments.[22] It is arguable that the Arabs would not welcome so much close engagement, but in any case we had no intention of offering it.

Of most crucial importance in the previous waves had been U.S. efforts to work in concert with Europe, international financial institutions, and private enterprise to pour vast economic resources into the new democracies. The idea had been to give promising political developments a sound basis in economic restructuring and greater engagement with the global economy. Over a ten-year period between 1989 and 1999, the West directed more than $100 billion to Eastern Europe alone.

During that time period the relevance of economic reform to successful democratization was captured in the so-called Washington consensus, an agreement among international financial institutions and world powers, led by the United States, to push for a regimen of reforms that would change the structure of economies, societies, and, hence, politics. That consensus has come under much criticism for its excesses, and the pain that many countries had to endure as a result. But it offered the benefit of clear direction to the international community and countries facing change—a sense of where they all wanted to go and how they would get there.

Democracy and stability in the Middle East need the same kind of direction, and a similar level of investment. Without economic change, democratic stirrings would not stand a chance. None of the democracy waves comparable to the Arab Spring succeeded without economic reform. Recall that it was stagnant economic growth, chronic mass unemployment, and the resulting despair that fueled protest against sclerotic Arab dictatorships in the first place.[23] And America had blamed 9/11 on the same lack of opportunity and economic stagnation.[24] Yet now that economic frustration was creating an opening for democracy rather than recruiting foot soldiers for Islamic extremism, Western support was nowhere to be found.

Nowhere was this Western insouciance more evident than in Egypt. None disputed that Arab democracy would be won or lost in Egypt. This is the most populous and, intellectually and politically, the most influential Arab country. The outcome in Egypt would decide whether the original message of the Arab Spring would take hold or be swallowed up in power games waged between military establishments and Islamist movements.

Egypt had started a tentative economic reform process during the last decade of Mubarak's rule.[25] Those reforms were in large measure responsible for the emergence of protests—some 4,000 labor strikes and protests between 1998 and 2011.[26] The reforms removed the safety net for workers but expanded the private sector and the middle class, who, like middle classes everywhere, clamored for greater freedoms. Middle-class Egyptians were the first in the country to embrace the Tunisian example, organizing anti-Mubarak demonstrations that drew huge numbers of the frustrated poor who blamed the elderly longtime president for the jobs and social services lost to economic reform.

Mubarak's reforms had not gone far enough by the time protesters occupied Tahrir Square in January 2011, and whatever gains they had made were washed away by the economic impact of the protests, Mubarak's fall, and the instability that followed. Political upheaval plunged Egypt's economy into crisis. In the first year after Mubarak stepped down, the country's economy contracted by 0.8 percent,[27] its GDP falling by 4 percent and manufacturing by 12 percent. The economy lost a million jobs; unemployment rose to 15 percent (25 percent for young people).[28] Investment fell by 26 percent, with foreign investment dropping off the table ($6.4 billion in 2010, but only $500 million in 2011).[29] The drastic drop in domestic and foreign investment presented the government with a gaping hole of $11 billion in its financing in the second half of 2011.[30] International arrivals have nearly halved—a grave problem when, like Egypt, 11 percent of your GDP comes from tourism. Not surprisingly, the government's budget shortfall ballooned, to $11 billion (10 percent of GDP, the largest in the Arab world). Combined with capital flight, which continues unabated thanks to persistent political instability, this has caused a sharp fall in foreign reserves from a high of $43 billion to $15 billion.[31] Given that two out of every five Egyptians live on less than $2 a day, the impact of such jolts has been profound.

It gets worse: Half of Egypt's 83 million people are under the age of 24. Among the country's unemployed, as many as 90 percent are young and two-thirds have never worked. The government is hopelessly bloated and corrupt—for every one government employee per capita in Turkey there are eleven in Egypt, where do-nothing state jobs have long served as a thinly veiled form of welfare. The woeful educational system turns out a workforce of graduates who are not competitive in today's global economy.

Egypt faces a vortex of poverty and instability unless it fixes its economy and finds jobs for its rapidly growing population. To keep up with the youth bulge, the economy must grow faster (in the range of 10 to 11 percent a year) and for much longer than perhaps has been seen anywhere in the world. (Actual growth in 2012 is expected to be 1.5 percent.)[32] Failing that, Egypt could face social misery, and worse, radicalism. If the past is any guide, falling wages, downward mobility, and growing inequality are drivers of Islamic activism.[33] The deadly attacks on American diplomats in Egypt, Libya, Tunisia, and Yemen by anti-American mobs in September 2012 are just a preview of the kind of radicalism that could take hold of the region if economic stagnation and social misery are to be the lot of its people. Between 1974 and 1984, Islamic fundamentalism exploded in Egypt, especially among urban youth. During that same decade, public-sector white-collar workers (those working in state-owned enterprises) saw their real wages shrink by 8 percent, and, for those in government administration, by 23 percent.[34]

The level of growth needed would require radical change. Egypt would have to open its economy, shrink its bloated and corrupt public sector (public debt stood at 80 percent of GDP in 2011), reform its laws and financial regulations, invest more in education and infrastructure, and promote privatization, trade, and direct foreign investment.

Unfortunately, the country has been reluctant to do any of this. Egyptians are not ready for economic change, at least not at the pace that was seen in Latin America or Eastern Europe when they went through reform. They want jobs and better services, but their political discussions do not include a serious debate over what to do with the economy.

On the street and in factories the perception was that with Mubarak gone there would be money flowing from the top down. But labor unrest and street agitation squeeze businesses. One ceramics manufacturer told me that he gave his factory workers a 40 percent raise only to have them strike for another 20 percent. He appealed to the government for help. The answer came back: "You are rich, they are poor; give them what they want." He could not, and started winding down his business. The impasse is driving Egyptian politics into a binary choice between populism, under which the public sector will grow again to feed the frustrated poor, and a return to the law and order of Mubarak days—either way, democracy will be the victim.

Egyptians are suspicious of the West and jealously guard their national rights and sovereignty. They do not want the IMF telling them what to do, and their first impulse was to refuse its loan offers. They thought they could get away with this because Qatar and Saudi Arabia had promised Cairo $11 billion in economic assistance, but none of it ever materialized. One senior administration official told me that the interim government said to Washington and the IMF in private, "We don't want your help, and if we agree to your help we don't want you to tell anyone about it."

This is a shame because such changes have a record of working. Reform was not easy. Eastern Europe had to endure 20 percent inflation along with drops of 20 to 40 percent in GDP. There were many setbacks, social hardships, and acts of political resistance. But in the end, economies were transformed, and Eastern Europe is better off for it. The same is true of Latin America.

Democracy (and also political and religious moderation) depends on economic growth, and economic growth depends on reform. It is that simple. Reforming Egypt's economy will not be easy. The country lacks leaders resolved to push painful change, however badly needed, and there is no unified vision of the future. Egyptians want prosperity but are not ready to sign up for real economic reform and the belt tightening and economic hardships that go with it. Many think Mubarak already tried and failed at those kinds of reforms. President Muhammad Morsi, a sixty-one-year-old engineering professor with a PhD from the University of Southern California, talks about development and the economy all the time. He says that he favors the private sector and a business-friendly environment, and wants to work with international financial institutions to reform Egypt's economy. His presidential campaign banners touted him as "Egypt's Erdoğan." But he represents a Muslim Brotherhood that has a strong populist wing and has promised an economic safety net for the poor.[35]

The single biggest obstacle to economic reform and democracy alike is the Egyptian military. Something of a state within the state, it controls vast holdings in every economic sector from manufacturing to construction, agriculture, and tourism.[36] It runs four-fifths of all industrial concerns and accounts for upward of 30 percent of the economy.

The generals have a different view of Egypt's future and are jealously guarding their economic assets, which means resisting reform. They think that Egypt's strategic importance would bring in enough aid for it to function—they have a hard time seeing why things could not go back to the way they had been under Mubarak. A senior American diplomat told me, "The military and its new government are not keen on reform, they think we should pay up for the country's upkeep, and are resentful that we are not [doing so]."

The military does not want to give up its control of the economy, and that is a large reason it does not want to give up political power. It used its influence over the interim government in 2011 to say no to the IMF. And when it looked likely that an independent Muslim Brotherhood government would take over, the military tried to wrest control of the parliament and the constitution-writing process and tightened its grip over the judiciary, in part to have veto power over economic reform.

Egypt eventually entered talks with the IMF for a $4.8 billion assistance package (which would demand some reforms). The Muslim Brotherhood delegation that visited the White House in April 2012 was surprised to learn that the IMF had offered a package twice as large, but the Egyptian government (at the military's prodding) had said no.

Many Egyptians, the Muslim Brothers foremost among them, say that they want democracy and prosperity. But unless the military's grip on the economy is loosened, democracy will not stand a chance, and poverty will remain Egypt's lot. Breaking the hold of the military over the economy will not happen absent fundamental reform with strong international backing. So far, Washington has neither endorsed economic reform forcefully nor used its considerable leverage (in the form of massive military aid) to nudge the military to consent to change.

Many hope that Egypt will embrace the "Turkish model," mixing democracy and capitalism with a somewhat toned-down brand of Islamism to produce an open and prospering society. But the Turkish model was built on the back of a series of IMF-prescribed reforms and the EU's deep economic and political engagement with Turkey. Absent similar fundamental economic reforms, Egypt looks to be going the way of Pakistan, its economy reliant on U.S. aid, constantly on the brink of disaster, and avoiding it only thanks to timely infusions of Arab aid and rescue packages put together by international financial institutions. Meanwhile, the country gets poorer, its problems grow, and its escape from the cycle of crisis and poverty becomes more daunting and less likely. Anti-American extremist forces would then reap the fruits of political frustration and social misery. On the political front, the military's "deep state" controls key sectors of the economy and wields considerable influence over the bureaucracy, the judiciary, and the still-potent security services. Prospects for civilian rule, let alone true democracy, are dim. The Obama administration may have bet on democracy turning Egypt into Turkey, but Turkey got where it is thanks to sustained European engagement. There we have fallen short.

It is true that the global financial downturn and the Greek crisis had left little for Cairo, but that is no excuse. Egypt is a hinge upon which the fate of the whole Middle East may turn. America spent trillions addressing security problems in the region after 9/11, problems that Washington believed were caused by the failings of dictatorship. Did America not go to war in Iraq to bring democracy to the broader Middle East and end the grip of Islamic extremism on Muslim hearts and minds? Now that democracy was on the horizon, we did not want to invest in it. "In short," writes David Sanger of the *New York Times*, "America would talk about democracy promotion. But it would no longer be democracy's venture capitalist."[37] Venture capitalism or something like it, however, is just what the Middle East needs. The region boasts plenty of entrepreneurial energy, but it can find no outlet as long as the twitching hand of the sclerotic state chokes off economic liberty.[38]

The United States does not need to get it right everywhere, but it cannot afford to get it wrong in Egypt. It definitely cannot afford to stand back and simply watch events unfold without trying to influence them. A year and a half after Mubarak's exit, the Obama administration still had no clear strategy for Egypt. Economic reform's potential as a key driver of other changes has been largely overlooked. Change the economy in a freedom-friendly direction, and the generals and Islamists will have to adjust. In the words of the international relations scholar Michael Mandelbaum, "The knowledge and skills needed to practice democracy . . . come from the experience of operating a particular kind of economic system. . . . The school for democracy [is] the free-market economy."[39]

Egypt's best chance for real change came early, right after Mubarak left. That is when America and its allies should have put a big financial package on the table in exchange for big changes. We should have stressed the need for economic reform emphatically, bending all efforts to convince Egyptians that their problems will never be solved until they scale back their overgrown central state, improve its efficiency, and allow more scope for free enterprise. We should have put economic reform at the top of our talking points with Egyptians across the political spectrum, the generals included. The administration is gradually warming up to the idea, but it still does not see the economy as the fulcrum for change in Egypt and is not making the necessary big push for it to happen.

That we have settled for doing so much less than we did after 1989 in Asia, Eastern Europe, and Latin America speaks volumes about our disengagement from the region. If the potential for democracy held by the Arab Spring was not enough to compel our engagement, it is not clear what would be.

The Arab Spring was a classic "black swan," an unlooked-for but massive strategic shift that made the first big cracks in the hard crust of brutal dictatorship that had long encased the Middle East's basket-case economies and scary social trends. It did what the Iraq war had been meant to do but had fallen short of. It was America's opening to try in this region some of what it had tried two decades ago as the Iron Curtain fell and dictatorships crumbled one after the other. Back then, America jumped at the chance to leverage the West's victory in the Cold War in ways that would change the world for the better. We led an international alliance to build market economies and consolidate democracy across many parts of the world. The chance to do the same in the broader Middle East, to build prosperous economies and nurture democracy—to try to move the region into a new historical phase and onto a safer trajectory for all concerned—has not evoked a comparable response. Reformist hopes are never a sure thing, but surely this is an opportunity tragically lost.

Obama never offered a vision or a grand strategy to guide America's response to the cascade of events unfolding in the Middle East. He responded to the Arab Spring without a consistent strategy or much enthusiasm or engagement, as if the protests and the political changes they produced were merely an unwelcome distraction instead of a historic opening. France and Britain (and Hillary Clinton) goaded Obama into intervention in Libya,[40] but there, as in Egypt, American interest evaporated once the dictator was removed. America proved even more reluctant to get involved when it got to Syria. Rebels there have received moral and material support (largely nonmilitary and humanitarian aid) from America but no promise of intervention. In Bahrain, the administration protested the crackdown on protesters but did nothing more; and in Yemen, Washington backed a plan to stabilize the ruling regime with a formula that amounted to "No more President Ali Abdallah Saleh, but no democracy either." Evidence of repression in Saudi Arabia was simply ignored.

To be sure, Obama's initial instinct was to support protesters demanding an end to dictatorship. He saw the Arab Spring as a turning point in history, and he wanted America to help Arabs realize democracy. His strident rhetoric in support of protesters and his personal stance in pushing Mubarak off his throne were as revolutionary as what was happening on the Arab street. But his administration backed away from that bold stance. It started talking about balancing interests against values, and in practice increasingly put interests before values. The administration would not support democracy for all Arabs (Bahrainis, Saudis, Yemenis were out of luck), but only for those Arabs whose cause fit American interests. By the summer of 2012, that was a club of one: Syria. To the rulers and people of the Middle East alike, "Obama's wavering policies could be interpreted not as encouragement of epochal change so much as an effort to continue as long as possible the policies of the past."[41]

Obama has been understandably reluctant to sign up for more wars in the Middle East. But his handling of the Arab Spring and Middle East policy has been defined by decisions that had nothing to do with armed intervention but were all about whether to support the possibility of building democracy in the wake of revolution.

In their book *Bending History*, Martin Indyk, Kenneth G. Lieberthal, and Michael E. O'Hanlon explain Obama's failure to rise to the challenge of the Arab Spring by arguing that the candidate who ran on the power of ideas became, once in office, a reluctant realist. His focus shifted away from the grand visions and hopes that marked his campaign and settled on the immediate tasks required for keeping America safe in a highly dangerous world. Realist or not, Obama's legacy in the broader Middle East will not be a Reaganesque one of having overseen one of the great historical transformations of our time. Instead, it will be far narrower and closer to the legacy of George W. Bush, whose war on terror provided the basis upon which Obama shaped his own approach to America's role in the world.

If there is a discernible American strategy for the Middle East, it is counterterrorism—continuing the war on al-Qaeda and its franchises and offshoots using Special Forces and drones. This is to be expected— after all, there is still the threat of terrorism coming from the region. But counterterrorism will not transform the Middle East. To fully appreciate the impact of American foreign policy on the region one has to consider the responses to democracy and terrorism side by side, as the Janus faces of American engagement. It is not just that we did not have a proper response at the right time to the Arab Spring, we have doubled down on counterterrorism. And when the two have come into conflict, as in Yemen, the latter has trumped the former. For, as surprising as it may seem to those who expected Obama to be a kind of "anti-Bush," it is Bush's preoccupation with homeland security as the be-all and end-all of grand strategy that serves as the best guide to how Obama sees American engagement in the Middle East.

America's fascination with drones is easy to understand. They are efficient and cheap and a far easier way to wage the war on terror than a counterinsurgency campaign involving tens of thousands of troops and nation-building to go with it. So it was not a surprise that drones quickly became the central pillar of America's successful counterterrorism strategy in Afghanistan and Pakistan, and then Yemen.[42]

Other counterterrorism advances also came online right around the time Obama became president, most notably an enhanced cyberwar capability.[43] The combination of drones, Special Forces, and cyberwarfare presented the new president with a viable high-tech clandestine alternative to traditional military means to combat terrorism—Counterterrorism Plus. All told, as in the counterterrorism expert Peter Bergen's estimation, Obama is actually one of America's militarily most aggressive presidents—comfortable with making tough decisions such as killing bin Laden or expanding drone programs.[44]

When it came to drones there were four formidable unanimous voices in the Situation Room: the CIA, the Office of the Director of National Intelligence, the Pentagon, and the White House's counterterrorism adviser, John Brennan. Defense Secretary Robert Gates may have said no to military involvement in Libya, but he was fully supportive of more drone attacks. Together, Brennan, Gates, and the others convinced Obama of both the urgency of counterterrorism and the imperative of viewing America's engagement with the Middle East and South Asia through that prism. Their bloc by and large discouraged debate over the full implications of this strategy in national security meetings.

Quietly, and without any fanfare or debate, counterterrorism became the cornerstone and principal objective of American policy in the Middle East and South Asia.[45] However, the policy of disengagement paired with drone strikes is not likely to prove viable in the long run. We have learned from our experience in Pakistan that drones are a difficult sell, though local populations may put up with drone campaigns longer if there is deep engagement with the United States and economic assistance to add other dimensions to the relationship.

Drones rely heavily on cooperative regimes that can tie America's hands in terms of supporting change. Yemen is a good example. Washington was rightly concerned that al-Qaeda would take advantage of the pro-democracy protests that engulfed Yemen throughout 2011 and eventually forced President Saleh out of office. But Washington had to balance its support for political change with its desire to keep in place the security apparatus that supported drone attacks on al-Qaeda targets. Washington left the political negotiations around Saleh stepping down to Saudi Arabia and the Gulf Cooperation Council and focused its attention on al-Qaeda. The outcome kept the Saleh regime in place but without Saleh himself, a sop to the protesters. In the bargain, America protected and expanded its drone program. (It was in the midst of protests that a drone strike killed the Yemeni-American al-Qaeda leader Anwar al-Awlaki, who had been identified as, among other things, a player in the failed Times Square attack.) The message was that even after Arabs themselves did what America had been asking of them for so long—break with Arab nationalism and its dictatorships—America is still sticking with the same game plan, fighting al-Qaeda. Drones, not democracy, drive American policy.

There is no doubt that drone attacks have worked locally (in Afghanistan, Pakistan's FATA region, and Yemen) to quickly decimate al-Qaeda's ranks. Yet it is open to question whether the drones' success in one location masks the creation of bigger problems elsewhere. The record in Pakistan and Yemen shows that drone attacks disperse al-Qaeda farther afield; the metastasis of terrorism in turn requires more drone attacks in more places. That is no success at all.

Drones are also not as innocuous as they sound. Drone strikes are aerial attacks that happen in collusion with a local government or in violation of a country's sovereignty and in either case run the risk of inflaming public opinion. They provoke anti-Americanism and the extremism that goes with it, and once those sentiments are inflamed it will be difficult to sustain the program—Pakistan and Yemen both provide ample evidence of that. Compared with other methods of striking from a distance, drones can indeed be surgical. But drones are like an economist's fiscal tool, clean and efficient until they encounter real-world politics.

When we were planning for Hillary Clinton's October 2009 trip to Pakistan, her first as secretary of state, Holbrooke was adamant that we organize a town hall with women. He said that whenever Hillary got together with women the atmosphere was electric—"Just look at what happened in South Korea," he would say. She could connect with women around issues that mattered to them, and that could produce a critical breakthrough in Pakistani public opinion.

It made sense, and the embassy invited a large group of affluent, English-speaking women—the type who cared about women's rights, democracy, and cultural freedoms. Four young women journalists would interview Clinton, and then the crowd would get to ask questions. The atmosphere was indeed "electric," but not because Clinton was bonding with the crowd. These modern Pakistani women were brimming with anger. From the get-go every other question was about drones, the civilians they killed, and the humiliation they visited on Pakistan by violating its sovereignty. Sitting through that inquisition, I could not see a future for a foreign policy built on drones.

In April 2012, Pakistan's parliament recommended that the government end the drone program. The next step could be street protests—which have been on the rise since September 2012, when a YouTube video clip insulting the Prophet Muhammad went viral. That would not only make the program untenable but also radicalize politics. Drones could be promoting the very problem that they are intended to solve.

At a time when the Arab world is grappling with economic and political change, American foreign policy is marching to a different drummer. The White House favors containment rather than engagement, and drones are the main tool. And the policy is spreading fast, from Afghanistan and Pakistan to the Middle East. Yemen is the Middle Eastern target for the drone strategy, but if al-Qaeda proliferates in Syria, or in an Iraq now stripped of U.S. troops, or elsewhere—Somalia or Libya—the program could extend to those places as well.[46] Al-Qaeda thrives in failed states. The right strategy for America is to shore up states battered by the winds of change.[47]

Some have argued that the Arab Spring has not given America much to work with. It has not produced liberal forces marching toward democratic capitalism. Libya is hardly a state, Syria is falling into civil war, and Egypt is descending into the unknown, caught for now between Islamic fundamentalists and their only real rival for power, a clique of authoritarian generals. Nor do democrats seem to predominate in Yemen or Bahrain. Others argue that locals themselves have waved away U.S. involvement. Egypt has been cool to the IMF and has been growing more anti-American. In fact, some say, it is a good thing that America has stayed away, making sure that it is not an obstacle to change.

But not being an obstacle to change is not enough. America should be making sure that change moves in the right direction, is not reversed, and does not go off the rails. Our policy, in the end, will be judged by whether the Arab Spring produces better Arab states that do right by their people and live up to their responsibility to the international order and its institutions. Only then will we have brought our values and interests into alignment. On that score, Obama's disengaged attitude toward the Middle East has served neither America's values nor its long-term interests.

THE GATHERING STORM

At a private meeting in London in January 2012, a senior Saudi prince with influence over the oil kingdom's foreign policy told an audience of prominent Americans that he did not like the term "Arab Spring" because it did not feel like a spring. "What about Arab Awakening?" asked one of his listeners. He did not like that either; the Arabs had not been asleep. "What would you call it then, Your Highness?" The prince thought for a moment. Then he said, "Arab headaches—that is what they are."

We are now fairly certain that in the new Middle East, the fruit of the Arab Spring will not be a rising liberal Arab order, but an ascendant Islamist one that, if it is able to assert itself, will be a rival to Iran and Turkey and an enemy to the United States and Israel. The shape of this reality will be decided by intensifying regional rivalries playing out amid rising sectarian tensions and the still-bleak economic picture. America will have to contend with these dynamics, which will affect American interests and set the context for American policy.[1]

As we look down that difficult road, we can sum up our interests in the Middle East under three headings: oil, Israel, and terrorism. Americans have come to believe that their country is engaged in the Middle East because we want a cheap and stable supply of oil. That is true, but in reality even if the Middle East had no oil, it would still hold our attention. America cares deeply about Israel, and Israel is in the Middle East. Wishing to change Arab attitudes toward Israel was one big reason why the George W. Bush administration pushed for the war against Saddam Hussein. Those on the right who favored the war saw extremism, anti-Americanism, and antagonism toward Israel as different faces of the same problem, which they blamed on decaying states built on Arab nationalism. As we have seen, that bellicose ideology, which captured the Arab imagination after the Suez Crisis of 1956, launched much of the region into decades of economic stagnation under brutal dictators such as Saddam. Ironically, Arab nationalism made a wasteland of Arab intellectual life, and even after the ideology lost its grip on the popular imagination, the states that it built suffocated whole societies and pushed numerous young people into the arms of Islamic extremists. Destroy those states, free Arab society, and bring democracy to the Middle East, the logic went, and extremism will begin to evaporate while the Arab-Israeli conflict grows more tractable. How unsound this reasoning was became apparent very quickly in 2011.

What is true, what must be openly discussed, is that it was largely in response to our dependence on the Middle East for oil and our concern for Israel's security that we became so focused on the rise of Islamic fundamentalism, the specter of al-Qaeda, and the rise of a nuclear Iran as a threat. The 9/11 attacks lent new urgency to our worries in these areas, but the roots of concern run deeper, and the lingering fear continues to preoccupy us even after the killing of bin Laden, the visible weakening of al-Qaeda, and the Arab world's tentative turn to democracy.

The Obama administration may talk of pivoting to Asia—and, by implication, washing our hands of the Middle East—but that goal will likely run up against the reality of challenges that oil, Israel, and terrorism and the host of issues tied to them will put before us. Moving on from the Middle East was an aspiration divorced from hard facts facing American foreign policy. Continued worry over terrorism is still a consuming concern that belies our proclaimed desire to deploy our resources elsewhere in the world.

Let us consider oil, our most obvious reason for being in the Middle East. By the end of the First World War, Great Britain had one overriding interest in the Middle East, and that was oil. The Royal Navy's switch from coal to oil made the precious liquid a strategic commodity of the first rank. Moreover, the British government stood to benefit from the taxes that British oil companies would pay into London's exchequer.[2]

Americans inherited this concern for oil along with management of the region when the British moment in the Middle East ended with the Suez Crisis in 1956. During the Cold War, America jealously guarded the Persian Gulf against Soviet designs. But in time, America also came to worry about Arab threats to cut off oil. One such disruption in 1973, led by Saudi Arabia to punish America for its support of Israel, wreaked havoc on the American economy. Before long, the price of oil had quadrupled as oil-producing countries banded together as OPEC to get a better deal for their precious export.[3]

The "oil shock" of the 1970s jolted America into action. Since then, we have coddled dictators, built military bases, gone to war, and generally kept deepening our engagement in the Middle East—all to secure oil. The costs of this strategy have been anti-Americanism, war, and terrorism. The columnist and author Thomas Friedman, a longtime observer of the region, thinks that our problems in the Middle East would go away if we ended our dependence on oil—if we kicked the habit and "went green." For some time now, he has rallied the American Left to embrace alternative energies as the remedy to our Middle East headaches—"go green and end the green menace," one might call this. Every time someone asks Saudi oil minister Ali Al-Naimi about green energy making oil obsolete, he simply laughs and says, "It's not going to happen." Getting off oil is a far-fetched, long-run answer to an immediate strategic problem.

The Right's solution is to find more oil at home, a sentiment most clearly captured by the battle cry "Drill, baby, drill!" And this might well work. According to a 2011 report from the Congressional Research Service, the sum of all fossil-fuel reserves plus technically recoverable but undiscovered oil and natural gas in the United States and Canada nearly equals the sum of such resources found in Saudi Arabia, Iran, Iraq, Kuwait, Libya, and Qatar put together.[4] If you add Mexico, then North America's total exceeds that of these Middle Eastern oil and gas producers. The past decade has seen the rapid expansion of oil and natural gas production via methods such as slant drilling and hydraulic fracturing (fracking) in U.S. shale deposits, including the Bakken Formation beneath North Dakota and Montana and the Marcellus Formation that extends from a corner of Tennessee in the south as far north as western New York State and as far east as New Jersey. Buoyed by such finds (some say the most significant since the discovery of the vast East Texas Oil Field in 1930), America could be on the road to becoming energy self-sufficient. By as soon as 2020, the United States could be the world's leading producer of oil and natural gas. There is also a great deal more oil and gas stored in Canada's Alberta tar sands and the outer continental shelf than anyone had realized—the problem is that the environmental costs of getting to it are as yet not fully known.

Still, besting Saudi Arabia or Qatar in oil and gas production will not change America's strategic conundrum. Energy self-sufficiency is a solution to an imaginary problem. Today we depend on the Middle East for only about 30 percent of our imported oil. The rest of our imported oil—and note that we are depending somewhat less on these sources as places such as North Dakota are now shipping the prized light, sweet crude[5]—comes from Canada, Mexico, Venezuela, and Africa. We take only a tenth of the Middle East's petroleum exports; most go to Asia. Abu Dhabi's oil, for instance, is locked down by long-term contracts with Japan and South Korea. And yet despite this, we cannot escape the strategic headaches caused by Middle Eastern oil.

The reason is that the oil market is fungible—a shortage or a high price in one corner means higher prices everywhere else. If the Asian states lose their Middle East supply, their demand for oil will not go away—it will simply push prices higher. But that is not a problem that will be solved solely by drilling or fracking our way to greater oil and gas independence. Nor can we think that oil-supply problems suffered by our allies and major trading partners will somehow leave our own economy unaffected. As such, we may cut our imports of Middle East oil further, but we must still keep viewing stability in the Middle East as a vital American interest. Protecting that interest will become more difficult as complicated changes continue to cascade across the region.

How complicated? Consider the fact that the administration's decision to escalate pressure on Iran to compel its compliance on the nuclear issue in early 2012 had an immediate blowback in the form of higher oil prices—at the inconvenient moment when the U.S. economy was starting to show signs of growth after years of sluggishness and depressed labor and housing markets.

The oil-producing countries ranged around the Persian Gulf have also become more dependent on their petrodollars, just as they have become weaker and vulnerable to political tumult. They need our greenbacks probably worse than we need their oil. Opulence is not power; to the contrary, it has cut these regimes from their traditional moorings. Behind the gilded veneer of wealth and power are hollow political structures and teetering institutions that increasingly lean far too heavily on American military might.

In late 1973, as the Arab oil embargo following the Yom Kippur War was causing great pain in the West, America warned King Faisal of Saudi Arabia that if he did not lift the embargo, America would invade his country to resume the flow of oil. The king replied, "If you do that, we will set the oil fields on fire. We came from the desert and will return to the desert." That may have been a slightly credible threat then; it is a wholly incredible threat now.

Gone are the days when Saudi royals could handle the nomadic life of mounted desert tribesmen. The Saudi rulers need stable oil markets even more than we do. Their lavish urban lifestyles depend on oil, as does whatever shaky degree of control they have over their restless people. Forty-five percent of the kingdom's GDP goes to supporting the royal family with its battalions of princes (60,000 by last count). In 2004 Saudi Arabia needed oil to sell at $20 a barrel to support its entitlement programs and defense spending. To keep the Arab Spring out (and also pay for massive defense spending), the Saudi monarchy promised its population $60 billion in subsidies—it now needs oil to sell for at least $80 a barrel to meet its obligations. That number is expected to go up to $325 a barrel by 2030.

On par with oil, and perhaps even more important to America's involvement in the Middle East, is Israel's security. Israel is not entirely a foreign policy concern for the United States. If that were true, we would have hardly sided with a small state with no natural resources or market to speak of, and would have long ago thrown in our lot with the far larger and resource-rich Arab world.

In reality, Israel is an American domestic political issue. Many Americans care deeply about Israel for religious and cultural reasons—Israel receives broad support from evangelical Christians, a community that is far larger than the American Jewish one. We do not have vital strategic interests in the Jordan Valley, but the need to behave as if we do has put us in an unenviable position in the midst of the Arab-Israeli dispute.

The United States will continue to support Israel, and that will weigh on Arab public opinion, fueling anti-Americanism and making it difficult for America to realize many of its goals in the region. It is therefore in America's interest that the Arab-Israeli dispute be resolved. Then America's support for Israel would not be at odds with the desire for stronger ties between the United States and the Arab and Muslim worlds. But how to do it? Whereas the Bush administration tried to solve the problem by changing the Arab world, it is more realistic to actually push for a real peace deal.

But we have failed to do so. The Arabs too have failed—either to defeat Israel or persuade it to make peace. With turmoil swirling all around the Middle East, there is now even more reason to sue for peace. America once had the luxury of standing between its Arab and Israeli allies because the region was locked in a predictable status quo. In today's fluid environment America cannot count on being able to continue as before or rest assured that trying to do so would not in fact fuel instability and imperil its allies. Resolving the Arab-Israeli dispute is perhaps the single most important thing America can do to contribute to regional stability and thereby help the Arab world find its way to peace and security. That would douse the flames of anti-Americanism. But this is unlikely. The Arab-Israeli Gordian knot will not be easily untangled; the corrosive impact of this reality will keep America in the Middle East for far longer than it hopes.

Oil, Israel, and terrorism will remain the mantra of our Middle East policy regardless of what other cause we embrace there or how much we say we are done with the region. The hard fact about the Middle East is that this trifecta is interconnected. We cannot pick and choose which part we want to deal with. If neither us nor our vital allies bought oil from the Middle East, so we could claim to have no more direct or nearly direct dependence on oil, the Middle East could move into someone else's orbit, probably China's or Russia's, which would erode our standing in the world and disturb the global balance. Or the Middle East could collapse into economic misery. Social scientists like to talk about "the oil curse"—when countries have lots of oil to sell and hence lots of money sluicing around to fund misgovernment and corruption—and yet not being able to sell their oil would be even worse. That outcome would not produce a peaceful and stable Middle East we can forget about. On the contrary, we would then face a far unrulier region dominated by conflict and extremism. That would make life harder for Israel as well as Europe, which not only sits next to the Middle East but has many people of Middle Eastern origin within its borders. If our allies suffered from Middle Eastern problems, we would hurt too. The sham of a "hands off the Middle East" policy would swiftly become apparent, and we'd be back in the region in no time.

The way to think about the Middle East is not to discount our dependence on it, but to take proper stock of *why* we have been so deeply engaged with it. There is more: now is the time to plan, to be prepared for addressing our vital interests in a drastically more complex and fragile environment. America's challenge is to achieve sustained, smart engagement. Exit is not an option, and whatever President Obama may believe, "leading from behind" our allies won't do.

The Middle East is going through a difficult phase—and that is saying something, considering that, in recent memory, the region has not had it easy. The Arab Spring has set loose long-simmering frustrations over political repression, economic stagnation, and cultural and religious expression. For the first time in a long time, there is real politics in the Arab world, and the street truly matters. There is also real conflict, and the potential for much more of it. The peoples of the Middle East have given themselves a fresh chance to tackle many problems, and that is a good thing. In the long run, it could help the region a great deal. But there is a danger that, given the current combustible mix of poor economies, Islamism, ethnosectarian score settling, and intensifying national rivalries, the region could end up much worse off, and that mix does not augur well for American interests or Israel's security. Never before has America encountered so much change and uncertainty in so many countries all at once in the Middle East.

The fundamental circumstances affecting the broader Middle East are worrisome, but not necessarily fatal. The region has too many people and too few resources.[6] The Middle East is running out of water, low on food and electricity, and increasingly unable to address citizens' demands for basic public services and infrastructure. The population, moreover, skews very young, so all these problems will only get worse as large generational cohorts come of age and seek better life prospects. Jobs are already scarce, which is one reason why there is growing poverty and political agitation across the region. But down the road, across the region, there will not be enough water, food, or electricity either.

Pakistan is generally considered a South Asian country but can be seen as part of the broader Middle East as well. In its travails we can glimpse the shape of things to come. Electricity shortages are already a staple of Pakistani daily life. A combination of corruption, mismanagement, and the sheer number of users places crushing demands on the country's outdated power grid. Power outages lasting more than twenty hours a day in sweltering summer heat are common.[7] Global climate change is melting the Himalayan glaciers, which in the short run means flooding in the Indus Valley that destroys homes, displaces people, and wrecks farmland.[8] After the deluge looms a time of severe droughts and food shortages. All this in a country of 180 million—the world's fourth most populous, and expected to be home to 325 million by 2050.[9] And Pakistan is not alone.

Yemen, too, is running out of water. Iraq is short of electricity, and Egypt is short of both electricity and food: its 83 million people rely on imports to eke out their diets, and high food prices were among the reasons crowds poured into Tahrir Square to pull down the Mubarak regime. Protests in Syria came on the heels of the worst drought in generations.[10] By 2030, there will in all likelihood be many more Yemenis, Iraqis, and Egyptians than there are today, just as there will be more Pakistanis. If food shortages helped spark the Arab Spring, we can only dare to imagine what water and electricity shortages added on top of them will do.

On the brighter side, a more youthful population could also be an engine for growth. Look at China or Vietnam, whose economic booms owe much to each country's large supply of young workers. The cheap and ample labor they supplied gave China a competitive edge that fueled double-digit economic growth, plenty of jobs at the bottom of society, and even more wealth at the top. The economic analyst Ruchir Sharma writes that cheap labor willing to move to industrial centers is necessary for rapid growth.[11] Since 1978, that has been China's elixir of growth, which in peak years soared to stratospheric rates of 13 percent and higher.[12] Now it can also be the Arab world's.

Today, China's labor advantage is not what it once was; manufacturers are looking for other parts of the world where young labor is abundant. The Arab world could be a good candidate. If jobs were to flow west from China, unemployment in the Arab world could decline, and with steady growth at least some Arab countries could find their way to the club of middle-income countries. Tunisia, Jordan, and Morocco are all good candidates.

Although development may not depend that much on what political scientists call "regime type" (dictatorship versus democracy), it does depend on stability. We know that economies will not prosper amid the kinds of conflicts that now haunt the Arab world. We can expect a series of Arab states to fail, generating crises that could tax our resources and demand our attention for years to come. And we are in danger of adding Iran to the tally. We can already see the potential for a belt of failed states containing hundreds of millions of people and stretching from Pakistan and Afghanistan through Iran and on to Iraq, Syria, and even Egypt. We may be able to deal with one at a time, but a confluence of crises could put to the test our ability to manage our interests in the region.

This may be the worst imaginable outcome, but even if only part of it comes to pass it could burden us with untold costs. Imagine the myriad problems that such a result would have in store for us: there will be wars and humanitarian crises to attend to as well as terrorism, piracy, drug trafficking, and other illicit activities to fight. We would be doing this fighting in high mountains and low deserts, cities, towns, and villages from Libya to Pakistan, from the air, on the ground, and on the seas. Our European allies would be supportive, China and Russia may lend us a hand, but what would be missing is real allies in the region. None of the main players in the region will be up to task; in fact they will be the source of much of the trouble.

Egypt may still be in search of stability, and even if it has found it we may no longer see it as a reliable ally—we may find little in common with what is likely to be an Islamist-dominated and prickly, nationalistic state. Egypt, indeed, may become a source of many problems, both deliberate (Cairo could stir up anti-Americanism) and inadvertent (famine could stalk the banks of the Nile as Egypt collapses into a fragile state).

Then there is Saudi Arabia. So much in the Middle East rides on the country's stability, including prospects for a steady oil supply and reasonable energy prices. You don't have to look too closely to realize that betting on Saudi Arabia's continued stability is a risky proposition. What are the odds that a thoroughly undemocratic and fabulously wealthy state built on unquestioning loyalty to a ruling family, backed by lavish entitlement programs and puritanical faith, will chug along unscathed as whirlwinds of change swirl around it? Maybe the Saudis will buck history and bend its rules at every turn—but is that likely? The more the region around Saudi Arabia falls into chaos, the less the kingdom will be willing or able to act as the pillar of American policy. It was not until 1965, when King Faisal brought a semblance of fiscal responsibility to state finances, that America actually thought Saudi Arabia could survive as a country. The past fifty years have lulled us into a false sense of comfort about Saudi Arabia's exceptional stability. But we should know better than to bet that the country's luck will continue indefinitely. We should definitely know better than to bet our regional policy on it, especially now in this period of profound change across the region.

As different as it is from the Kingdom of Saudi Arabia, the Islamic Republic of Iran is also something of a dubious historical relic—an ideological state languishing under a bloated public sector, standing outside the global economic and political order and increasingly at odds with its own people. We know from experience that such states, whether communist or Islamist, don't have an indefinite lease on life. They are brittle entities, all too prone to become victims of their own economic floundering and political brutality.

Unlike Egypt or Saudi Arabia, of course, Iran is not a country that America is counting on to support U.S. interests in the broader Middle East—although as the veteran political analyst Leslie Gelb puts it,

Washington and Iran do have a surprising number of significant common interests and could in principle (however unlikely it may seem right now) be fast friends. Much of U.S. policy in the region since 1979 has been aimed at containing Iran and combating its nefarious influence outside its borders. America's tight relationship with the Persian Gulf's Arab states and the chain of American bases across the Persian Gulf from Oman to Kuwait all came about in an effort to deal with a troublesome Iran. But let us recall that before 1979, Iran was in fact an important U.S. ally. Is it so strange to think that, even after the massive shift wrought by the rise of the Islamic Republic has been taken into account, a substrate of common national and geostrategic interests remains, at least in potential form, and can be accessed if circumstances change?

Consider that even since 1979 America has at least been able to take Iran's stability as a given, and has drawn benefit from this. The Iranian state has been a menace to be sure, but not so Iranian society. Iran is arguably the one country in the region outside Israel where the general public is pro-American (or at least not reflexively anti-American). Iran has so far not produced warlords and drug kingpins. Nor is it a free space in which terrorists and pirates may nest at will, or whose main export is massive humanitarian crises. In short, Iran is not a weak or failing state, and while it produces threats, they are of a sort easier to see and even, I would argue, to deal with than the kind of inchoate, unpredictable threats and problems that typically emanate from failed states.

If the current mix of confrontation and economic pressure continues, however, as we've seen, state failure is exactly where Iran is heading. The outcome of our policy will be not a stable, friendly Iran, but an *un*stable, *un*friendly Iran. The gradual implosion of the Iranian state and society under international pressure will only add to regional instability.

There is now also another gladiator in the arena to consider: Turkey. Buoyed by a dynamic economy and a decade of political stability under Erdoğan's Justice and Development Party (AKP), Ankara is building its influence in Lebanon, Syria, and Iraq, and increasingly also in Egypt and Libya. The Turks like to do business in the Middle East, but economics is merely the foundation for a more ambitious role as undisputed regional leader and bridge builder between East and West. The Turks have one foot in Europe and one in Asia, they belong to NATO and have special ties with the EU, and now they are also the richer, stabler, and more solidly democratic elder brother who wishes to guide the Arab world toward greater stability and prosperity.

Ankara's decision to become engaged in the broader Middle East is the most welcome development of the past decade. We should thank Europe for that. By closing the door to Turkey's hopes for full EU membership, Europe unwittingly made Ankara look east and south. Ruled by a party of moderate Islamists and able to boast years of economic success, Turkey now feels comfortable about returning to the Middle East after close to a century of absence. At the end of World War I, the new Turkish Republic turned west, imagining a European future. Turkey disowned its Islamic and Ottoman legacy just as its rebellious Arab subjects made it clear that they wanted nothing more to do with Turkish rule. Then, Turks were not fellow Muslim Middle Easterners but all-too-recent imperial overlords who had blocked the path to Arab empowerment.

But now the Turks are returning and being welcomed like long-lost relatives who come back from a distant land bearing all the signs and trappings of success. In the time that Turkey was gone, the Middle East changed. It has forgotten about the inequities of Ottoman rule that gave birth to Arab nationalism and the horrors of World War I, or the heroics of the wartime Arab Revolt against Turkish rule led by the maverick British officer T. E. Lawrence. There are no more grudges against Turkey. Instead, Arabs are mesmerized by Turkey's success, wanting to hear all about how it happened and whether there is anything in it for the region.

Over the past decade, Turkey has increased its economic and diplomatic activity across the Arab world and the broader Middle East, but it still does not have enough Arabic speakers or deep knowledge of the Arab world. Turkish troops and assistance have gone to Afghanistan. Turkey has cultivated trade ties with Iraqi Kurdistan; tried but failed to broker deals between rival factions in Lebanon and Iraq; and participated in international efforts to deal with contentious issues involving Libya, Syria, and Iran.

The West alternately worries about and dismisses "neo-Ottomanism"—the desire to rebuild the cultural and political web of influence that once joined the Arab periphery to the metropole of the Turkish sultans.[13] Turkey's tendency to evoke Ottoman times may strike listeners as ominous, but it is unclear that Turks mean their rhetoric as anything more than historical color—somewhat like the occasional evocations of Charlemagne, the Holy Roman Empire, or the Hanseatic League that were heard among Europeans when they were discussing the European Coal and Steel Community and the Common Market. American diplomats tend to look askance at Turkey's ambitions and have been known to mock foreign minister Ahmet Davutoğlu as a neo-Ottoman "Energizer bunny" who can turn every diplomatic contact into a forum for his vision of Turkey's old-yet-new regional role. But over time Washington has warmed up to Davutoğlu and found Turkey to be the perfect instrument for its policy of "leading from behind" our allies in the Middle East—which, whatever its flaws, would be utterly unworkable without Turkey.

Obama seems to recognize this. He phones Erdoğan often and has probably conferred with him more than he has with any other world leader. The Turkish prime minister has worked closely with the White House on Syria and Iran, even carrying a personal message from Obama to Khamenei in March 2012 on the eve of the crucial talks with Iran. For America, Turkish influence in the Middle East is an important stabilizing force. Turkey is prosperous and democratic. It is a longtime NATO member and has deep economic ties with Europe. Despite Erdoğan's worrisome authoritarian tendencies—muzzling the press and putting journalists in jail—and periodic overtures to his Islamist base, Turkey retains a competitive political system with values that are closer to those of the West than those of the Arab world. Unlike Arab states or Iran, moreover, Turkey is not running against history, but with it. We can safely imagine Turkey becoming even more stable, democratic, and capitalist.

Some in Washington think the new axis of power in the region pits Ankara-Riyadh-Doha (add Cairo and Damascus to that once Egypt gets on its feet and Syria's Sunni majority topples Assad) against Tehran-Baghdad-Beirut (until Hezbollah is declawed). They argue that America ought to work with and through the Sunni axis against the Iranian one. The logic seems self-evident, but the picture is not likely to be that clear.

There is still reason to doubt that Turkey could or would serve as anchor for American policy. Turkish enthusiasm for the Middle East was at its peak when the region looked to be opening up economically and inching its way to democracy. Ankara could then imagine a region built in Turkey's image; Istanbul would be the region's economic hub and Ankara its political center. Foreign Minister Davotuğlu, Turkey's most articulate strategic thinker, did not envision neo-Ottomanism to be about troubleshooting, peacekeeping, and scurrying from crisis to crisis to tackle the region's problems.[14] Turkey will have to do some of this, especially when trouble is at its door as in Syria, but Ankara's appetite for diving headfirst into the region's problems is dwindling. Davotuğlu's slogan for Turkey's turn to the Middle East was "zero problems with neighbors." Now with states across the region imploding into protest and conflict, it looks as if Turkey may find itself with neighbors that offer zero aside from problems.

Turkey may also lack the capacity to do more troubleshooting. In the near future it will have to contend with succession in its ruling party, and the Turkish economy is beginning to show signs of slowing down, along with many other once high-flying emerging markets.[15] This does not mean that Turkey will become unstable, only that it may not be willing or able to act as regional ombudsman or America's go-to ally.

In short, America will be compelled to do more in this region, and it will have to do it increasingly on its own. If it needs help, it will have to rally allies. Leading others from behind will not work largely because there are no obvious allies able to put out ahead. Add to this the fact that in the end, it is we alone who must defend our position and protect our interests against encroachment by our global rivals, especially China.

If there is any American strategy at play in the Middle East these days it can be summed up as follows: Keep Egypt from getting worse, contain Iran, rely on Turkey, and build up the diplomatic and military capabilities of the Persian Gulf monarchies. In other words, play defense with regard to the Arab Spring, play offense when it comes to Iran, and maintain continuity in waging the war on terror. But the United States must do all this in a changing geostrategic environment.

Over the past decade, the center of gravity of the Middle East has been steadily shifting east and south, first from the Levant and eastern Mediterranean (the region running from Turkey in the north to Egypt in the south and stretching east to the borders of Jordan and Syria with Iraq), which was for decades the eye of the storm in the Middle East, to the Persian Gulf, and then from the Arab world north and east to Iran and Turkey. Since the Iraq invasion of 2003, conflict in and around the Persian Gulf has consumed most of America's attention and resources. It is in the Persian Gulf that the United States has deployed to fight in Iraq, contain Iran, and keep oil flowing to world markets. The newly salient fault line between Shias and Sunnis runs through the Persian Gulf, and it is also here that oil money gives new kids on the block such as Oman, Qatar, and the UAE their outsize influence on Arab politics.

Since 2003, a Persian-versus-Arab competition for power in the Persian Gulf (with clear sectarian overtones) has become an important regional dynamic, influencing the turn of events in Syria, Lebanon, and the Palestinian territories, where distant Iran, Saudi Arabia, and Qatar are more influential players than neighboring Egypt or Jordan. The fate of Syria and future of Lebanon, in large measure, hang in the balance of Iranian-Saudi relations; it was Qatar that brokered a peace in Lebanon in 2008; and it is Iran and Saudi Arabia that are deepening the sectarian divide in Syria and vying to decide the region's stance on the Palestinian issue.

Shia-Sunni sectarian rivalry will not always lead to bloody conflict and is by no means the only dynamic at play in the Middle East, but its influence over events large and small, and more broadly over the balance of power in the region, is unmistakable. And the Arab Spring has accelerated this dynamic. Sectarianism will not explain every development and every alliance in the region, but until the imbalance in distribution of wealth and power between Shias and Sunnis is set right, sectarianism will remain an important determinant of regional politics. The Shia-Sunni rivalry and the Arab Spring have brought into sharp relief how much tension centers on the Persian Gulf. It is here that the Shias are concentrated in numbers, and that Iran faces Sunni champion Saudi Arabia. The Persian Gulf is a Shia lake, surrounded by Shia-majority Iran, Iraq, and Bahrain, with significant Shia populations also living in Kuwait, Saudi Arabia's eastern oil region, and the UAE. The more besieged the Shias feel—and the sight of a U.S.-backed Sunni regime such as Bahrain's shooting Shia protestors cannot help in this regard—the more likely they will be to seek shelter under Iran's wing.[16] Iran may pull back from Sunni lands (Syria or Yemen), where its tenuous influence depends on denunciations of Israel, but Iranian influence will only expand among the Shia. Iran's zone of influence will grow in and around the Persian Gulf exactly when we see it to be on the decline in Syria. This reality not only makes the Persian Gulf the geostrategic epicenter of the broader Middle East, but also should give pause to any American strategists who think they can count on stable Persian Gulf monarchies as pillars of U.S. policy.

Washington has found itself unwittingly on the Sunni side of the street. That might have been inevitable given that Iraq now matters less to America while the threat that Iran and Hezbollah pose to Western interests puts them in America's crosshairs. The combustible mix of the Arab Spring and sectarianism has undermined another American foe in Syria, whereas in Bahrain an American friend quickly stamped out protests. America looks to be doing the Sunnis' work for them—caging Iran and pulling down Assad. America of course does not think that it is lining up as a player in the region's sectarian scrum, but it might as well be doing just that, for the result is the same.

That may not be the best outcome, and Washington should take great care lest it sleepwalk into a sectarian blind alley. It will not serve America's interests to become involved on one side of the most deep-seated and long-running division in the region without a clear sense of its dynamics, how it may end, and what its implications may be for the United States.

To start with, the energy calculus in the Persian Gulf may change to reflect sectarian rivalries. Shia-majority Iraq could challenge Saudi Arabia for primacy as an oil exporter, thereby loosening the Saudi grip on the West's strategic imagination. Once the mammoth Iraqi oil fields begin pumping to their potential (and also develop excess capacity on par with Saudi Arabia's), world markets could soften and Saudi Arabia's economic stability and global political influence wane. Saudi Arabia has 262 billion barrels of oil reserves. It also has pumping capacity (10.8 million barrels a day) that dwarfs Iraq's (2.4 million barrels a day) and Iran's (4.2 million barrels a day). But as suggested above, this imbalance in pumping capacity could change. Iraq has an estimated reserve of 144 billion barrels, but some put its true reserve as high as 300 billion. Add Iran's 136 billion, and the geostrategic stakes in the Sunni-Shia rivalry along the Persian Gulf shoreline begin to come into focus. That these three countries together account for a third of the world's proven oil reserve bears heavily on worries about steady supplies and stable prices.

There are also rivalries and disagreements between the flag bearers of the Sunni rise, Turkey and the Persian Gulf monarchies, especially over how to handle Iran. They all view Iran and its Shia allies with suspicion, but Turkey, unlike the Persian Gulf monarchies, does not see Iran as a strategic threat and does robust business with Tehran. Furthermore, Turkey and the Persian Gulf monarchies are now rival claimants to leadership of the region's Sunnis.

The Arab Spring has animated this jockeying for power and influence by aggravating sectarian tensions. This is not just a matter of governments, but of popular attitudes. Sunnis all over the region are cheering for the Sunni rebels who are fighting to topple Assad's minority Alawite (read Shia) regime in Syria. Similarly, Shias in Iraq, Iran, and elsewhere are identifying with coreligionists in Bahrain who are being held down by a Sunni monarchy and the minority that it represents.

The toppling of Saddam enfranchised Iraq's Shias. Iran likewise felt emboldened after Saddam's removal, and when Hezbollah made a strong showing in its 2006 conflict with Israel in southern Lebanon, the Shias seemed decisively on the rise. Fast-forward to 2012, however, and the picture changes. American pressure regarding the nuclear issue is squeezing Iran, and its main ally is on the ropes in Damascus.

Syria is being torn from the clutches of the Assad regime to become a Sunni-led country. Elsewhere, the Arab Spring's biggest upshot so far has been the unleashing of Sunni Islamism—the Sunni expression of Islam and its unabashed claim to sectarian supremacy and political power—in Egypt, Tunisia, Morocco, and potentially many other Arab countries. In public discourse and official statements, a certain Sunni triumphalism is now palpable.

Leadership of the Sunni world is a plum eagerly sought by many. It is clear that Turkey, in keeping with neo-Ottomanism, sees itself as the protector of Sunni prerogatives in the region.[17] A sense of Sunni identity is embedded in the ruling AKP's conception of Islam and its place in politics inside Turkey as well as across the region. Back in 1997, before the AKP as we know it had come into being, I sat down with a group of Islamist political activists (several of them are now leaders in the AKP and the Turkish government). One of them tried to explain the dilemma they faced in Turkey by drawing a parallel with Syria. He said, "We do not want Turkey to become Syria, a Sunni-majority country ruled by an Alevi military. In Syria, an Alawite military dominates; here an Alevi military is trying the same thing." (Turkish generals with origins in the Alevi community, a religious minority with Shia affinities, were then seen as Kemalism's staunchest defenders and Turkish Islamism's worst enemies.) The sense of Sunni defensiveness and embattlement that he expressed brought me up short.

The large majority of Turks—especially those on the Islamic side of the aisle—are not just Muslim, but distinctly Sunni in their identity. Just as Turkey's Sunnis identify with Syria's Sunnis, Turkey's Alevis feel solidarity with Syria's Alawites—although their faiths are not the same and their rituals differ. Alevis, for instance, congregate in *cemevis* to pray, and the community has so far refused the Turkish government's entreaties that it too worship in mosques—that is, blend in with Sunnis.[18]

By some estimates, Alevis make up as much as a quarter of Turkey's population (Alevis themselves claim the share is much higher), and they include Turkish citizens of both Kurdish and Turkish ethnicity.[19] To get a fuller picture of the ethnosectarian identities that exist in today's Turkey, one should also take into account the additional 3 to 5 percent of the population who are Shias of Azeri lineage, the ethnic cousins of Iranian Azeris and much of the population of independent Azerbaijan. None of this is to suggest that Turkey suffers from acute sectarianism—it does not—but sectarian shadings and undercurrents are present. If the rest of the region blows up into sectarian violence, these could become more prominent and more problematic features of Turkish life. Already Turkey's role in the Syrian crisis has brought to the fore uncomfortable debates about where Alevis pray. Alevi intellectuals have taken the lead in criticizing the AKP government's support for the uprising in Syria, and debate over Turkey's role in the conflict now has a clear sectarian undertone. Deniz Baykal, former leader of the opposition Republican People's Party, or CHP, has called for constitutional changes that would protect Turkey from "Syrian contamination" by fully recognizing the religious rights of the Alevi sect and reorganizing the State Directorate of Religious Affairs to accommodate Alevis.[20] The ruling AKP has rejected such suggestions. Prime Minister Erdoğan has shot back, saying, "If we are Muslims then our temple ought to be one and the same" (i.e., no constitutional recognition of Alevi rights).[21] At the same time, the government is conscious of the brewing sectarian tension in light of developments in Syria. At a public rally Erdoğan brushed aside criticism by his main rival, Kemal Kiliçdaroğlu (current leader of CHP), of Turkey's posture toward Syria, saying that of course as an Alevi, Kiliçdaroğlu would have a soft spot for Assad.[22]

Much has been written about the personal relationship between Erdoğan and Assad—they had been known to vacation together—and how that had improved the once-tense relations between Turkey and Syria before the Arab Spring. Such coverage is overblown. The truth of the matter is that neither Erdoğan nor anyone in his party has ever thought of Alawites as true Muslims or considered their control of Syria legitimate.

The AKP party's Sunni base may support greater Turkish involvement in Syria—and that may sit well with Erdoğan's ambition to lead the Sunni world from the Balkans to Central Asia and deep into the Middle East. But fear that deeper involvement in Syria's troubles could inflame Turkey's own sectarian tensions has stayed his hand. And so will Turkey's business interests.

The coming apart of Syria has reactivated Turkey's Kurdish separatist PKK (Kurdistan Workers Party), which has strong ties with Syria's Kurds. As Damascus loses control of its Kurdish region and refugees flow into Turkey, the PKK—with the Syrian government's encouragement—has found more room to operate. The resulting terrorist attacks in Turkey have put the country on edge, raising the specter of a risky Turkish intervention in Syria. What's more, Iraq's Kurds are sympathetic to the separatist movement, and their leader Masoud Barzani has provided it support, to Turkey's annoyance. Relations between Turkey and the Kurdish region of northern Iraq have been warm—this year, after oil giants Chevron, Gazprom, and Total signed oil deals with Barzani, Turkey announced it would build two new pipelines to export the new oil through Turkey. But the PKK is now coming between Erdoğan and Barzani.

Similarly, China, which has been doing growing trade with Turkey, is irked at Turkey's stance on Syria in support of the United States. That has not impacted business between the two countries so far, but it is a dark cloud over the horizon. Syria is putting at risk Turkey's domestic stability and economic interests, and that is likely to serve as a brake on Erdoğan and Davutoğlu's embrace of the Sunni surge in Syria and Iraq.

Turkey's main rival for leadership of the Sunni world is Saudi Arabia. The rivalry is not new. During the first decade of the twentieth century, the Ottoman-appointed governor of the Hejaz (the mountainous Red Sea coastal province of today's Saudi Arabia where Mecca and Medina are located, and which at the time was the seat of power on the Arabian Peninsula), Sharif Hussein of Mecca (the great-grandfather of King Abdullah II of Jordan), challenged the Ottoman sultan in Istanbul, claiming autonomy for Hejaz and religious authority for himself despite the sultan's nominal status as caliph of all Muslims. Hussein's case rested on his claim of blood kinship to the Prophet Muhammad himself (something to which the Ottoman sultans had no pretensions) and his status as "guardian of the two holy places," meaning Mecca and Medina.

The rivalry reached its symbolic climax in a dispute over who had the authority to declare a jihad either for or against the Allies or the Central Powers during the First World War. In the end, Sharif Hussein threw in his lot with the British, who thought in turn that his fatwa would carry the most weight not only with Arabs but also among the many Muslims of British India and Britain's African colonies. Given this thumbnail history (readers may be familiar with some of it from well-known sources such as T. E. Lawrence's *Seven Pillars of Wisdom* or David Lean and Robert Bolt's 1962 cinematic masterpiece *Lawrence of Arabia*), it is not hard to see how neo-Ottoman Turkey's recent rise has grated on Saudi sensibilities and breathed new life into the old competition between Mecca and Istanbul.

Turkey and Saudi Arabia may cooperate on Syria, but they are vying against each other for influence over Egypt and Iraq. Turkish foreign minister Davutoğlu's idea of an "axis of democracy" running between Ankara and Cairo runs athwart Saudi hopes of embracing Egypt as a means of containing the Arab Spring and the democratic aspirations it released.[23] Saudi Arabia looks to Egypt with worried eyes. A chaotic Egypt will present the Saudis with myriad problems, and a democratic Egypt may be no less a thorn in the kingdom's side. It is hard to imagine that the oil princes relish the prospect of a large Arab country filled with Sunnis just across the Red Sea playing host to Saudi dissidents, holding competitive elections, allowing mass demonstrations, and the rest. Unlike Iran, Egypt cannot be dismissed as a bearer of Persian and Shia deviationism. Saudi Arabia has already had to close its Cairo embassy for a time.[24] Saudi rulers can feel at ease only with an authoritarian Egypt.

Turkey is less sectarian in its outlook than Saudi Arabia and has many more areas of common interest with Iran than do the Saudis, and what we may see is not a hard-and-fast Sunni alliance arrayed against Iran, but a degree of cooperation between Ankara and Tehran that would allow Turkey to set itself apart from Saudi Arabia.

An Iranian businessman who plies his trade in Iraqi Kurdistan told me, "All those Turkish businesses that you see doing business in northern Iraq are not really Turkish; many are Iranian or part Iranian." He said:

The Revolutionary Guards could not do business in Iraq after 2003 because the Americans would not let them. So [the Guards] formed shell companies in Turkey. Those companies are either Revolutionary Guards–owned or they are partnerships between the Guards and Turkish businesses. Together they do business in Iraq. You go to meetings in Istanbul with these Turkish companies to talk about business in Iraq and there are Iranians in the room. The Turks know it, they are all making money; it contributes to the Guards' budget.

America should favor a prosperous and democratic Turkey rather than a conservative and authoritarian Saudi Arabia assuming the mantle of Sunni leadership. Saudi Arabia and other Gulf monarchies will be caught between containing the Shia power centers (Iran, Iraq, Lebanon) and coping with the surging Sunni Islamism of the Muslim Brotherhood and Salafis, which have a populist and antimonarchical bent. In order to have any hope of surviving, these monarchies will have to gravitate toward Islamism and feed Sunni extremism across the region. Here again, Pakistan tells a disturbing premonitory tale. There, the Saudis pumped money in to empower Sunni extremists (and fund a nuclear program) as a way of flanking Shia Iran. If the troubles that Saudi-backed Sunni extremism have brought to Pakistan, its neighbors, and the world at large are any indication, we should hope that Ankara rather than Riyadh emerges as the Muslim world's Sunni big brother. Turkey too will find itself having to tack in the direction of the Islamism that is sweeping the Arab world. That will not suit Ankara's global ambitions, and we will have to do what we can to see that Turkey does not veer too far off course in order to align itself with the Arab mood. Neo-Ottomanism can be a positive force only if it avoids marching under the banner of Islamism.

The Persian Gulf monarchies' efforts to surf the new wave are already in full swing. Qatar and Saudi Arabia have been aiding Salafi forces in Libya, Syria, and Lebanon. Yet Washington relies heavily on gas-rich Qatar, a tiny emirate that has big regional ambitions and deep pockets to go with them. Occupying a small peninsula that juts off the Arabian coast into the Persian Gulf, Qatar has long-running rivalries with the UAE and especially Saudi Arabia (there have been armed border skirmishes). The ruling al-Thani family provides bases for the U.S. Central Command (CENTCOM) and also owns al-Jazeera, the Arab world's most popular and influential satellite TV channel. This unusual combination of U.S. military muscle and influence over Arab public opinion via the power of television gives Qatar an outsized presence in Arab politics. Al-Jazeera tends to follow the interests of the Sunni regime, showing blood-curdling news footage from Syria to rally Arab public opinion against Assad but remaining largely silent about Shia protests against a Sunni monarch in nearby Bahrain.

Qatar took a leading role in brokering a truce between Lebanon's bickering factions in 2008, averting open conflict there. More recently, Qatar played a key role in Arab League deliberations over whether to push for intervention in Libya and Syria. That sort of regional engagement is attractive to Washington. Doha, America thinks, has the cash and the desire to move policy. But that is a risky proposition. Should America trust a small country that may have the will to make its voice heard diplomatically but lacks the diplomatic and military capacity to see its favored policies through to completion?

Nor are Qatar's power plays always in line with U.S. objectives. A small fish that wishes to swim beside a whale may know a few tricks, but does it have the stamina to swim against the tide? In a region awash with anti-Americanism, Qatar has decided to balance its close ties with Washington with hedging on the other side. It was not until al-Jazeera broadcast images of the Arab Spring to the world that Washington found something to like about the network. Over the years, al-Jazeera has consistently criticized American policy—and on many occasions deservedly so. In return, Washington has blocked its broadcast on American cable channels, and it was perhaps a convenient coincidence that in both Iraq and Afghanistan American firepower zeroed in on the al-Jazeera bureaus. The network's anti-American slant was fine with the al-Thanis and their lieutenants, who pointed to it in order to reject charges that they were U.S. stooges.

Qatari hedging does not end with al-Jazeera, however. The emirate has also lent support to Islamist forces (both the Muslim Brotherhood and, more worryingly, Salafis) in Libya, Egypt, and Syria.[25] Qatar Airways announced a deal with Iran to take over a fifth of that country's domestic airline industry at a time when a lack of spare parts and rising air accidents rooted in American sanctions were causing ordinary Iranians much angst.[26]

The Persian Gulf monarchies have not made it past the dangers that the Arab Spring represents, and indeed are particularly vulnerable to them. The UAE's decision to close the offices of the National Democratic Institute (a pro-democracy organization backed by the U.S. government) in March 2012 betrayed an awareness of this. The Persian Gulf's ruling elites are eager for American military protection, but not for American values.

Saudi Arabia in particular is vulnerable to Arab Spring aftershocks. The House of Saud was quick both to jack up domestic entitlement spending and to urge the region's other monarchies not to give in to protesters.[27] The kingdom's rulers have pumped billions into the economies of Bahrain, Egypt, Jordan, Morocco, and Yemen. The dole has bought Saudi Arabia some relief—bolstering ruling regimes in Bahrain and Jordan, and strengthening the military's hand in Egypt while giving Yemen a soft landing after Saleh's exit.

That has worked for now, but the fundamentals are not in favor of long-run authoritarian stability. As we have seen, the region's monarchies are now more dependent on oil than at any other time in their history, and soon they may be more dependent on the flow of oil from the Persian Gulf into world markets than their thirsty customers.

Saudi financial support to its fellow monarchs is not a one-time intervention. Absent real reform, Arab economies are going to remain bottomless money pits, and Saudi Arabia cannot afford to keep them all serviced amply enough to maintain its influence on the shape of Arab political life. The Middle East is not Europe, and Saudi Arabia (or even the whole collection of Arab petromonarchies) is not Germany. Certainly Abdullah bin Abdulaziz cuts no Angela Merkel–like figure. The notion that America can expect the Middle East to manage its own financial crises the way Europe does is misplaced and dangerous.

We cannot think with glee of getting off Middle Eastern oil and seeing energy prices drop, but then continue to rely on the Persian Gulf's oil monarchies to realize our security and diplomatic goals in the region. If oil prices fall sharply, Saudi Arabia runs into big trouble. We might not shed many tears for the Saudi princes and their religious policemen, but can we think that cataclysmic change in the Persian Gulf will somehow not affect us?

Oil experts estimate that risk accounts for at least a fifth of the current price of oil—jittery buyers paying a premium to hedge against future supply cutoffs. Our policy in the region, threatening war with Iran, contributes to that premium. If we were to free ourselves of Middle East worries or somehow find our way to peace with Iran, the biggest losers would be Saudi Arabia and Russia, each of which has an economy that is dangerously dependent on high oil prices.

If the Chinese and Indian economies slow down over the coming decade, the Persian Gulf will face a precipitous drop in the price of oil. If fracking and other new fossil-fuel extraction technologies do around the world what they are doing in America, the resulting fall in energy prices could produce a Persian Gulf that is in deeper economic and social trouble and with fewer prospects for recovery than its larger Arab neighbors in the Levant and North Africa. Saudi Arabia could then be in worse shape than Egypt—it will have a harder political landing, and worse yet, the Saudi economy and labor force would not be in the position to pick up the pieces by attracting foreign investment to manufacture goods for export and integrate happily into the world economy. The Persian Gulf will not be able to do as Southeast Asia did after the financial crisis of 1998.

There is a lot of talk around the Persian Gulf region of "life after oil." Dubai and Bahrain have experimented with building financial sectors and every emirate is investing in tourism. As yet, however, there is no sustainable model—the non-oil economy still needs oil revenue to survive. The smaller emirates have built sovereign wealth funds that will provide income long into the future. That is a cushion to protect against dropping oil revenues, but only if the population feeding off that income does not grow inordinately. Despite rising oil wealth, Saudi Arabia's per capita income ($20,000) has not changed since the 1980s.[28] If its population keeps growing at the current rate of 2 percent annually—which means that Saudi Arabia's population will double in fewer decades than it should—then GDP per capita may start to decline.

A larger question is whether a youthful populace living off a sovereign wealth fund will remain satisfied with idleness and lack of productivity and not turn to political activism. Can the appeal of Xbox always be counted on to exceed the appeal of Tahrir Square? Despite expensive investments the Saudi educational system is not producing skilled labor. Much of the productive work is still done by foreign guest workers while locals hold do-nothing government jobs or occupy themselves with religious activities. Saudi Arabia is awash with holders of doctorates in religious subjects.

There has been a buzz about the new King Abdullah University for Science and Technology (KAUST), a Saudi version of MIT intended to turn out world-class scientists and engineers who will build the kingdom a highway into the future. Billions have gone into the new venture, luring leading American universities to partner with KAUST. But the project remains a white elephant, disconnected from the rest of the Saudi educational system, the prospects for realizing its goals uncertain as of yet. Like many other megaprojects in the Persian Gulf, the emphasis is on audacity rather than substance. What the region needs is change that is built from the ground up.

Already there are too many frustrated unemployed and underemployed youth in Saudi Arabia, spending too much time watching al-Jazeera and networking on Facebook or Twitter to remain immune to the lure of change on display in Tunisia, Egypt, or Syria. Forty percent of young Saudi men are unemployed—and their ranks will swell in the coming years—and a staggering 40 percent of all Saudis are under the age of fifteen.[29] Protests could easily return to the kingdom, and if Bahrain erupts again, then protests could take on a sectarian cast, triggering agitation among Saudi Arabia's own Shias.

Jacked-up entitlement spending has poured oil on the troubled waters for now, but it cannot correct worrisome long-term trends. If oil prices do not keep pace with the country's current standards of living, the only alternative would be to whittle down entitlement programs and wean the economy off oil. The Saudi state could not accommodate that change easily if at all.[30] It could crack, and if it survives it would be only after becoming more representative.

To avoid a crisis point the Saudi economy and society will have to undergo fundamental structural change. The rulers are not ready for anything so drastic, but are experimenting with new ways of doing things. One approach is to educate women and give them more freedom in hopes that they will become more gradual change agents. There are now more women in universities—at some schools they outnumber men—and they are winning new rights: to drive, to vote (albeit in what are still fairly meaningless elections, since they account for only a minority of council seats), and to hold previously forbidden executive positions. But the social impact of this change is as yet unclear. The Saudi economy cannot create enough jobs for men; it will be hard-pressed to furnish enough for legions of new female applicants. Having more men pushed into unemployment, moreover, will not bode well for social and political stability.

Over the past decade, Islamic finance—whose compatibility with sharia law both in terms of banning interest and keeping the sexes apart in bank branches accounts for much of its attraction—has employed a growing number of women. Islamic financial institutions have developed banking and financial services for women, becoming a source of what in the West would be called "pink-collar" jobs. Some Saudi women are now crossing over to regular banking and elbowing men out of white-collar jobs. One senior male Saudi banker told me, "Women are more diligent, work harder, and stay at the office until the work is done. In short, they are better employees. I would much rather hire women than men, and I expect I will be hiring more [women] in the future." Educated Saudi women will continue to create new workplace pressures that the current Saudi system is ill equipped to address.

Since 9/11, America has encouraged reform in Saudi Arabia. First we thought reform would stem the rising tide of extremism; now we think it may ensure the kingdom's stability. But there is no soft landing for Saudi Arabia. Its political system is too rigid, too dependent on the hard-line cabal of influential Wahhabi clerics, and too dominated by the large class of princes of the House of Saud to be able to change. If it tries to change, it will break. Saudi Arabia's rulers know this; they know their youth want economic prosperity and political empowerment, and that is why they have positioned their country squarely against the Arab Spring.

And it is not just the youth who are restless. I have often thought about a conversation I once had regarding Saudi Arabia's future. It was 2007, and I was in the country to give some talks. Iraq was then in the grip of sectarian violence, and everyone I met in Saudi Arabia seemed worried about the Shia-Sunni conflict and the rising tide of Iranian influence. Saudi Arabia has a significant Shia minority, concentrated in the country's vast oil-rich Eastern Province.[31] Since the Iranian revolution of

1979 first raised the specter of sectarianism in the region, unrest among Shias has been a sensitive topic in the kingdom.[32]

One afternoon, I went to a date plantation outside the city of Dammam in the heart of the Eastern Province to meet community leaders. The plantation belonged to a local Shia leader, and he gathered several of his friends and colleagues to talk about the impact of Iraq and the challenges facing Saudi Shias. I asked them what they wanted of their government. A well-educated middle-aged engineer who had worked for decades at the Saudi oil giant ARAMCO replied, "It is not true that we want to break away from Saudi Arabia, we just want the right to practice our faith." I asked him, "If that is all you want, then why are you such a threat to the kingdom?" He leaned forward in his chair and said:

> We are not the only minority in this country; Wahhabis are a minority too. Most Saudi Sunnis are not Wahhabi. If Shias get their way, those other Sunnis will want to practice Islam their own way. Here in Dammam they come to us, they say they want to celebrate *milad al-nabi* [the Prophet's birthday] but they cannot, here it is forbidden. If Shias get permission to observe Ashura, then other Sunnis also want permission to observe *milad al-nabi*. Before Saudis captured Mecca [in 1925] every noon there were five *adhans* [calls to prayer] in Mecca, one for Shias and four for each of the four schools of Sunni law. Now there is only one, the Wahhabi one. We want five calls to prayer every day in Mecca.

The fanatical Wahhabi warriors, the so-called brothers or *ikhwan* who won the Arabian Peninsula for the Saudi clan at the end of World War I, were particularly hard on the Shia. Many were put to the sword, but the pogrom failed to subdue the Shia. They have remained the one Muslim community to successfully resist Wahhabi hegemony—and their continued presence means the standing possibility that they will push for a modicum of pluralism.

In addition to religion, there is the factor of regionalism. The Hejaz was once a separate kingdom with its own far-flung ancient trade routes, a long Red Sea coastline, a Turkish- and German-built railroad to Damascus, and the great religious centers of Mecca and Medina to lend it towering spiritual prestige. In fact, the Hejaz is the cradle of Islam, and it was where the trade wealth, the high culture, and the political power of the Arabian Peninsula were focused. The Hejaz's dominant position changed only when the House of Saud (a clan from the high-desert province of Najd to the east) and its Wahhabi armies conquered the region and bested its Hashemite rulers (the ancestors of today's king of Jordan) after World War I. Hejazis have a proud cultural heritage and resent the cultural domination of Najd enshrined in the Saudi state.

And Hejaz is not alone. Asir (on the border with Yemen) and Ha'il (in the heart of the kingdom) also claim a proud heritage in defiance of Najdi cultural hegemony. Could a Shia campaign for autonomy in matters of religious observance encourage the long-murmuring, never-stilled voice of Hejazi nationalism to make itself heard more loudly? The House of Saud created a single country, but its roots may be shallower than we think. Shias cannot break away from Saudi Arabia, but they might be able to break it up.

This is why Saudi Arabia fears Iran and its nuclear ambitions. It is not that a nuclear Iran would invade Saudi Arabia as Saddam overran Kuwait in 1990. Nor is it a question of Iran twisting Saudi Arabia's arm on oil prices or the Palestinian issue. Saudi Arabia is afraid, rather, that a bullish Iran armed with nuclear weapons will ask for the broadcasting of Shia prayer calls in Mecca, and then for a Shia mosque there. Next, Iran might seek to build a massive shrine and pilgrimage destination dedicated to certain Shia saints who are buried in Medina. The first Saudi king razed the cemetery where they lie into rubble decades ago, but if it were to be rebuilt, Shia pilgrims would doubtless return there in huge numbers, much as they did when the fall of Saddam restored access to the holy cities of Iraq. The Saudi rulers and their clerical allies find such a prospect deeply frightening and disconcerting: it would threaten the end of Wahhabism. Saudis fear not so much Iran, but the pluralism that Iran has promised to force on their country if ever the chance arises—a pluralism that would speak loudly to the multitude of Saudi citizens whose ethnic and sectarian aspirations do not line up with the Saudi-Wahhabi ideology of state.

In Saudi Arabia, the pillars of American policy in the region rest on quicksand. When Saudi Arabian troops arrived in Bahrain to help the monarchy there suppress its pro-democracy opposition—claiming that it was putting down an Iranian-backed Shia power grab—Iranian parliamentary speaker Ali Larijani observed that "Saudi Arabia has now moved all its pawns, and its queen is exposed."[33] Saudi Arabia has embarked on an audacious foreign policy offensive to contain and defeat the Arab Spring across the Arab world and snuff out Iranian influence in the region. Saudis are deeply involved in the politics of Arab countries from Morocco to Yemen, spending billions to decide political outcomes. They are involved in the internal struggles of Sunni regimes with their Shia populations in Yemen (against the Shia tribal Hooti rebellion), Bahrain, Syria, and Lebanon, and against Iran at the international level. This offensive is stretching Saudi Arabia's military, diplomatic, and economic capacity, an overreach that could indeed expose the kingdom's "queen."

The specter of cataclysmic change demands continued engagement from America. Gone are the days when the United States could easily safeguard its interests by relying on a handful of pliant dictators. America is inclined to hold on to that old and tired strategy even as it claims to be welcoming the winds of change sweeping across the region. But the ground is shifting in the Middle East. Power is moving from rulers to the masses, from the secular elite to Islamist challengers, and from the Arab heartland to the Persian Gulf (Iran's lair) and Turkey. These transitions will be fraught with conflict that will cause instability and put American interests at risk. The least good option is to double down on the monarchies of the Persian Gulf and in so doing take sides in the sectarian power struggle driving the region's conflicts. It is better that American policy rely on a broader set of countries, and then not just on their rulers but also their people. That nimbleness is all the more important as the complexities of the Middle East will also become fodder for the approaching American rivalry with China.

THE CHINA CHALLENGE

In the spring of 2012, I asked a senior member of President Obama's cabinet, who had just returned from high-level talks in China, where he thought the Chinese leadership was on the host of issues that worried America: Afghanistan, Pakistan, Iran, the Arab Spring. "We don't know," he said. "What most worries us is that we don't know what they want, and what they are afraid of."

Others wonder the same about us. They don't know what we are thinking and where we are heading. We have abandoned Iraq and Afghanistan to instability, pushed Pakistan away, destabilized but not "denuclearized" Iran, let down countries of the Arab Spring, and still managed to also alienate authoritarian allies in the Persian Gulf. We have done all that and then declared our intention to shrink our presence in the Middle East, because we don't see an upside to investing in the region's future. We think the future lies in the east, and that the great game of global power politics will be against China in the Asia-Pacific.

President Obama's "pivot to Asia" policy is at its core a policy of containing China—it is a "forward-deployed diplomacy to face China in its backyard."[1] Hillary Clinton used the term "pivot" first, in an article in *Foreign Policy* magazine, to argue the administration's case that America ought to pay less attention to the Middle East and more attention to Asia.[2] She wrote that China (and not the Middle East) is the real strategic challenge facing America. What is needed, she went on, is a "reset" of global strategy in which Washington deemphasizes the Middle East and camps at China's doorstep to make sure that Beijing's influence remains limited. "The future of the United States is intimately intertwined with the future of the Asia-Pacific," she declared.[3] Global politics "will be decided in Asia," went the subhead, "not Afghanistan or Iraq, and the United States will be right at the center of the action."[4]

But it would be folly for America to build its new strategy thinking that the Middle East has nothing to do with China. Folly to think that we can abandon one to contend with the other, or that what happens in the wake of our departure from the Middle East will stay in the Middle East. The Middle East remains the single most important region of the world—not because it is rich in energy, or fraught with instability and pregnant with security threats, but because it is where the great power rivalry with China will play out and where its outcome will be decided. The various strands of our Middle East policy—in Afghanistan and Pakistan, with regard to Iran and the Arab Spring—already intersect with our broader interests with regard to China. In China's eyes, the region is growing in importance—and in the coming decades it will matter more to Beijing than Africa or Latin America. If we could tell what the Chinese were thinking, or what they were afraid of, we would see the Middle East right at the heart of it. A retreat from the Middle East will not free us to deal with China; it will constrain us in managing that competition.

We not only have to remain fully engaged with the Middle East, we have to increase our economic and diplomatic footprint there to match our show of military force.

I am hardly the first to see rising China as a global challenge—the most significant strategic challenge facing the United States today.[5] Economically, China accounts for growing shares of global output and consumption and has a voracious appetite for commodities that it feeds via trade and investment links reaching deep into every continent. China has risen by participating in the global economy, but that interdependence does not necessarily mean that China's rise will be peaceful or that its coexistence with the United States at the helm of the global order will be harmonious.[6]

China is building up its military; its navy has extended its reach as far as the Gulf of Aden (to suppress Somali pirates) and the shores of Libya (to evacuate Chinese citizens endangered by the fighting there). Chinese warships now routinely make port calls in the Middle East.

Building bases on a series of islands along its own periphery and extending deep into the Indian Ocean will give China the necessary foundation for building a dominant naval position in some of the world's most strategic waters. China is expanding its second-strike nuclear capability, improving the effectiveness of its anti-ship missiles, and building its capabilities in new domains such as cyberspace and outer space.[7] The goal is to replace America as Asia's preeminent power and to fold all of East Asia into a Chinese sphere of influence. Some may dismiss such fears as exaggerated, but there is no doubting that China's ambitions are increasingly running up against American interests. Hillary Clinton confirmed this trend when she told an audience in Senegal that the continent's infatuation with China was misplaced. Africa should not look to China, but to "a model of sustainable partnership that adds value, rather than extracts it." Unlike China, she continued, "America will stand up for democracy and universal human rights even when it might be easier to look the other way and keep the resources flowing."[8] China was stung by that volley and joined the rhetorical battle, highlighting the growing competition for influence and access between two powers across the globe.

The rise of China as an economic and military powerhouse is changing the global balance of power and challenging the United States with a return to a bipolar world.[9] The boundary lines will not be as stark as during the Cold War; there are fewer ideological differences, no clear sense of "us and them" jealously guarded by threat of war and nuclear annihilation. But we are inching our way to something similar—a global rivalry that although not ideological is real and is still about global power.

America's interest lies in an open international economic system—built on the principle of free trade and open exchange of goods, services, and money. Our great fear is that China sees its interests in exactly the opposite way: carving out various regions of the world into spheres of influence from which America would be excluded.[10] We would like to avoid this outcome by encouraging China to fully embrace the rules and institutions that govern global economics and international politics—in short, the normative global order that we helped create and have enforced for more than sixty years, and which China had no part in creating. We hope China will enter into more multilateral treaties, participate in more multilateral organizations, embrace shared global values, and live by them at home and abroad. We would like China to act as a partner with the United States in addressing global issues. But this may all be too much to ask, at least in the short run. And if China's growth is going to challenge international norms then it is bound to run up against the global order, which means conflict with the United States. Conflict is not in our interest, but we are preparing for it. The Middle East will have much to do with whether that will come to pass.

We have been joined at the hip with China when it comes to economic concerns; trade, investment, and the financing of U.S. debts with Chinese surpluses have interwoven the U.S. and Chinese economies in intricate ways.[11] We have sought its support in tackling thorny issues from Libya to Iran to Pakistan. But when it comes to global affairs we see a clear line separating our interests from those of China. The Chinese see us as a challenge too—they are the rising power and we the established one; they are elbowing their way to the top and we do not want to make room.

From Beijing's perspective, American reassurances to the contrary notwithstanding,[12] "pivoting to Asia" sounds a lot like "containing China."[13] It looks to them like Obama has settled the long-running debate in America over whether to "engage" or "contain" China in favor of the latter. America has sharpened its rhetoric on China and declared its intention to confront its ambitions in Asia and Africa. America's vision is "that we continue to be what we have been now for seven decades: the pivotal military power in the Asia-Pacific region, which has provided peace and stability." The emphasis on "military" is what worries China.[14] We are forging new military ties with India, Vietnam, and the Philippines; wooing Myanmar and Mongolia; and pursuing a free-trade pact (the so-called Trans-Pacific Partnership, or TPP for short) with several Asian countries to link them closely with America. Beijing sees all these efforts as components of a strategy to put China in a cage. "China's greatest strategic fear," writes Henry Kissinger, "is that an outside power or powers will establish military deployments around China's periphery capable of encroaching on China's territory and meddling in its domestic institutions. When China deemed that it faced such a threat in the past, it went to war . . . . in Korea in 1950, against India in 1962, along the northern border with the Soviet Union in 1969, and against Vietnam in 1979."[15] China is not thinking of war with America, but its instinct is to build its capability to resist American pressure and push back against American encirclement, and that could be a slippery slope to confrontation.

Signs of China's greater influence are all around for American leaders to see. As one high administration official noted, "We go to country after country through airports built by China, and meet [those countries'] leaders in new buildings paid for by China." In Pakistan, Holbrooke was told time and again, "We can point to the bridge that China built here; we cannot point to a bridge that you have built." Yet America's attention has turned to China's regional backyard. Recent sage advice on how to handle China from Kissinger as well as Zbigniew Brzezinski has focused on maintaining the balance of power in the Asia-Pacific—popularly viewed as the arc from the Sea of Japan to the Straits of Malacca.[16]

China, however, already sees East and West Asia (the term it uses for the Middle East) as linked. For instance, in July 2012, after months of coaxing, the Chinese finally agreed to talk to U.S. emissaries about Afghanistan and Pakistan. But the U.S. diplomats arrived in Beijing not long after tensions over the South China Sea had surged, with Chinese and Philippine warships engaging in a standoff over Scarborough Shoal, a tiny collection of reefs and rocks plus a lagoon sitting only 120 miles west of Luzon (the largest island of the Philippines, on the eastern edge of the South China Sea). The Chinese blamed the United States for the crisis and refused to engage on the question of Pakistan, telling their American interlocutor: "There are now new issues like the South China Sea coming over the horizon that demand our attention." The Chinese don't divide the world into a set of separate policy domains; to them, the Middle East and Asia (and Africa and Latin America) are interconnected.

The Obama administration took the Scarborough Shoal contretemps as a sign that China's rise would no longer be as peaceful or harmonious as before, and likely come at the cost of American interests and those of its regional allies. American interests rest with strong Southeast Asian states prospering on the back of open commerce. China's aggressive posturing over the South China Sea (and the rich oil and natural gas deposits lying beneath it) challenges that vision. It has rattled Beijing's Asian neighbors, and some among them, like the Philippines and Vietnam, have looked to Washington for help.[17] But what Obama and his advisers got wrong is their assumption that Chinese assertiveness is limited to Asia, and that Asia, in China's view, is the Asia-Pacific.

There are two conceptions of Asia in Chinese thinking. The first is indeed the Asia-Pacific: the area from Myanmar eastward, or, in other words, the regions we call Southeast Asia (Myanmar, Thailand, Vietnam, Indonesia, Philippines, Singapore, etc.) plus Northeast Asia (Japan, North Korea, South Korea). Then there is the larger conception of Asia as the entire vast landmass—the world's largest both in area and population—that stretches from the Pacific Ocean to the Mediterranean Sea. China has come to accept America's dominance in the Asia-Pacific for now, but not so in the countries of South and Central Asia and the greater Middle East. Our strategy should be to challenge the Chinese conception of where America can and should be present. We achieve that by maintaining a strong presence in the western parts of Asia and not just in the form of military bases, but by becoming embedded in the region's economy and political life.

America is an integral part of the Asia-Pacific thanks to its many trade deals and military bases, and also its bilateral alliances and the multilateral institutions it has helped create and now participates in. Our goal is to keep the region stable, open, and free of conflict. We see benefit in the region's prosperity and openness to American business and trade. The wealthier the Asia-Pacific has become the more important it is for us to make sure that it will remain free of hegemonic control by any one power. The same logic should apply to the Middle East. Yet today the Middle East accounts for 5 percent of U.S. trade and only 1 percent of its direct foreign investment ($54 billion out of $3.4 trillion), a paltry amount compared with the Asia-Pacific, which accounted for 16 percent of American investment abroad.[18] We are now doing less trade with the region than China is. The big story of the past decade that we missed amid our preoccupation with wars in the Middle East is the explosion of Chinese trade with the region. China's trade with Iran has grown from $1.3 billion in 1999 to $45 billion in 2011; with Saudi

Arabia from $4 billion in 2001 to $50 billion in 2011; and with Egypt from less than a billion in 2001 to $9 billion in 2011. Since 2006 China has been exporting more to the Middle East than the United States does, and the same is true for imports since 2009.[19] In 2010 Chinese exports to the region were close to double that of the United States (China is now the largest exporter to the region), and Chinese direct foreign investment took off, leaving America far behind: 30 percent of China's global contracts in that year were with Arab enterprises.[20] We have essentially ceded the Middle East to China and others to profit from just as we geared up to prevent the same happening in the Asia-Pacific and Africa.

In the past, America has resisted being pushed out of Asia by a hegemonic force. From 1941 to 1945, America fought a world war with Germany and Japan, then we faced down the Soviet Union for decades to prevent such an outcome.[21] America now fears that China may wish to exclude the United States from Asia exactly when the sagging U.S. economy badly needs all the ties that can be mustered.[22] That fear is behind the expansion of free-trade arrangements (with Japan and South Korea) and new business ties in Asia (with India and countries of Southeast Asia)[23] and, more broadly, behind the "rebalancing" exercise and the effort to convince the countries of the Asia-Pacific that China is *not* going to grow till it blocks the sun; we will be there to check its ambition. We also want China to know that we will stand athwart its path to hegemony. But to be convincing, we have to do that not just in East Asia but everywhere else, too, starting with West Asia.

The global oil company BP forecasts that between now and 2030, 95 percent of the increase in world demand for oil will come from China and India (which by 2030 could surpass China as the world's most populous country). Even if they grow at a slower pace, the two Asian giants will still account for a significant share of global energy consumption. North America, by contrast, will become energy independent. In 2030, natural gas will account for a far bigger share (and likely majority) of global energy consumption, but less so in China or India. For starters China will still lack the necessary pipeline infrastructure to distribute natural gas nationally (building a national grid connecting supply sources to hundreds of thousands of cities, towns, and villages will take considerable time and investment), and that will limit its ability to harness its own shale gas reserves as well.

By 2030, the oil- and gas-producing countries of Central Asia and the Middle East will be totally dependent on Asian buyers—the oil-induced strategic nexus between America and the Persian Gulf will be coming apart. That trend is already evident. Japan is buying natural gas from Qatar at $15 to $17 per million BTUs (about a thousand cubic feet), whereas the cost in America for the same amount of gas is just $3 (one reason to be hopeful that U.S. manufacturing will become more competitive). Qatar and other Middle Eastern gas producers can expect a shrinking demand from the West—Asia is now their market. They are looking east just as China is looking west. Persian Gulf monarchies are investing in refineries, banks, and manufacturing in China, deepening economic ties between East and West Asia.

Pondering this picture, the Obama administration and some observers have assumed that America can leave the Middle East and wash its hands of Middle Eastern problems. If we don't need their oil, then surely we don't have to deal with their headaches? That would be wise if Chinese interest in Middle Eastern energy sources did not threaten to put at a disadvantage the very allies—India, Japan, South Korea, and even much of Europe—that America needs to balance China.[24] If these countries became dependent on China for their energy supplies they would have to align their foreign and economic policies with China, which would mean moving away from the United States. That would put a big dent into our plans for containing China in the Asia-Pacific and ensuring the region's continued prosperity and openness. The best way for China to break American containment in its backyard is to squeeze the energy lifeline of America's Asian allies, and that would have to happen in the Middle East. It is these same countries, which have been asking us to pay more attention to the Asia-Pacific, that will soon be asking us to refocus on the Middle East.

In April 2012, Turkey's prime minister, Recep Tayyip Erdoğan, visited Urumqi, the capital of China's far western province of Xinjiang, home to the Turkic-speaking and historically Muslim Uyghur ethnic group. With four ministers and thirty Turkish business executives in tow, Erdoğan visited factories, mosques, and bazaars. To set the proper tone for the first visit of a Turkish premier to China in twenty-seven years, Erdoğan had decided to first make a stop in predominantly Turkic and Muslim Urumqi. But unlike Charles de Gaulle in Quebec, Erdoğan had not gone to Urumqi—site of Uyghur versus Han Chinese communal unrest not long ago—to support local nationalist aspirations. On the contrary, he told an audience there that Turkey believed in "one China." There would be no Turkish support for Islamic activism and Uyghur separatism. This was a major shift for Turkey. Only three years before, Erdoğan had angered Beijing by referring to China's crackdown on Uyghur separatists as "genocide." Beijing had asked Erdoğan to retract his comments; he declined then, but was now in effect doing just that.

Turkey was not interested in local politics, but stood ready to invest in the local economy—to help develop a free economic zone in Urumqi. Turkey's economic reach into Central Asia would now extend to Xinjiang, and that could in time help China further extend its own reach into Central Asia.

Erdoğan's trip to China was a follow-up to the February 2012 visit to Turkey by the incoming Chinese president Xi Jinping. On his way back from Washington, Xi made two stops. One was Ireland, where China hopes to capitalize on shrinking American and European investments—especially in the pharmaceutical industry—in order to seize a commercial beachhead on Europe's western flank. The other was Turkey, where China sees an opportunity to enter Europe from the east, and also to find a foothold in the Middle East and the Caucasus. It is rare for an incoming Chinese president to make such an exploratory visit—it signaled the centrality of Turkey to the new president's plans for China. China is pivoting west, angling to poach on the lucrative economic relations between the United States and the EU, and to push into western Asia. Turkey is the critical launching pad for both ambitions.

Erdoğan's performance in Urumqi sat well with China's leaders: "It is what we would have wanted to see, confirming the new economic and strategic opportunity," was how one senior Chinese official put it. Erdoğan had set the stage for the real reason he was going to China: to conclude a sweeping and historic agreement between China and Turkey. After Urumqi, Erdoğan went to Beijing. There, he and Chinese premier Wen Jiabao signed on to deals on a wide range of economic projects, an ambitious twenty-five, to be precise. The two countries agreed to build cars and consumer goods together, but also to invest massively in new infrastructure for Turkey—some of which would serve China's larger geostrategic interests. China agreed to sell energy-hungry Turkey two nuclear power plants, build oil refineries, develop new port facilities, dig a canal in Istanbul to reduce congestion on the Bosporus, and lay down a railway from Istanbul through eastern Turkey with plans to connect (likely through Iran, where China is also building railroads)[25] to lines in China proper that reach all the way to the coastal cities that are the hubs of Chinese industry and commerce.[26] There was even talk of China building a third bridge over the Bosporus to connect Istanbul's European and Asian halves. Between 2000 and 2012, Turkish trade with China grew more than twentyfold to $25 billion, and it was poised to multiply again.[27]

At the Beijing offices of the Turkish Industrialists and Businessmen's Association (TUSIAD) there is unbridled enthusiasm for the burgeoning business ties: "Our trade is $25 billion. China exports $23 billion to Turkey, but we export only $2 billion to China. We want to export more to China, but China is also happy to make up for that imbalance with FDI [foreign direct investment]." That means more Chinese companies opening shop in Istanbul and across Anatolia. TUSIAD has been wooing Chinese companies, beating the pavement in Beijing and Shanghai, looking for Chinese customers for Turkish goods and Chinese investors for Turkish ventures. Erdoğan's trip was a shot in the arm. "Now that there is government to government agreement there is official support for the business relationship. This is now a whole new game." TUSIAD's vanguard in Beijing acknowledges that there are hurdles to clear—for instance, Turkey has been slow to give Chinese nationals work visas—but it hopes bureaucratic snags will not stand in the way of a boom in trade. Indeed, China is now so important to Turkey's aspirations that the promise of a rich relationship will move mountains in Ankara—and even change Turkish foreign policy. Rebuffed by Europe and hungry for investments and markets, Turkey is fast moving into China's orbit. And

Turkey is not alone. Egypt's new president Mohammad Morsi, too, has written off the West as a source of investment and financial assistance. He is looking to China for help. In August 2012 he flew to Beijing (ahead of a stop in Tehran) to cultivate economic ties with China. The Arab world's most important country, with the largest population, sitting at the crossroads of Asia, Africa, and Europe, thinks it has a thing or two to offer to China.

For Turkey, the Chinese connection brings new markets and much-needed foreign investment to sustain its economic boom at a time when Europe (Turkey's major trading partner) is going through a downturn, and when the Arab world (where Turkey had hoped to grow its exports) is being buffeted by political instability. Turkey has set itself the goal of becoming, by the time of the Turkish Republic's centennial in 2023, the world's tenth-largest economy (it is now the sixteenth largest). Everything in Turkey is now geared to achieving this—both the government and the private sector have made it their mantra. Massive investments, mountains of commodities, and lucrative new markets will all be needed. In Turkish eyes, East Asia and especially China hold the key. One senior Erdoğan adviser put it this way: "To realize our goal we need China's investments to build new bridges, roads, telecommunications and new technologies, but also business and trade. China is building up Africa, why not Turkey? China is the only country in the world that is willing to make that kind of investment." And what of Turkey's future in Europe? I asked. "Europe will not make that kind of investment. Turkey's future needs China."

The turn to China is part of a bigger push east for Turkey. Ankara has also signed an ambitious free-trade deal with South Korea and is encouraging investments from Singapore (which has even opened an office for its economic development board in Turkey) and Japan, which is looking for the same investment opportunities that China is keen on. The expanded trade deals with East Asian economic powerhouses will complement trade deals Turkey is planning with Southeast European, Caucasian, and Central Asian states. Through their investments in Turkish manufacturing, East Asian countries can reach deep into Europe and the broader region around Turkey.

Turkey's "neo-Ottoman" vision is in one sense rather literal. Because borders in this region are so artificial—drawn by colonial powers at the end of the First World War—there is a natural wish to transcend those boundaries somewhat and for Turkey to return to the regional family it left when the Great War ended and the Ottoman Empire collapsed. No single measure has done more to move Turkey and the region toward that vision than Turkey's decision to abolish visa requirements for citizens of the broad region around it. That has spurred unprecedented travel and trade all centered on Turkey—a vast market of singular importance to China and its East Asian neighbors.

Turkey's ambitious development plans rely heavily on Iraqi oil and East Asian markets and investments. As energy and investment enable Turkish growth, they will also bring together the two wings of Asia with Turkey as the critical linchpin. Proven oil and gas reserves in Iraq's Kurdish region, where Turkish influence is ubiquitous, equal those of Libya, and the low cost of exploration matches that of Saudi Arabia. The Kurdish region expects to pump 1 million barrels a day by 2015 and double that by 2020.[28] China is eyeing that production. So many Chinese companies have showed up in Irbil in the last year that local firms are looking for Mandarin speakers to serve the burgeoning Chinese business.

China sees rising Turkey as an economic partner, a new market for Chinese goods and technology (China is particularly proud of selling its old nuclear technology to Turkey), and a good place in which to invest. Turkey has a growing middle class and consumer market, and soon it will be Europe's fifth-largest economy. Its transport corridor and commercial ties make it a convenient gateway to large European and Middle Eastern markets as well as smaller ones in the Balkans, the Caucasus, and Central Asia. Turkey also offers China potential access to energy sources in Iraq and the Caucasus. China is also keenly interested in Central Asia, and there Turkish influence runs deep. A Chinese-Turkish partnership could rival the influence that Russia and Iran exert in Central Asia and the Caucasus. China has a sizable footprint in all these markets, but Turkey can provide China with an even greater presence. Turkey's special economic relations with Europe, its open border and relaxed visa policy with its neighbors, and its port, road, rail, and pipeline infrastructure all add up to this: if China is in Turkey, then it will automatically be in many other places, too.

It looks, in other words, like Asia is getting smaller as Turkey moves east and China moves west. The two booming emerging markets now bracket the continent, and as economic integration takes root the vast expanse between the Mediterranean and the Yellow Sea will shrink into one geostrategic space. That should be how America thinks of Asia, as the geographic region, economic zone, and strategic space between Turkey and China.

Over the past decade western Asia has emerged as the energy hub for the rapidly growing economies of the Asia-Pacific and South Asia, China chief among them.[29] These economies need the vast oil and gas reserves of Russia, Central Asia, and the Persian Gulf and the transport corridor of Iran, Afghanistan, and Pakistan to fuel their growth.

Coal still accounts for 70 percent of China's energy consumption and 80 percent of its electricity supply,[30] but oil is catching up fast and is already the main topic of concern when China considers its global outlook and interaction with international markets.

James Fallows of the *Atlantic* explains China's growing hunger for oil as a peculiar facet of its growth. "As fast as [China's] economy grows, its energy consumption grows faster still. Each percentage point increase in economic output leads to a more than proportional increase in demand for energy."[31] Two decades ago, China produced all the oil that it needed and even exported some.[32] China started importing oil in 1993. By 2005, its demand for crude had doubled, and it had become the world's second-largest oil importer, behind only the United States. China's demand for oil will double again in the coming fifteen years or so. Well before then, in 2020, China is projected to be importing 7.3 million barrels of crude a day—half of Saudi Arabia's planned output.[33] By this time, China will be the world's number one oil consumer, and the manic rate of urbanization is likely to keep China deeply dependent on oil. In the next decade alone, the rise of new Chinese cities, according to a McKinsey report, "will account for around 20 percent of global energy consumption and up to one-quarter of growth in [global] oil demand."[34]

To sate its burgeoning hunger for energy, China has gone on the prowl for coal, oil, and gas around the world.[35] Around 1999, China adopted the "Go Out" policy of encouraging diplomats and state-owned companies to secure long-term oil contracts.[36] Chinese interests looked first to low-hanging fruit (places where there is little competition or Western presence) in Thailand and Peru, and then sought larger deals in Sudan and South Sudan. China has invested $44 billion in oil projects beyond its borders, half of it in Africa. Between 2002 and 2003, trade between China and Africa doubled to $18.5 billion, most of it oil imports.[37] But none of this is enough. China needs the larger supplies of Russia and the Middle East. It craves the stability of long-term supply contracts but also seeks to invest in "upstream" oil and gas exploration, which it has done in Iran. Iran's rich oil and gas reserves remain a significant opportunity for the Go Out strategy.[38]

East Asia is emerging as the ultimate energy importer, whose needs are perfectly matched with the supply potential of western Asia (comprising the Middle East and Central Asia). The Middle East exports around 30 million barrels of oil per day, and East Asia imports the same amount.[39]

Securing fossil fuels at the source is not China's only concern. It is also worried about the security of its supply routes.[40] The first step in America's pivot to Asia has been to build up military ties with Australia, the Philippines, Vietnam, and India. In a military competition, America has the clear advantage of using its superior sea power to squeeze China's oil supplies. China, meanwhile, is worried about the U.S. Navy's control of the Persian Gulf. Also a worry is the narrow, five-hundred-mile-long passage between Sumatra and the Malay Peninsula known as the Straits of Malacca. This shallow, heavily traveled, easily blocked stretch of water—in the Phillips Channel just south of Singapore it is less than two miles wide—is the eastern doorway to the Indian Ocean and one of the world's critical maritime chokepoints. More than 85 percent of the oil and oil products bound for China pass through the Straits from west to east. For Chinese strategists, resolving what they call "the Malacca dilemma" is a major preoccupation.

The Chinese are concerned about American strategic relations from Japan to India, for they see in U.S. dealings the outlines of a noose that could choke China's access to energy.[41] In the run-up to World War II, America, Britain, and the Netherlands did deny energy- and resource-poor Japan access to oil, rubber, and iron shipments from Southeast Asia and the Dutch East Indies. This is a lesson that is not lost on China's strategic decision makers. During the Cold War, the Soviet Union cast hungry eyes on the Persian Gulf with the idea of doing something similar to the West. Access to energy, and therefore the Middle East, will be at the heart of the next global rivalry.

In response to its concern, China is building a blue-water navy and has invested in the "string of pearls" strategy of building bases in the Indian Ocean (in places such as Sri Lanka) to protect its sea routes to Africa and the Middle East. There is already a brisk competition between China and India over which country will dominate the Indian Ocean. The two Asian powers eye each other with suspicion even as they cooperate to address the menace of piracy.[42] But China in particular is also worried about U.S. control of the high seas, which, added to America's dominant position in the Persian Gulf, puts China's energy supplies at risk. The Scarborough Shoal row, in which China's assertion of primacy over the South China Sea met with resistance from some Southeast Asian nations with U.S. backing, brought the problem into sharp relief. At that point, America had already announced that it would deploy 2,500 U.S. Marines to Australia and help the Philippines to upgrade its navy.

In order to escape the Malacca dilemma, China has turned to a series of overland pipelines linking the eastern industrial centers of Shanghai and Guangzhou with western China and Turkmenistan, respectively.[43] China has also looked to Myanmar as an alternate route that avoids the Straits. There, Beijing has had to compete for influence with Delhi. India, too, is growing rapidly, and is looking to the same Middle Eastern and Central Asian sources to sustain its economy. India, however, already has a sizable navy and is America's strategic partner; the Bush administration sought to bolster India as a counterweight to China by forging closer ties with Delhi through measures such as a deal regarding nuclear power for civilian uses.

China and India have a contentious history. They fought a short, sharp border war high up in the Himalayas in late 1962, and India remains China's strategic nemesis. They do plenty of trading now, but their rivalry will come to the fore as they vie against each other to gain access to western Asia's energy resources on the best terms. In its extensive efforts to secure its access to Middle Eastern and Central Asian oil and gas, China is acting upon its fear of India as well as its fear of the United States.

Myanmar also poses a challenge to China's plans. In early 2011, Myanmar's military regime began a surprising series of reforms that have led to a thaw in relations with Washington. This cannot be pleasing to China, which had been treating Myanmar as effectively a client state. In fact, fear of excessive dependence on Beijing seems to be one of the motives driving the reform advocates within Myanmar's ruling regime. In mid-2012, Myanmar suspended work on the massive Myitsone Dam that China had been building across the Irrawaddy River—another signal that Naypyidaw is trying to put some modest distance between itself and Beijing.

Farther to the west, China has earmarked $12 billion to develop the port of Gwadar on Pakistan's Arabian Sea coast. The idea is to create a place where petrochemicals piped down from Central Asia (Kazakhstan and Turkmenistan) and minerals shipped from Afghanistan can be loaded onto tankers and cargo ships bound for China. The Gwadar project has been hampered by instability and security challenges—the product of clashes between local Baluch separatists and the central government—of the kind that U.S. multinationals such as ExxonMobil have long had to cope with in Indonesia or Nigeria. But China continues to invest in Gwadar and work to bring the port facility under its control.[44]

Little wonder, then, that China has been interested in still other pipelines. These include one going from Iran into Pakistan and then perhaps eventually through the Hindu Kush mountains into Xinjiang. Another would start in the Central Asian gas fields of Turkmenistan and then snake its way through Afghanistan and Pakistan to Gwadar or into Xinjiang. Here again, however, there is U.S. competition. Washington is talking about a pipeline from Turkmenistan to India (not China) as part of America's "New Silk Road" initiative to bring commerce and economic development to Afghanistan and other countries along the historic overland trade routes between China and Europe. The New Silk Road is a lofty idea that would work if there were true American commitment to Afghanistan's stability and substantial financial commitment to build infrastructure, develop industry, and facilitate trade, not to mention commitment to improved relations with Pakistan and engagement with Iran. Without this commitment, at best the idea will become the basis for a Chinese regional economic system.

Two decades ago, China's large industrial and population centers lay almost exclusively along its east coast. That region remains a dynamo, but people and production—and the hunger and thirst for energy inputs—are moving west.[45] China now needs more and more energy for its middle and western regions, and that is another reason why pipelines into China's southwestern provinces of Yunnan (from Myanmar) and Xinjiang (from Pakistan) are increasingly attractive.[46]

Political scientist Kent Calder writes that energy interdependence is tying eastern and western Asia together in new ways. The Chinese-Turkish deal further shows that East Asia's need for closer ties with West Asia is matched by West Asia's need to trade with the East. In 1980, East Asia accounted for 20 percent of the Middle East's imports; that number has now doubled to 40 percent and is likely to grow further.[47] China now carries on a robust trade with the Persian Gulf monarchies and is rapidly filling the gap left by the withdrawal of Western interests from Iran and Pakistan. China's economic reach in Asia is vast and rapidly growing. Its political touch and military sting are sure to be felt soon.

China's rise has so far not been as disruptive as that of Japan or Germany (or Russia) in the last century. The economic rise of those countries had, to put it mildly, a distinctly militaristic edge. The hunger for resources and markets drove those powers to start expansionist wars. The Chinese mantra since Deng Xiaoping launched economic reforms in 1978, in contrast, has been "a peaceful rise in a harmonious world." There is a detectable air of caution and patience in China's strategic thinking, but that barely masks the country's determination in protecting its interests and realizing its goals. Beijing has ambitions but doesn't want trouble.[48] Given China's manifold domestic challenges and all that it still must do to consolidate its economic gains, Beijing knows that it "is not in a position to be arrogant or boastful" (the words are those of Deputy Foreign Minister Dai Bingguo). And yet, China still sees its interests as separate from those of the rest of the world, and its hunger for resources and markets could end up in military conflict.[49]

The "we don't want trouble" approach sounds nice, in other words, but it may prove increasingly hard to sustain, exhibit one being the current saber rattling in the South China Sea. But the current spat over the South China Sea is not all that puts the United States and China on a collision course or makes China's rise a source of global tension, for that matter. China is, after all, increasingly an imperialist power. Imperialism emerged in the nineteenth century as growing European economies looked around the world for commodities and markets to fuel their gathering industrialization.[50] European powers then—much like China today—invested heavily in securing trade routes and building infrastructure for resource extraction.

Journalist Steve Coll has described what he calls China's "mercantilist approach to energy" and the premium that it places on physically owning oil supplies. This flies in the face of the fungibility of the global oil market. Whereas America thinks of global oil markets as an integrated whole, governed by rules of free exchange, China seeks a direct supply-and-demand relationship between itself and wherever the oil comes from. That harkens back to nineteenth-century colonialism. The upshot will be greater Chinese control of the supply–demand relationship and deepening political involvement with, and dependency on, energy-producing regions and countries. The scent of nineteenth-century colonialism is not lost on Coll, who calls China's approach "neo-colonial."[51]

"Peaceful rise" will not go hand in hand with mercantilism. And if a peaceful rise does not work, then, as Henry Kissinger has warned, America's relationship with China could start to look like a version of the Anglo-German rivalry that haunted Europe on the eve of World War I.[52] Germany was the rising, insurgent power then, hungry for energy and other commodities that would aid its expansion, eagerly seeking markets for the products of its burgeoning factories. Germany's mercantilist approach collided with Britain's dominance over the global economy—a dominance that was secured not only by the reach of a British Empire "upon which the sun never set," but also by a Royal Navy that protected the commercial interests of many other nations before German expansionism.[53] Germany turned to militarism, forming its High Seas Fleet, which supported the growth of its influence beyond continental Europe and set in motion a race to war in the first decade of the twentieth century.

Similarly, America's response to China's mercantilist push against open trade and commerce puts us on a collision course with China. The Middle East will be at the center of that clash when it happens.

The example of European imperialism holds other lessons too. The initial outflow of capital from Europe to the New World (British capital played a large role in building the iconic cattle-ranching and railroad businesses of America's Old West) was soon followed by the flow of capital back to Europe as cheap commodity prices and industrial exports sold to the New World yielded European countries huge profits. Things did not run smoothly everywhere, however. Some local populations balked at the unfair terms of trade with Europe, and European powers reacted in some cases with the use of force and even outright territorial-political conquest. Imperialism evolved into colonialism, which made sense because European powers were struggling not only to deal with restive locals but also to protect their holdings from rival powers.

Yesterday's imperialism has gradually shifted east as a latecomer to the party, China, has begun investing heavily in Africa, Latin America, and western Asia.[54] It is building railways and ports in sub-Saharan Africa and Afghanistan, much as Britain and France once did in India or Africa.[55] Chinese managers and workers are moving to Africa, living and working in colonies that are reminiscent of British cantonments in colonial India. These Chinese are there to stay for the long haul.

China is also doling out cash to rulers, such as Venezuela's Hugo Chávez, as Britain, France, and the Netherlands once did. In the "game of nabobs" that Britain played with its European rivals in India, the object was to win the allegiance of local rulers in order to control trade routes. In a contemporary version of the ploy, Beijing's deep investment in Cambodia has separated that country from its Southeast Asian neighbors on issues that matter to China, creating discord in the ranks of ASEAN just when the United States is trying to rally the regional grouping to resist Chinese domination of the South China Sea. The game of nabobs goes on.

Across Africa and Asia today, country after country is happy to have Chinese money building railways and ports for moving commodities to China. As for what floods of cheap Chinese imports are doing to local manufacturing, that is another, less happy story. In Nigeria and Pakistan, Chinese textiles are driving local producers out of business. One Pakistani textile manufacturer told me: "Everyone worries that if we open trade with India its textiles will put us out of business, but the Chinese are already doing that." Soap manufacturers and even producers of crockery are saying the same. According to some estimates, China now accounts for a staggering 90 percent of that market in Pakistan.

We know from history that the imperialist formula of monopoly control over commodity exports plus plentiful manufactured goods imports will lead to political trouble. The initial enthusiasm for Chinese investment will give way to anger at the net outflow of wealth to China as it extracts commodities and dumps cheap manufactured goods in country after country. To sustain the economic arrangement, China will have to get involved politically. It will have to delve into the domestic politics of countries, taking sides in messy internal fights, but also take a position on regional disputes. And when its interests warrant making important decisions for desired outcomes, persuasion will be the method of choice, and force the method of last resort.

China will also encounter other global players looking for the same commodities and resources. America, Europe, India, Japan, and South Korea, as well as other emerging nations, will all be looking for the same iron, copper, manganese, bauxite, rare earth metals, and oil. The gold rush boom in Mongolia—which has attracted $15 billion in foreign investment and is pitting the United States against China in the vast but sparsely populated country of 3 million people—along with the South China Sea disputes provide a window into this. After all, China has already seized the Spratly Islands, a collection of rocks near undersea oil deposits. Elsewhere, China has the first mover's advantage in Africa and is trying to elbow its way to domination in Southeast Asia. But to protect its investment and prevent supplying countries from playing it against its rivals, China will have to exercise more political control. As China faces the same kind of challenges protecting its assets that once led Europe to embrace colonialism, a "peaceful rise" may grow considerably less peaceful.

The Chinese, however, are not looking that far ahead. For now, the U.S. security presence in the Persian Gulf and other regions is providing the stability upon which Beijing can free-ride as it develops its interests abroad. China gets to have it all. It enjoys the luxury of engaging a region's troublemakers and unstable states—Iran or Pakistan, for instance—while at the same time benefiting from advantageous trade conditions.

As we have seen, America has been lobbying the Saudis to sell China more oil in order to gain Chinese help in reining in Iran and Pakistan. But why should that be? Why shouldn't Beijing be offering *us* concessions in order to get America to maintain its costly investment in regional security? Many observers muse that in the not-too-distant future, when any U.S. need for Middle Eastern oil is a fading memory and the only customers for Persian Gulf oil are in East Asia, China will be in the unenviable position of relying entirely on U.S. security to protect the Gulf's crucial wellheads. And yet, it is not that simple. China is happy with free-riding now because its relations with America have been, generally speaking, quiet. Since 9/11 we have been focused on the Middle East, ignoring China's rise for the most part. But as China finds itself in America's crosshairs, the benefits of freeing its Middle East interests from the clutches of American influence will outweigh the security dividend it gains from American presence in the region. China will soon welcome the American exit from the region even at the cost of shouldering the security cost itself. American retreat from the Middle East will be welcomed in China as a strategic boon; and this is exactly why it should not happen. This is already evident in the Chinese attitude toward Central Asia. This region is not only a source of valuable energy for China, but owing to its cultural and ethnic ties to the Turkic Muslim minority living in China's westernmost provinces, it is also of security and geostrategic interest to China. Beijing has sought to tightly integrate Central Asia into its economic orbit. This has also meant ally-ing with Iran and Russia—the other key players in the region—to limit American presence in the region. The Chinese-founded and -backed Shanghai Cooperation Organization (SCO)—a rival to American power wrapped as a counterweight to NATO and the Gulf Cooperation Council (GCC)—reflects this approach. It should be America using its presence in the Middle East to deny China hegemony over commerce. That would be for the greater good of the global economy.

America may not have announced that it is closing any bases in the Persian Gulf—for now it is our diplomatic and economic footprint that is visibly shrinking—but President Obama has declared that with mounting economic pressures at home America is considering a different sort of military footprint in the Middle East, one that will be designed not to wage new land wars, but primarily to carry out precision counterterrorism missions. The example of America's precipitous withdrawals from Iraq and then Afghanistan looms large and could well extend to the Persian Gulf in years to come unless we have a global agenda associated with our military presence in the Middle East—as was the case in Europe and East Asia during the Cold War. The military presence should be tied to a growing diplomatic and economic engagement, the goals of which are treaties, alliances, and multilateral organizations. All this would promote regional stability and the inclusion of the Middle East in the international economic order.

This is not America's current trajectory. China without America in the Middle East will have a free hand to impose its own economic system on the region, and when conflicts arise, to referee them from the exalted perch of the Middle Kingdom—as it is now doing between warring Sudan and South Sudan.

In this endeavor China would need allies and local enforcers. Those in America who argue that we should reduce our footprint in the Persian Gulf because we will no longer need its oil and gas should consider what could fill the vacuum: a greater role for Iran and Pakistan, backed by China. That should give us pause, given the illiberal nature of both countries and the state of our relations with them.

For a period in the 1970s, the Shah's Iran did in fact serve as the gendarme of the Persian Gulf. Britain had pulled back from the "east of Suez," and America, preoccupied with and then exhausted by its war in

Vietnam, was none too keen to step into the breach. The Shah offered to take responsibility for Persian Gulf security.

The deal was that Western powers would recognize Iran's regional role if Tehran would recognize the sovereignty of Bahrain and other Persian Gulf emirates and use some of its newfound oil wealth to build up Iranian naval strength so it could contribute to the defense of American interests. Soon, Iranian ships were patrolling the Gulf, and when a communist-backed rebellion in the Dhofar region of Oman threatened the pro-Western monarch there, it was Iran that sent troops to wage a counterinsurgency campaign (which is the main reason why Oman remains to this day the most Iran-friendly of the Persian Gulf emirates). The Persian Gulf security arrangement worked until the Shah fell in 1979. But it had not all been smooth sailing. In 1974, Iran had occupied three strategic islands at the mouth of the Straits of Hormuz, claiming them as Iranian territory. Even today, the dispute continues to mar relations between Iran and the United Arab Emirates.

Pakistan too has played a security role in the Persian Gulf region. After extremists occupied the Grand Mosque in Mecca in 1979—posing the most serious threat to the Saudi monarchy since its creation—the kingdom turned to Pakistan for help. Pakistan sent divisions of troops to Saudi Arabia to serve as the monarchy's praetorian guard. The Muslim and highly experienced Pakistani forces gave Saudi rulers peace of mind throughout the 1980s, and a good reason to deepen security ties with Pakistan—setting the stage for what many believe was Saudi investment in Pakistan's nuclear program.

The Pakistan option is still Saudi Arabia's trump card when its interests diverge from those of the United States. In March 2011, when the Arab Spring was in full swing and just after protests rocked Saudi Arabia and Oman and nearly toppled the pro-Saudi monarchy in Bahrain, Prince Bandar bin Sultan flew to Islamabad to ask for help. He wanted assurances from Pakistan that it would deploy troops in Bahrain and Saudi Arabia if and when protests grew out of hand (he knew the United States certainly would not). He was asking, in other words, for a return to the Saudi-Pakistani security arrangement of the 1980s.

The help ultimately arrived in Bahrain, the Gulf state where the regime had come closest to falling. With the Pakistan army's blessing, thousands of Pakistani veterans and experienced tribal fighters were recruited through newspaper ads to join the Bahraini security forces, which were desperate to beef up their capabilities ahead of surging unrest.

However, it is worth noting that managing Persian Gulf security with Iran and Pakistan for allies could prove a difficult undertaking for Beijing. Back in the 1960s and 1970s, Iran and Pakistan were the best of friends. At the time, the main strategic fault line in the region was between Iran and Pakistan on one side, and Afghanistan and India on the other. By the 1990s, however, Iran and Pakistan had grown apart. Pakistan saw Iran's revolution as a menace—it was stoking sectarian tensions between Shias and Sunnis. Sectarian violence plunged Pakistan into sporadic chaos throughout the 1990s, as radical groups on both sides, backed by patrons in Iran and Saudi Arabia respectively, carried out bombings and assassinations in campaigns of violence that continue to this day.[56] Iran and Saudi Arabia first crossed swords over regional power in Pakistan in the 1980s and 1990s. Saudi Arabia mobilized Pakistan's radical Sunni groups to stand in the way of Iran-backed Shia politicians and militias seeking to influence politics next door.[57] Saudi Arabia won that battle.

Iran and Pakistan were also at odds over Afghanistan. During the 1980s, Pakistan worked closely with Saudi Arabia and America to drive the Soviets out, and then Pakistan forged a partnership with the Saudis over its Taliban project in Afghanistan in the 1990s. Iran moved closer to India, and the two backed the Northern Alliance as it resisted the Taliban and therefore the Pakistani-Saudi plan for dominating Afghanistan.

Today, American efforts to peel India away from Iran are happening at the same time that Washington has been breaking with Islamabad over counterterrorism issues. That has created an opening for Iran and Pakistan—both of which resent the American presence in the region—to ponder working together in Afghanistan and over regional issues. But Pakistan still has close ties to Iran's archrival, Saudi Arabia. There is as yet no clear strategic realignment with Iran, but there is a lot of jockeying for position. China could face difficulty managing the complex web of alliances and rivalries in this region—especially Saudi anxieties over Iran. For now, the souring of U.S. relations with Pakistan has created grounds for improved relations and increased strategic coordination between Tehran and Islamabad, both of China's allies.

Those alliances are powerful. In November 2009, when the Obama administration was busy pressuring Pakistan into cooperation on Afghanistan, Chinese and Pakistani officials gathered in Islamabad to celebrate the launch of a new high-level Chinese-Pakistani project: manufacturing up to 250 JT-17 fighter jets in Pakistan. It was a $5 billion deal, and only the first part of a broader joint initiative to develop military hardware.[58] The project is significant, not only as a token of Chinese support for Pakistan in its military and strategic rivalry with India, but also in what it says about the depth of ties between China and Pakistan.[59]

Pakistani prime minister Yusuf Raza Gilani likes to repeat the Chinese ambassador's cloying description of Sino-Pakistani friendship as "higher than the Himalayas and sweeter than honey."[60] Pakistanis also say that China is an "all-weather" friend as a way of suggesting that America is at best only a "fair-weather" friend.[61]

In the atmosphere of bitterness and recrimination that followed the discovery of bin Laden living in the very lap of its military establishment, Pakistan has fallen back on the old idea that China stands by Pakistan through thick and thin. Pakistanis will tell you readily of China's critical assistance during the 1965 war with India (although Iran played just as supportive a role), or that China helped Pakistan during the 1971 war, the Kargil War of 1990, and even today: China is the only country to support Pakistan after the Abbottabad fiasco.[62]

China may be an "all-weather" friend, but China still does not like blizzards or tornados. China does not like it when Pakistan pushes too hard with India, or provokes American anger. China wants Pakistan as a strategic base, not a source of fresh headaches. Waves of extremists trained in Pakistan may stoke fires of separatism in Xinjiang, and, as happened before, countless Chinese engineers can be abducted by Pakistani tribesmen for ransom; yet China's true anger at Pakistan is directed at its threat of a regional power play. China wants to use Pakistan to serve Chinese interests, and it will not be made a pawn in Islamabad's regional games. So it was that even as China was stepping up its investment in Pakistan's military capability, it was winding down its support for Pakistan on the Kashmir issue.[63]

China has been a source of moral support too, the country that Pakistan turns to when faced with Indian threats or U.S. pressure. Over the past decade, China has encouraged this feeling by deepening its strategic investment in Pakistan. Along with fighter jets, pipelines, a port, and bridges, China is building roads and power plants and has promised civilian nuclear reactors like the one going to Turkey. There are free-trade agreements that promise to expand commerce between the two countries to $15 billion by 2015. China already accounts for 11 percent of Pakistan's imports.[64]

Chinese businessmen are ubiquitous in hotels in Lahore and Karachi, exploring investment prospects even in software companies. China Mobile has bought a controlling share of PakTel; Chinese arms manufacturers sell $7 billion per year in military hardware to Pakistan. In fact Pakistan accounts for the bulk of China's weapons sales worldwide, and China is Pakistan's largest defense supplier. Beijing sells it aircraft (including those that can deliver a nuclear payload), ships, and advanced warning systems. There are plans for the sale of submarines. China is helping Pakistan build an indigenous military-industrial complex through joint projects that cover not only fighter planes but also tanks, guided-missile frigates, ballistic missiles, and even satellites for communication and remote sensing.[65] China clearly wants a strong Pakistani military—and in particular a strong Pakistani navy—as a strategic asset in West Asia.

The cooperation also extends to Pakistan's controversial nuclear weapons program. The infamous A. Q. Khan, father of the Pakistani A-bomb, openly acknowledged Chinese assistance in the form of weapons-grade uranium, technical drawings of nuclear weapons, and tons of uranium hexafluoride that Pakistani centrifuges could spin into yet more weapons-grade uranium.[66]

Pakistan grew closer to, and warmer toward, China while General Pervez Musharraf was president, but now the ties between the two countries have a distinct business component. President Zardari travels to China twice a year. He says it is "to learn," but the wealthy Zardari is also known to have personal investments in China. He is showing the way, as it were, to tighter business ties that complement the growing military and development ties between the two countries.

China also values Pakistan as a thorn in the side of India. Pakistani mischief preoccupies India, taxes its military resources, and could potentially deny India the security it needs to achieve its desired economic growth. China does not encourage war between India and Pakistan, but a credible Pakistani threat, backed by nuclear weapons, is an asset to China. India hopes to win China with promises of access to the vast Indian consumer market, but China sees India more as a rival in selling cheap exports and buying commodities than as a market for Chinese wares. And of course India is now America's close strategic ally in the great game of containing China.

The strategic location of Pakistan—and a possible Chinese naval base at Gwadar—not too far east of the Strait of Hormuz is a fact of enormous importance to Beijing as it contemplates its strategy for West Asia and the Gulf region, and ponders how to counter U.S. and Indian strength in the area. As Robert Kaplan writes:

> The Indian Ocean accounts for fully half the world's container traffic. Moreover, 70 percent of the total traffic of petroleum products passes through the Indian Ocean, on its way from the Middle East to the Pacific. As these goods travel that route, they pass through the world's principal oil shipping lanes, including the Gulfs of Aden and Oman—as well as some of world commerce's main chokepoints: Bab el Mandeb and the Straits of Hormuz and Malacca. Forty percent of world trade passes through the Strait of Malacca; 40 percent of all traded crude oil passes through the Strait of Hormuz.[67]

As trade in energy supplies and goods between East and West Asia as well as between Africa and Asia continues to grow, the figures cited by Kaplan will only increase as well.

India too, of course, sees the Indian Ocean basin as a strategically critical area. Set to become the world's fourth-largest energy consumer (only the United States, China, and Japan are bigger), India will soon be importing 90 percent of its oil from the Persian Gulf, on a route that goes directly past Pakistan's Makran coast. India also imports coal from Africa and Southeast Asia, and that too has to cross the Indian Ocean.

Even if India were to switch to natural gas, given its limited pipeline capacity, it would have to rely on tankers coming from the Persian Gulf or Indonesia.[68]

Gwadar is therefore a centerpiece in the "string of pearls" strategy, which would give China strategic control over Indian Ocean trade, as well as a staging ground for protecting its supply routes against pirates or more global rivals. Gwadar is for now a desolate place—more like an abandoned construction project than a bustling port—but then, the Chinese are in Pakistan for the long haul. Gwadar's value will come into play down the road.

Iran is a long-term friend of China as well. It was among the first Middle Eastern countries to follow America's lead and open up to China in the 1970s.[69] But relations between the two ancient nations go much further back. As Iranian diplomats learned to their delight back in the mid-1970s, China to this day preserves priceless manuscript collections of classical Persian literature—some of it no longer extant in Iran itself—that go all the way back to the time of the Great Silk Road, when caravans hauled goods back and forth across Asia on the same route that took Marco Polo from Persia to China and brought the Mongols into the Middle East.

This historic bond is reinforced by a common view that not only as modern nation-states but as ancient civilizations, China and Iran deserve their respective places in the sun. Iranians swoon when Chinese leaders wax poetic about the rights of old nations, the travesty of the abuses that China and Iran suffered at the hands of Western powers, and the putative malign role of those same powers in continuing to block China's and Iran's rise to the top.

Iran's leaders like the idea of a strong China as a balance against America. A bipolar world is a safer place for Iran. Iranian rulers fantasize about a world in which China would confront America, as did the Soviet Union at one point, shielding Iran from American pressure.

Chinese trade has kept the Iranian economy afloat despite severe Western economic sanctions, and Chinese arms sales and technology transfers have been critical to modernizing Iran's antiquated military.[70] But China has a long way to go to rival American power, and unlike the

Soviet Union, China is not gunning for confrontation with America. Beijing's counsel to Tehran is to be supple and not to provoke Washington.

In Iran, China has both strategic and economic interests.[71] Iran is a heavy hitter in the Middle East, a local power with a long history in a region full of "tribes with recently acquired flags," and the influence to go with that status. The Soviet Union's fall helped restore Iranian influence across a vast region, from the Caucasus through Central Asia. When the United States and NATO took down the Taliban after 9/11, Afghanistan too fell under renewed Iranian influence. Iran's soft power on the Arab street waxed with anti-Israel bluster and extended westward into Iraq, Syria, and Lebanon. Iran's economic zone now stretches from Herat in western Afghanistan west to Suleimaniya and Basra in Iraq.

That Iran has defied American wishes is not unwelcome to China. Beijing gets that its rivalry with America is global, and does not like seeing uncontested U.S. hegemony in any region. And the more China covets Middle Eastern oil, the more it feels keen to check American influence.

But China does not want to see Iran become like Iraq—so defiant and risk prone that it invites U.S. military action followed by U.S. control of the spoils. So the Chinese caution Iran, nudging it to talk to the West and to accommodate at least some Western concerns.[72] Beijing has supported sanctions against Iran—and benefited from the effect of sanctions in driving away Western economic interests, leaving the field to China. In an ironic twist, it appears that China has supported sanctions in order to do more business with Iran and to tighten its own economic hold over the country. But as with North Korea, when it comes to the Iranian nuclear program (or support for Hamas and Hezbollah), Beijing does not share American interests.

Iran, as the Chinese are keenly aware, is also rich in oil and gas. It holds 10.3 percent of the world's proven oil reserves and 15.8 percent of its gas reserves (second in size only to Russia's). In 2010, China was Iran's largest energy customer (accounting for 16.2 percent of Iran's energy exports), and Iran was China's largest energy supplier (accounting for 17.4 percent of China's energy imports). These numbers have grown since sanctions have cut Iranian energy exports to Europe and the rest of Asia. The Chinese too cut some of their formal oil imports from Iran, but that drop is more than made up for by off-the-books exports of Iranian oil to China via Iraq and some of it through Dubai.

More important, Iran has the only major oil and gas reserves in the region that are outside Western multinational control. It presents Chinese state-controlled oil companies with a unique opportunity to build "upstream" capabilities. China has signed on to develop the North Azadegan oil field and to explore for natural gas offshore in the North Pars field under the Persian Gulf.

Then there are the deepening economic ties that have unfolded apace with tightening Western sanctions. As Western businesses left, Iran turned to China to fill the void. Chinese goods flowed into Iran to replace European, Japanese, and Korean imports. Chinese oil conglomerates stepped in to take over energy and infrastructure contracts abandoned by French and Japanese companies. Iranians did not like the China option, but they had no other recourse. Iran's bureaucrats doubt that Chinese companies can get the job done—the North Azadegan field is five years behind production schedule, and China's record exploring oil and gas in the South China Sea has not inspired confidence either. Many Iranians, moreover, find the Chinese hard to work with—the cultural gap is wider than the one that separates Persians from Europeans. Despite their legendary toughness and wiliness as negotiators, Iranian businessmen find that their Chinese partners give less and squeeze more and drive exceptionally hard bargains. But China is willing to do business with Iran when no one else will, and the Iranians have nowhere else to turn.

Since 2009, China has emerged as Iran's largest trading partner. Bilateral trade between the two countries is estimated at $40 billion in 2012, and a good portion of China's surging trade with the UAE actually consists of goods that are promptly reexported to Iran—worth an estimated $7 billion this year alone. China pays Iran in yuan for its oil, depositing the money in Chinese banks. Iran's Central Bank keeps those yuans in China and sells them to Iranian businessmen, who then convert their Chinese currency into dollars and euros in order to do business in the international market.

Many Iranian manufacturers have now shifted all their production to China. A maker of kitchen utensils for the Iranian home market explained to me that he had had to shutter his factory in Iran because he could not obtain letters of credit in Western currencies and could not afford the high cost of energy and imports. He moved his production to China. He now ships his Chinese-made products back to Iran through Dubai and as a "Chinese" manufacturer is able to sell to a far broader market in the Middle East and Africa. He himself is prospering, but the Iranians who used to work for him back home are jobless. The sanctions have not stopped the nuclear program, but they have made Iran economically dependent on China. Could strategic dependence follow?

Washington sees its Iran policy as something separate from the pressure applied to Pakistan, but the fact is that U.S. policy is pushing the two isolated countries closer to each other just as it is confirming Chinese domination over their economies. Iran and Pakistan are to China's Asia strategy what Vietnam and India are to America's. The two countries, both with significant influence in Afghanistan and Central Asia, could serve as pillars of China's "Silk Road strategy." By establishing control over post-American Afghanistan, they could help see to it that Central Asian riches could get to Persian Gulf and Arabian Sea ports or go through overland pipelines into China. Add Turkey to the Iran-Pakistan duo, and China will have secured economic hegemony over a vast region that stretches from the northwest borders of India to the southeast corner of Europe.

We view Iran and Pakistan today antagonistically. Through the narrow lens of our current regional priorities they look menacing, and so we have isolated Iran and alienated Pakistan—and still failed to change them. But our priority will soon be China, and that means it will not be in our interest to leave these countries out in the cold to serve as pillars of China's power play in the Middle East. Addressing China's challenge requires us to build bridges, not push away Iran and Pakistan.

The region will not be better off under China's thumb. Indeed, it is not as a favor to our regional allies that we should keep our presence there. It is because by staying there in a meaningful way (not just with jet fighters and aircraft carriers but through economic and civilian engagement) we would be denying China dominance. We would also be sitting in a chokehold position next to China's energy lifeline—something that the Chinese have been trying to avoid. Chinese leaders may believe in their country's peaceful rise and discount the conflict-rousing implications of their mercantilism, but they also believe that America's intentions are not peaceful. That could mean military confrontation down the road, and short of that, it could mean serious friction with implications for both the American and Chinese economies—a new kind of cold war.

In the short run, China is content with the U.S. security dividend. American military power, diplomacy, and development aid keep the Persian Gulf and the broader Middle East in some semblance of order. To keep Washington happy—and dissuade America from creating instability—Beijing is willing to provide the United States with measured support on Iran and Pakistan. Beijing would not like to see Iranian obduracy or Pakistani adventurism invite greater American military involvement in the region. Resistance to America on the part of Saddam Hussein's Iraq and Taliban-run Afghanistan led not to less but to *more* American presence in the region. The fruit of an American war with Iran or Pakistan would be regional instability and (eventually) governments in Tehran and Islamabad that would be closer to Washington than Beijing (Maliki and Karzai's governments in Iraq and Afghanistan are undeniable evidence here). That would not serve Chinese interests. It is better for Beijing if for now Iran and Pakistan give in far enough to international pressure to keep America at bay.

Stability in the Middle East is good for China because it should help hold down the price of oil. America was once a source of that stability, but its policies, and more so its talk of a desire to unburden itself of the Middle East, are now fueling jitteriness in oil markets. For Beijing, U.S. policy represents a potential source of what economists call "externalities." In other words, if the United States shifts its policy toward confrontation and away from stability in the Persian Gulf region, China will have to pay the resulting higher-risk premium on oil. This will erase some of China's comparative trade advantage. Beijing does not want to see this happen. In the short run, therefore, it advises Iran and Pakistan to keep things cool and avoid raising tensions with America. In the longer run, it may mean that China would welcome a smaller U.S. role in the region.

China's tactical support of U.S. aims sometimes looks to Washington like a convergence of interests. For example, concerned with possible

American military strikes against Iran's nuclear program, China signed on to UN sanctions and leaned on Tehran to take its talks with the P5+1 seriously. Similarly, as U.S. relations with Pakistan frayed in 2011 and 2012, putting Pakistan's stability at risk and raising serious prospects of a clash between Washington and Islamabad, China turned away Pakistani requests for aid, lobbied Islamabad to make up with Washington, and dropped its usual cagey stance in order to agree to informal talks with America on Pakistan.

America looks to China for help in managing Iran and Pakistan, whereas China sees Iran and Pakistan as part of its policy of managing America. If America were not in the Middle East, China would not feel the compulsion to placate Washington; it would more brazenly protect its narrow economic interests—and the costs to America (and its allies) could really add up.

China could start by cutting India's access to energy and markets in Central Asia and the Middle East, doing to India what China fears America could do to it. Japan and South Korea could suffer too. All the talk these days in American foreign policy circles is about how to leverage U.S. relations with Japan and South Korea to pressure China. But those two Asian countries depend on the same Middle Eastern energy sources as China, and the more China's influence grows in the Middle East the more they will have to fall in line with China to protect their energy supply. If America wants Japan and South Korea to stay independent of China and be able to stand up to Beijing, then it must protect Tokyo and Seoul's position in the Middle East—not from the Arab suppliers, but from China.

Over time, a region dominated by China will begin to look like China. Its push into the broader Middle East in search of energy and markets will shape that region in China's image: illiberal and mercantilist. For its part, America has laid its chips on the Gulf's Arab monarchies (no liberal bastions themselves). China looks to them, too, to sell it oil and gas, but the pillars of China's Middle Eastern strategy are Turkey, Iran, and Pakistan—the Northern Tier countries that America befriended during the Cold War. In those years, Washington took up London's old position in what Rudyard Kipling famously called "the great game," which was to keep Moscow away from the warm waters of the Mediterranean Sea and the Indian Ocean, and don't let the Russian bear get his paws on the oil fields of the Middle East. Now China is rebuilding old Northern Tier multilateral organizations for its own strategic ends.

The SCO seeks to achieve this end. Both Iran and Pakistan belong to the SCO. The organization's June 2012 meeting was dedicated to discussing regional security in the Afghanistan-Pakistan corridor and to expanding Chinese-Russian cooperation on economic issues in Central Asia in anticipation of the U.S. withdrawal from Afghanistan.

In one way after another, America is pushing the Middle East further into China's bosom. More broadly, it seems, America has done all the fighting while China has done all the business. For more than a decade now, America has poured blood and treasure into Afghanistan to defeat the Taliban and pacify the country. But once mineral riches were discovered in an Afghanistan now made safer for geological exploration by U.S. and NATO involvement, who got the first mining contract? China, which also promised to build highway and rail routes for shipping copper ore—to China. It is the same story in Iran and Pakistan. America wrestles with thorny security problems, while the Chinese ink deals.

What would be the upshot if America remained fully engaged in the Middle East? What would that mean for China's role in the region, and for our relations with China? We could protect the region from China's heavy hand and from illiberal institutions that it would promote and support. We could ensure our Asian allies' access to steady energy supplies, and in the process limit China's ability to realize its broader strategic interests in Asia and globally.

American presence in the Middle East at a time when China too is expanding there would force China to abide by international rules and institutions of the kind they have had to submit to in the Asia-Pacific. That would enforce America's larger goal of persuading the rising giant to live within the bounds of a rules-based system—the one based on Western liberal values and reflecting the fundamental tenets of the international system. To that end we should be building multilateral institutions in the Middle East of the kind we have built and supported in Asia, such as ASEAN, Asia-Pacific Economic Cooperation, and the East Asia Summit—which China is doing in the form of SCO—rather than leave the region to its own fate. Those institutions would promote stability and also entrench rules and norms necessary to the orderly conduct of regional politics. Once we have built those institutions we should encourage China to join and to participate in regional security, diplomatic and economic discussions, and collective management. Just as China links what is happening in the South China Sea to developments in Pakistan or Iran, we should link Chinese actions in the Middle East to American relations in Asia and vice versa.

James Fallows writes of China's rise, "Either the growing power of the Chinese economy will change the rest of the international system, effectively making it more Chinese, or the growing prosperity of the Chinese people will change their own country's system, making it more international."[73] That is how our deeper engagement in the Middle East can have an impact: encouraging China to become international rather than allowing the Middle East to become Chinese.

We have the requisite military muscle and economic and political influence today to see to the orderly expansion of China's role in the region; we should put this capability to good use.

America does not need to pivot to Asia geographically; it needs to do so conceptually. That means it must recognize the Middle East as an integral part of Asia. In 2010, Hillary Clinton took the bold step of challenging China's claim to the South China Sea. In a speech at the ASEAN meeting in Vietnam, she defended all nations' right of access to that body of water. She added that it was a right that America was prepared to defend and finished by saying that all disputes should be settled through multilateral talks. That doughty stance on behalf of the liberal world order—"freedom of the seas" is among the great principles of classical liberalism—caused several nations in the region to take heart, show greater independence vis-à-vis China, and move closer to America.[74] The same bold thinking that governs America's China policy in East Asia should govern its approach to West Asia. China, more than counterterrorism and nuclear fear, should be the bedrock of America's Middle East strategy in the twenty-first century.

CONCLUSION: AMERICA, THE PIVOTAL NATION

There is a great debate these days about whether America is declining.[1] Those who warn that our best days are behind us blame this reversal of fortune—the loss of our superpower status, economic dominance, and unrivaled leadership in the world—on economic troubles at home,[2] imperial overreach abroad, or simply the fact that we are no longer alone in the pole position—there is China and its fellow BRIC (Brazil-Russia-India-China, a popular shorthand for rapidly growing economies) pack aspirants to great power nibbling at our heels.[3]

We have economic problems at home, to be sure, but we are still the world's largest economy and have the strongest military, and the idea of emerging markets supplanting America on the world scene is for now more fantasy than reality. We still have all the ingredients for global leadership,[4] and we certainly talk of how much our place in the world matters to us. The problem is that none of that is reflected in how we do business.

I don't believe America is declining. Far from it. Rather than why we are declining, the question everyone should be asking is why, despite our overwhelming power and potential, our influence is diminishing.[5] The answer lies in how we exercise our power and how we see our role in the world.

If we see global leadership slipping from our grasp, it is not because our economy was in recession for much of the past four years but because we have been uncertain about our role in the world. Over the past decade, first our exclusively military approach to foreign policy making did great damage to our reputation, and now the inconsistency evident in how we pursue our interests has cast doubt on our leadership. Our aim for the past four years has been to engage less, do less, and have a smaller footprint. But then we should be prepared to also matter less and influence less—to become irrelevant to outcomes, be they large or small. It has been a losing proposition for us, and that should matter to us. So it is that in the past decade we have gone from leading everywhere to leading nowhere. That is the surprising epilogue to our decade-long foray into the Middle East.

America should not settle for this result. American leadership is still critical to the stability of the world order and the health of the global economy—to expansion of trade and the continued development and prosperity of nations. There is no other power today that could play America's role on the world stage or is willing to step into America's shoes. Nor would the world be better off were that to happen, or even if any and all of the rising BRIC nations and those following in their footsteps tried their hands at it. The world America has built still needs America to lead it. America remains the world's pivotal nation.

But the world has changed and is changing still, and so should American leadership. The frustration Americans feel when they tally the cost of their foreign adventures only to see them fail is understandable. Too often in the recent past we have led with our military. That has been costly and fruitless. In the Middle East, in particular, where American leadership was put to the test in the past decade, that approach has been disastrous.

Rather than shun leadership in the world, it is time to think differently of how we approach influencing its affairs. It is time we returned diplomacy and economic engagement to their rightful place. Those facets of American power were central to its leadership in the past—defining both our vision and audacity—and they should be so again in the future.

Our world has been shaped by bold acts of American statesmanship. Harry Truman won the future for the free world with a massive commitment of American power and resources to build a transatlantic alliance that successfully contained and defeated the Soviet Union. George H. W. Bush similarly pushed hard for German unification, a risky proposition that at first even Germans were wary of. Successfully contending with the challenges that the greater Middle East poses to American security demands similar bold American leadership, the willingness to embrace a clear strategy and commit the full measure of American power to realizing it.

Historically, American leadership in the world has been a force for good. Without it, writes Robert Kagan, the world could be led "by some other kind of order, reflecting the desires and the qualities of other world powers," which may be illiberal and destructive; or, he writes, "perhaps [the world order could] simply collapse."[6] That is why we think of America as the indispensable nation.

It was only after what America did in Bosnia—compelling a confused and recalcitrant Europe to follow America's lead to end genocide in the Balkans—that it earned that sobriquet. The people of the Middle East heard President Obama say in his much-anticipated speech on the Arab Spring, "Our support for these principles [human rights and democratic, peaceful demands for political freedom and economic opportunity, and legitimate aspirations of people] is a top priority and central to the pursuit of other interests in the region. The U.S. will marshal all our diplomatic, economic, and strategic tools to support these principles."[7] What they understood was that the nation that had transformed other parts of the world for the better was now poised to help change theirs.

The Arab Spring was a ray of hope in a troubled region. But a brave call for freedom cannot alone change the reality of economic stagnation, social misery, and political frustration. Not without outside support. We don't have to look too closely to realize that the Middle East is going through a historical transformation. Islamism is rising, sectarianism exploding, and regional balances of power collapsing, and flash points in Lebanon, Iraq, Syria, and Bahrain are threatening conflagration on a regional scale. The last time change of this magnitude happened was in 1979, when the Iranian revolution inspired Islamic radicalism and upended regional stability. What is happening in the Middle East today is both more complex and potentially bigger, and demands greater American engagement.[8]

Solving the problems of the Middle East and the threat they pose to the world requires a fundamental change in the region's economic profile.[9] The international community would have to make a sizable investment—a Marshall Plan in scale—to bring about change of that magnitude. And that requires American leadership. Even if we cannot afford that right now, we still need a clear economic strategy for the region—a plan for using development aid, trade, and investment to help the region and also serve our interests.

That is familiar territory for the United States; it has secured stability, promoted prosperity, and built democracy in region after region of the world since the end of World War II. But when it comes to the Middle East, America has forgotten this legacy. It has relied more on war (and nowadays on drones) than on trade. The Bush administration contemplated a free-trade deal with Egypt but then shelved the idea when President Mubarak jailed dissidents. We have signed preliminary free-trade agreements with Jordan and Morocco, but they remain limited in scope and there have been no plans for deepening them. Pakistan has been clamoring for more trade instead of aid, but our response has been yes to aid but no to trade. American leadership of the kind that would transform the Middle East has to be anchored in economic interdependence that would promote growth in the region and make it a part of the burgeoning global economy. Change in the Middle East needs BRIC-like development, and that requires American investment.

In turn, growth relieves social pressure and creates upwardly mobile middle classes that tend to champion democracy and engagement with the world. America could help make all this happen. It could rally the international community, mobilize resources, and provide the kind of influence in the region's capitals that would persuade them to commit to (sometimes painful) economic change.

Economic engagement should go hand in hand with serious diplomatic engagement in the region. Our generals are prominent across the Middle East and should remain so, but so should our diplomats. We should be a participant in the flow of regional politics and not just a military arbiter. Our engagement should be directed at ensuring regional stability and promoting regional harmony. Seeing the region through the narrow lens of counterterrorism does not serve those goals.

Zbigniew Brzezinski writes that America has played a critical balancing role in East Asia, fostering peace and prosperity by maintaining a delicate balance between China and its neighbors.[10] But it is not just in Asia that America has kept the balance. In the Middle East, too, America has played a balancing role, between Iran and its neighbors on one side of the region, and Israel and its neighbors on the other. Without American engagement the region would have to arrive at its own balance, and that will be a violent and destabilizing process. Without American leadership in the Middle East, the region's future, left to China and Russia to figure out, or to Turkey, Iran, and Saudi Arabia to fight over, will not be hopeful.

The political scientist John Ikenberry lauds the liberal international order America has built.[11] The global order is today durable and stable thanks to the many multilateral mechanisms America helped build and continues to support: institutions such as the UN, the World Bank, and NATO that have fostered security and development, or the EU and NAFTA, which have promoted prosperity and lured the likes of Mexico and Turkey to embrace capitalism and democracy.[12]

America has lost some of its own authority to international institutions it created and sustained. But that is a good thing. It means that the liberal international order has legs; it will last longer and continue to define the world order around values and practices that will foster peace, freedom, and prosperity. As Ikenberry notes, "The underlying foundations of the liberal international order will survive and thrive" without America's guiding hand.[13] In the Middle East, though, where simmering instability threatens global security and prosperity, America has done very little institution building of the kind Ikenberry writes about. There is no equivalent to ASEAN or APEC (the Asia Pacific Economic Council), or rival to the SCO, which is backed by China, Russia, and Iran. Perhaps America should help create those kinds of institutions, which could foster order but also make the region's security and prosperity less dependent on the exercise of American authority. Only then should America think about pivoting somewhere else.

Whatever our new commitments, it is not likely that America can easily and quickly wash its hands of the Middle East. We cannot escape the blowback from trouble in this region. Even Asian leaders who are now the object of our greater attention are incredulous: "Are you sure you can do this with all that is happening in the Middle East?"

The answer should be yes. We have done it in the past and we can do it again. We can have a vision of the world that encompasses our interests in Asia and in the Middle East. That is the essence of global leadership.

ACKNOWLEDGMENTS

This book would not have been but for the generosity of many colleagues in Washington, Europe, China, the Middle East, Afghanistan, and Pakistan; senior and junior officials, journalists, and scholars. They shared their views of the past and the present, and provided essential information that helped my thinking and sharpened my arguments, and narrated telltale vignettes and backstories that have enriched this book.

No one was more instrumental in shaping the idea for this book than Richard Holbrooke. He was a source of inspiration and fount of ideas large and small about America's place in the world and how it ought to conduct its foreign policy. I owe to him the core ideas of this book and the details of many of the events narrated within it. He exhorted me to focus on the challenges facing American foreign policy, especially in the Muslim world, and I hope the result is true to his vision and legacy.

Thanks also to Rina Amiri, Peter Bergen, Ashley Bommer, Stephen Bosworth, Nicholas Burns, Kent Calder, Rajiv Chandrasekaran, Shamila Chaudhry, Alexander Evans, Leila Fawaz, Leslie Gelb, Fiona Hill, Ibrahim Kalin, Bijan Khajepour, John Lipsky, Maleeha Lodhi, Kati Marton, Sean Misko, Afshin Molavi, Nader Mousavizadeh, Meghan O'Sullivan, Tom Pickering, Joel Rayburn, Barnett Rubin, Jamie Rubin, David Sanger, Arthur Sculley, Emma Sky, James Walsh, Frank Wisner, and Emirhan Yorulmazlar for their wisdom and insights. There are many others to whom I owe a debt of gratitude but who shall remain anonymous.

Liaqat Ahamed, Ray Takeyh, Randa Slim, and Bilal Baloch read all or parts of the early drafts of this book and made valuable comments that have improved the narrative in important ways. I am grateful to them. Philip Costopolous read all of what I wrote with his customary care and attention to detail, and spared no effort to hone my arguments.

My talented research assistants, Artin Afkhami, Maliheh Birjandi Feriz, and Tara Sepehrifar, were immensely helpful in locating sources and finding relevant facts large and small that have enriched the pages of this book.

Throughout the time I worked on this book I benefited from the support of colleagues at the Fletcher School of Law and Diplomacy of Tufts University, where I taught when I first embarked on this endeavor, and the Paul H. Nitze School of Advanced International Studies of Johns Hopkins University, where I served as dean when I finally finished the manuscript. I also benefited from the support of colleagues at Brookings Institution, where I was senior fellow in foreign policy through most of the time I worked on this book. I would like to thank in particular Brookings's president, Strobe Talbot, and the institution's vice president and director of its foreign policy program, Martin Indyk. They were generous with their support and also with their insight. I am grateful for their friendship and interest in my work.

My literary agent, Susan Rabiner, was instrumental in giving this book direction. She gave this project the full measure of her attention from our very first conversation about it to when the final draft went to press. Her insights and suggestions were invaluable, and the book owes much to her caring interest. My brilliant editor at Doubleday, Kris Puopolo, took a deep interest in this book, and read everything I wrote carefully, and then took her pen to the entire manuscript, time and again improving each chapter, page, and paragraph. I am deeply grateful for her work on this book. Thanks also to Kris's assistant editor, Daniel Meyer, my publicists, Alison Rich and Todd Doughty, and the entire team at Doubleday for their professionalism and wonderful work.

My deepest appreciation is reserved for my wife, Darya, sons, Amir and Hossein, and daughter, Donia. Without their love and encouragement, not to mention patience and good humor, this book would not have been possible. I hope they will find the book worthy of that indulgence.

NOTES

INTRODUCTION

1. "Pakistan, China Have Shared Interests in Peace Promotion: PM,"
   Nation, May 15, 2012, http://www.nation.com.pk/pakistan-news
   -newspaper-daily-english-online/islamabad/15-May-2012/pakistan-china
   -have-shared-interests-in-peace-promotion-pm.

PROLOGUE: "A WEEK IN SEPTEMBER"

1. Rajiv Chandrasekaran, *Little America: The War Within the War for
   Afghanistan* (New York: Knopf, 2012), pp. 261–69.
2. On the history of how this idea has been used by Democratic Party
   leaders see James Mann, *The Obamians: The Struggle Inside the White
   House to Redefine American Power* (New York: Viking, 2012),
   pp. 37–38.
3. This theme is most clearly examined in Robert Kagan, *The World
   America Made* (New York: Knopf, 2012).

CHAPTER 1: AFGHANISTAN: THE GOOD WAR GONE BAD

1. James Risen, "U.S. Identifies Vast Mineral Riches in Afghanistan," *New
   York Times*, June 13, 2010, www.nytimes.com/2010/06/14/world/asia/
   14minerals.html?pagewanted=all.
2. This concept is best elaborated in Richard Haass, *War of Necessity, War
   of Choice: A Memoir of Two Iraq Wars* (New York: Simon & Schuster,
   2009).
3. Judy Hevrdejs, "Hamid Karzai: The World's Most Stylish Man?" *Chicago Tribune*, January 31, 2002, http://articles.chicagotribune.com/2002
   -01-31/features/0201310025_1_hamid-karzai-glenn-o-brien-hats.

4. A critical event in this retreat was the successful effort by Taliban leaders, but also Osama bin Laden and Mullah Omar, to slip out of the December 2001 U.S. and NATO dragnet at the Tora Bora cave complex about six miles north of the FATA line. In a bad sign for the future, the failure to nab bin Laden at Tora Bora was ascribed not only to U.S. command failures and NATO irresolution but also to Pakistan's failure to watch the border, as well as unreliability or perhaps even deliberate treachery on the part of native Afghan troops who were supposed to be acting as U.S. allies but instead created opportunities for bin Laden to escape. See Sean Naylor, *Not a Good Day to Die: The Untold Story of Operation Anaconda* (New York: Berkley, 2005).

5. Naylor, *Not a Good Day to Die.*

6. Angela Balakrishnan, "Afghanistan Troop Deaths Outnumber Those Killed in Iraq," *Guardian*, July 1, 2008, http://www.guardian.co.uk/world/2008/jul/01/afghanistan.iraq; Ahmed Rashid, *Pakistan on the Brink: The Future of America, Pakistan, and Afghanistan* (New York: Viking, 2012), p. 74.

7. Antonio Giustozzi, *Koran, Kalashnikov, and Laptop: The Neo-Taliban Insurgency in Afghanistan 2002–2007* (New York: New York University Press, 2009).

8. Steve Coll, *Ghost Wars: The Secret History of the CIA, Afghanistan, and Bin Laden, from the Soviet Invasion to September 10, 2001* (New York: Penguin, 2004), p. 134.

9. Ian S. Livingston and Michael O'Hanlon, *Afghanistan Index: Tracking Variables of Reconstruction and Security in Post-9/11 Afghanistan* (Washington, DC: Brookings Institution, January 30, 2012), p. 18, http://www.brookings.edu/~/media/Files/Programs/FP/afghanistan%20index/index.pdf.

10. Bob Woodward, *Obama's Wars* (New York: Simon & Schuster, 2010), pp. 88–90.

11. Rajiv Chandrasekaran, *Little America: The War Within the War in Afghanistan* (New York: Knopf, 2012).

12. Chandrasekaran provides a devastating account of Karzai's corruption and misrule in *Little America.*

13. Ibid.

14. Sheri Berman, "From Sun King to Karzai: Lessons for State Building in Afghanistan," *Foreign Affairs*, March/April 2010, http://www.foreignaffairs.com/articles/65984/sheri-berman/from-the-sun-king-to-karzai. For a broader discussion of this theme see Francis Fukuyama, *The Origins of Political Order: From Prehuman Times to the French Revolution* (New York: Farrar, Straus and Giroux, 2011), pp. xi–xiii.

15. Thomas Barfield, "Afghanistan's Ethnic Puzzle," *Foreign Affairs*, September/October 2011, http://www.foreignaffairs.com/articles/68204/thomas-barfield/afghanistans-ethnic-puzzle.

16. Gretchen Peters, *Seeds of Terror: How Drugs, Thugs, and Crime Are Reshaping the Afghan War* (New York: Thomas Dunne Books, 2009); Alissa Rubin, "War on Afghan Opium Yields Few Victories," *New York Times*, May 28, 2012, p. A6.

17. Antonio Giustozzi, *Decoding the Taliban: Insights from the Afghan Field* (New York: Columbia University Press, 2009).

18. For a fuller discussion, see Kimberly Kagan, "The Anbar Awakening: Displacing al-Qaeda from Its Stronghold in Western Iraq," Iraq Report, Institute for the Study of War and WeeklyStandard.com, August 21 2006–March 30 2007, http://www.understandingwar.org/sites/default/files/reports/IraqReport03.pdf.

19. How this strategy worked is best described in Michael O'Hanlon and Hassina Sherjan, *Toughing It Out in Afghanistan* (Washington, DC: Brookings Institution, 2010).

20. "President Obama's Secret: Only 100 al Qaeda Now in Afghanistan," ABC News, http://abcnews.go.com/Blotter/president-obamas-secret-100-al-Qaeda-now-afghanistan/story?id=9227861#.TyypheNWqf8.

21. "Ambassador Eikenberry's Cables on U.S. Strategy in Afghanistan," *New York Times*, http://documents.nytimes.com/eikenberry-s-memos-on-the-strategy-in-afghanistan#p=1.

22. James Dobbins, "Your COIN Is No Good Here," *Foreign Affairs*, October 26, 2010, http://www.foreignaffairs.com/articles/66949/james-dobbins/your-coin-is-no-good-here?page=2.

23. Chandrasekaran, *Little America*, pp. 68–81.

24. Rashid, *Pakistan on the Brink*, p. 76.

25. Ibid., pp. 19–20.

26. Geir Lundestad, *The United States and Western Europe since 1945: From "Empire" by Invitation to Transatlantic Drift* (New York: Oxford University Press, 2003), p. 160, cited in Robert Kagan, *The World America Made* (New York: Knopf, 2012), p. 63.

27. Fotini Christia and Michael Sempel, "Flipping the Taliban," *Foreign Affairs*, July/August 2009, http://www.foreignaffairs.com/articles/65151/fotini-christia-and-michael-semple/flipping-the-taliban.

CHAPTER 2: AFGHANISTAN: RECONCILIATION?

1. Strobe Talbott first referred to Holbrooke as the "unquiet American" in an obituary: "Remembering Richard Holbrooke," *Washington Post*,

December 15, 2010, http://www.washingtonpost.com/wp-dyn/content/article/2010/12/14/AR2010121406366.html. Later a biography of Holbrooke carried the same title: Derek Chollet and Samantha Power, eds., *The Unquiet American: Richard Holbrooke in the World* (New York: Public Affairs, 2011).

2. Mark Landler, "Afghan Shift Puts Top U.S. Civilians in Tricky Spot," *New York Times*, July 1, 2010, p. A14.

3. Author interview with Mark Landler, August 2010.

4. Rajiv Chandrasekaran, *Little America: The War Within the War for Afghanistan* (New York: Knopf, 2012), p. 230.

5. Les Gelb, "Richard Holbrooke's Lonely Mission," *Daily Beast*, January 16, 2011, http://www.thedailybeast.com/newsweek/2011/01/16/richard-holbrooke-s-lonely-mission.html.

6. Cited in William H. Luers and Thomas R. Pickering, "Envisioning a Deal with Iran," *New York Times*, February 2, 2012, http://www.nytimes.com/2012/02/03/opinion/envisioning-a-deal-with-iran.html?_r=1&ref=opinion.

7. Matthew Rosenberg, "When Afghans Look to the Border with Pakistan, They Don't See a Fixed Line," *New York Times*, October 29, 2012, p. A9.

8. Robert D. Hormats, remarks at conference titled "The United States' 'New Silk Road' Strategy: What Is It? Where Is It Headed?" September 29, 2011, School of Advanced International Studies, Johns Hopkins University, available at http://www.state.gov/e/rls/rmk/2011/174800.htm.

9. Obama even discussed the idea with journalists in August 2010. David Ignatius, "The U.S. Should Test Iran's Resolve to Stabilize Afghanistan," *Washington Post*, September 17, 2010, http://www.washingtonpost.com/wp-dyn/content/article/2010/09/16/AR2010091606067.html.

10. Christoph Reuter, Gregor Peter Schmitz, and Holger Stark, "How German Diplomats Opened Channel to Taliban," *Der Spiegel*, January 10, 2012, http://www.spiegel.de/international/world/0,1518,808068,00.html.

11. Ahmed Rashid, *Pakistan on the Brink: The Future of America, Pakistan, and Afghanistan* (New York: Viking, 2012), pp. 113–36.

12. Rod Norland and Alissa Rubin, "Taliban Captives Dispute U.S. View on Afghanistan War," *New York Times*, February 2, 2012, p. A1.

13. Later in 2010, Aisha, whose ears had been sliced off as well, received reconstructive surgery from plastic surgeons in Los Angeles. See http://www.theage.com.au/world/doctors-rebuild-face-and-future-of-afghan-child-bride-20101014-16lt2.html.

14. By this time there were a number of serious studies of how to carry out reconciliation talks, and some had influence on debates inside the White House. Lakhdar Brahimi and Thomas C. Pickering, *Afghanistan:*

Negotiating Peace (New York: Century Foundation, 2011); James Shinn and James Dobbins, *Afghan Peace Talks: A Primer* (Washington, DC: RAND Corporation, 2011).

CHAPTER 3: WHO LOST PAKISTAN?

1. Vali Nasr, "No More Bullying Pakistan," *Bloomberg View*, July 5, 2012, http://www.bloomberg.com/news/2012-07-05/u-s-apology-ends-doomed -policy-of-bullying-pakistan-vali-nasr.html.
2. Admiral Mullen's comments are quoted in Stephen Krasner, "Talking Tough to Pakistan," *Foreign Affairs*, January/February 2012, pp. 87–96.
3. Jeffrey Goldberg and Marc Ambinder, "The Ally from Hell," *Atlantic*, December 2011, http://www.theatlantic.com/magazine/archive/2011/12/ the-ally-from-hell/8730/.
4. Bruce Riedel, "A New Pakistan Policy: Containment," *New York Times*, October 14, 2011, p. A19; Zalmay Khalilzad, "A Strategy of 'Congage-ment' Toward Pakistan," *Washington Quarterly* 35, no. 2 (Winter 2012): 107–19. See also, Gerald Stang, "US Strategic Interests in South Asia: What Not to Do with Pakistan," *European Union Institute for Security Studies*, June 25, 2012, http://www.iss.europa.eu/publications/detail/ article/us-strategic-interests-in-south-asia-what-not-to-do-with-pakistan/.
5. "U.S. Embassy Cables: 'Reviewing Our Afghanistan-Pakistan Strat-egy,'" *Guardian*, November 30, 2010, http://www.guardian.co.uk/world/ us-embassy-cables-documents/226531.
6. See Matthew Teague, "Black Ops and Blood Money," *Men's Journal,* June 2011, http://www.mensjournal.com/black-ops-and-blood-money.
7. Thorough accounts of this relationship can be found in Dennis Kux, *The United States and Pakistan, 1947–2000: Disenchanted Allies* (Balti-more: Johns Hopkins University Press, 2001) and Teresita Schaffer and Howard Schaffer, *How Pakistan Negotiates with the United States: Riding the Roller Coaster* (Washington, DC: United States Institute of Peace, 2011).
8. Ahmed Rashid, *Descent into Chaos: The United States and the Failure of Nation Building in Pakistan, Afghanistan, and Central Asia* (New York: Viking, 2008).
9. Pervez Musharraf, *In the Line of Fire: A Memoir* (New York: Free Press, 2006), p. 201.
10. Steve Coll, "Looking for Mulla Omar," *New Yorker*, January 23, 2012, p. 52.
11. Declan Walsh and Eric Schmitt, "Militant Group Poses Risk to U.S.-Pakistan Relations," *New York Times*, July 31, 2012, p. A1.

12. David Rohde and Kristen Mulvihill, *A Rope and a Prayer: A Kidnapping from Two Sides* (New York: Viking, 2010).

13. Ahmed Rashid, *Pakistan on the Brink: The Future of America, Pakistan, and Afghanistan* (New York: Viking, 2012), p. 150.

14. Goldberg and Ambinder, "The Ally from Hell."

15. Barnett R. Rubin and Ahmed Rashid, "From Great Game to Grand Bargain: Ending Chaos in Afghanistan and Pakistan," *Foreign Affairs*, November/December 2008, pp. 30–44.

16. The best account of the war and Pakistan's role in it is Steve Coll, *Ghost Wars: The Secret History of the CIA, Afghanistan, and Bin Laden, from the Soviet Invasion to September 10, 2001* (New York: Penguin Press, 2004).

17. Bruce Riedel, *Deadly Embrace: Pakistan, America and the Future of Global Jihad* (Washington, DC: Brookings Institution Press, 2011).

18. Imtiaz Gul, *The Most Dangerous Place: Pakistan's Lawless Frontier* (New York: Viking, 2010), pp. 112–29.

19. Cited in Mohsin Hamid, "Why They Get Pakistan Wrong," *New York Review of Books*, September 29, 2011, http://www.nybooks.com/articles/archives/2011/sep/29/why-they-get-pakistan-wrong/?pagination=false.

20. Zahid Hussain, "Pakistan's Most Dangerous Place," *Wilson Quarterly*, Winter 2012, http://www.wilsonquarterly.com/article.cfm?aid=2097.

21. William Safire, "Wide World of Words," *New York Times*, April 26, 2009, p. MM16.

22. Pir Zubair Shah, "My Drone War," *Foreign Policy*, March/April 2012, pp. 58–62.

23. Jane Mayer, "The Predator War," *New Yorker*, October 26, 2009, http://www.newyorker.com/reporting/2009/10/26/091026fa_fact_mayer; David Sanger, *Confront and Conceal: Obama's Secret Wars and Surprising Use of American Power* (New York: Crown, 2012), pp. 243–70.

24. Krasner, "Talking Tough to Pakistan," p. 87.

25. Riedel, "New Pakistan Policy."

26. Seth Jones, *Hunting in the Shadows: The Pursuit of Al-Qaeda Since 9/11* (New York: Norton, 2012), pp. 417–32.

27. Peter Bergen, *Manhunt: The Ten-Year Search for Bin Laden from 9/11 to Abbottabad* (New York: Crown, 2012).

28. Sanger, *Confront and Conceal*, p. 10.

29. Eric Schmitt, "Lull in Strikes by U.S. Drones Aids Militants in Pakistan," *New York Times*, January 8, 2012, p. A1.

30. Karen DeYoung and Karin Brulliard, " 'A New Normal' for U.S., Pakistan," *Washington Post*, January 17, 2012; http://www.washingtonpost

.com/world/national-security/as-us-pakistani-relations-sink-nations-try
-to-figure-out-a-new-normal/2012/01/13/gIQAklfw3P_story.html.

CHAPTER 4: IRAN: BETWEEN WAR AND CONTAINMENT

1. Gordon M. Goldstein, *Lessons in Disaster: McGeorge Bundy and the Path to War in Vietnam* (New York: Henry Holt, 2008), pp. 178 and 186.
2. Ibid.
3. George Stephanopoulos, "The Must Read Book for Obama's War Team," ABC News, September 22, 2009, http://abcnews.go.com/blogs/politics/ 2009/09/the-mustread-book-for-obamas-war-team/.
4. See Obama's interview with Jeffrey Goldberg, "Obama to Iran and Israel: 'As President of the United States, I Don't Bluff,'" *Atlantic*, March 2, 2012, http://www.theatlantic.com/international/archive/2012/ 03/obama-to-iran-and-israel-as-president-of-the-united-states-i-dont -bluff/253875/.
5. Goldstein, *Lessons in Disaster*, p. 184.
6. Vali Nasr, "Obama Needs to Go the Whole Mile on Iran Diplomacy," *Bloomberg View*, March 13, 2012, http://www.bloomberg.com/news/ 2012-03-13/obama-need-to-go-whole-mile-on-iran-diplomacy-vali-nasr .html.
7. Michael R. Gordon and General Bernard E. Trainor, *The Endgame: The Inside Story of the Struggle for Iraq from George W. Bush to Barack Obama* (New York: Pantheon, 2012), pp. 312–28.
8. Stephen Graubard, "Lunch with the FT: Henry Kissinger," *Financial Times*, May 24, 2008, http://www.ft.com/intl/cms/s/0/6d4b5fb8-285a -11dd-8f1e-000077b07658.html#axzz1pIrOuTFv.
9. James Dobbins, *After the Taliban: Nation Building in Afghanistan* (Washington, DC: Potomac Books, 2008).
10. Barnett Rubin and Sara Batmanglich, "The U.S. and Iran in Afghani- stan: A Policy Gone Awry," MIT Center for International Studies, Octo- ber 2008, http://web.mit.edu/cis/editorspick_rubin08_audit.html.
11. Author interview with a former Iranian government official who was present at that meeting with Khamenei.
12. Author interview with President Khatami, Davos, Switzerland, January 2007.
13. Vali Nasr, "Who Wins in Iraq: Iran," *Foreign Policy*, February 13, 2007, http://www.foreignpolicy.com/articles/2007/02/13/who_wins _in_iraq.
14. Bassem Mrou, "Talabani Says Iranians Ready for Talks With U.S. on Regional Security," *Associated Press*, January 20, 2007, http://

news.google.com/newspapers?nid=1665&dat=20070120&id
=JZNPAAAAIBAJ&sjid=OCUEAAAAIBAJ&pg=3299,3780514.

15. Author interview with Iranian official, July 2007.

16. Cited in "Khamenei Denies Nuclear Weapon," *Iran Primer*, United States Institute for Peace, February 22, 2012, http://iranprimer.usip .org/blog/2012/feb/22/part-i-khamenei-denies-nuclear-weapon; Nick Cumming-Bruce, "Iran Calls Nuclear Arms Production a 'Great Sin,'" *New York Times*, February 28, 2012, http://www.nytimes.com/2012/ 02/29/world/middleeast/iran-calls-for-negotiations-on-treaty-banning -nuclear-weapons.html.

17. "In Heavy Waters: Iran's Nuclear Program, the Risk of War and Lessons from Turkey," Middle East and Europe Report no. 116, International Crisis Group, February 23, 2012, p. 2, http://www.crisisgroup.org/~/media/ Files/Middle%20East%20North%20Africa/Iran%20Gulf/Iran/116—in -heavy-waters-irans-nuclear-program-the-risk-of-war-and-lessons-from -turkey.pdf.

18. Mohsen Milani, "Tehran's Take," *Foreign Affairs*, July/August 2009, http://www.foreignaffairs.com/articles/65123/mohsen-m-milani/tehrans -take.

19. Vali Nasr, *The Shia Revival: How Conflicts within Islam Will Shape the Future* (New York: Norton, 2006), pp. 147–68.

20. Ray Takeyh, *Guardians of the Revolution: Iran and the World in the Age of the Ayatollahs* (New York: Oxford University Press, 2009), p. 245.

21. Shahram Chubin, *Iran's Nuclear Ambitions* (Washington, DC: Carnegie Endowment for International Peace, 2006).

22. Cumming-Bruce, "Iran Calls Nuclear Arms Production," p. A7.

23. Dennis Ross, "Calling Iran's Bluff: It's Time to Offer Tehran a Civilian Nuclear Program," *New Republic*, June 15, 2012, http://www.tnr.com/ article/politics/104085/calling-iran%E2%80%99s-bluff-its-time-offer -iran-civilian-nuclear-program?page=0,1.

24. Efrahim Halevy, "Iran's Achilles Heel," *New York Times*, February 7, 2012, http://www.nytimes.com/2012/02/08/opinion/to-weaken-iran -start-with-syria.html; James P. Rubin, "The Real Reason to Intervene in Syria," *Foreign Policy*, June 4, 2012, http://www.foreignpolicy.com/ articles/2012/06/04/the_real_reason_to_intervene_in_syria.

25. For a full discussion of Bush administration handling of Iran's nuclear program see David Sanger, *The Inheritance: The World Obama Confronts and the Challenges to American Power* (New York: Crown, 2009), pp. 1–108.

26. Ray Takeyh and Suzanne Maloney, "The Self-Limiting Success of Iran Sanctions," *International Affairs* 87, no. 6 (2011): 1297–1312.

27. Suzanne Maloney, "How to Contain a Nuclear Iran," *American Prospect*, March 5, 2009, http://prospect.org/article/how-contain-nuclear -iran.

28. Hossein Mousavian, *Iran's Nuclear Crisis: A Memoir* (Washington, DC: Carnegie Endowment for International Peace, 2012).

29. "Blair, Chirac Hope IAEA Confirms Iran's Voluntary Suspension," *Payvand*, November 19, 2004, http://www.payvand.com/news/04/nov/1163 .html.

30. Hossein Mousavian, "How the U.S.-Iran Standoff Looks from Iran," *Bloomberg View*, February 16, 2012, http://www.bloomberg.com/ news/2012-02-17/how-the-u-s-iran-standoff-looks-from-iran-hossein -mousavian.html.

31. Hossein Mousavian, "How to Engage Iran," *Foreign Affairs*, February 9, 2012, http://www.foreignaffairs.com/ARTICLES/137095/hossein -mousavian/how-to-engage-iran?page=show.

32. Author interviews with a former Iranian official, June 2010.

33. Robin Wright, "Stuart Levy's War," *New York Times,* October 31, 2008, http://www.nytimes.com/2008/11/02/magazine/02IRAN-t .html?pagewanted=all.

34. U.S. State Department cable, Cairo, February 9, 2009, from Ambassador Margaret Scobey to the secretary of state, http://wikileaks.org/cable/ 2009/02/09CAIRO231.html.

35. U.S. State Department cable, Paris, February 12, 2010, from the American embassy to the secretary of state, http://www.wikileaks.ch/cable/ 2010/02/10PARIS174.html.

36. Roger Cohen, "Iran's Day of Anguish," *New York Times*, June 14, 2009, http://www.nytimes.com/2009/06/15/opinion/15iht-edcohen.html?_r=2.

37. Trita Parsi, *A Single Roll of the Dice: Obama's Diplomacy with Iran* (New Haven, CT: Yale University Press, 2012), p. 115.

38. David Sanger, *Confront and Conceal: Obama's Secret Wars and Surprising Use of American Power* (New York: Crown, 2012), p. 184.

39. David Sanger, "Iran Deal Would Slow Making of Nuclear Bombs," *New York Times*, October 21, 2009, http://www.nytimes.com/2009/10/22/ world/middleeast/22nuke.html.

40. Author interview with German diplomat present at the meeting, May 2010.

41. Farideh Farhi, "Anatomy of a Nuclear Breakthrough Gone Backwards," *Middle East Research and Information Project*, December 8, 2009, http://www.merip.org/mero/mero120809.

42. Martin Indyk, Kenneth G. Lieberthal, and Michael O'Hanlon, *Bending History: Barack Obama's Foreign Policy* (Washington, DC: Brookings Institution, 2012), pp. 196–98.

43. John Parker, *Persian Dreams: Moscow and Tehran Since the Fall of the Shah* (Washington, DC: Potomac Books, 2008).

44. Mark Katz, "Iran and Russia," *Iran Primer*, United States Institute for Peace, http://iranprimer.usip.org/resource/iran-and-russia.

45. Parsi, *Single Roll of the Dice*, p. 193.

46. "The Iran Nuclear Issue: The View from Beijing," Asia Briefing no. 100 (overview), International Crisis Group, February 17, 2010, http://www.crisisgroup.org/en/regions/asia/north-east-asia/china/B100 -the-iran-nuclear-issue-the-view-from-beijing.aspx.

47. Dennis Ross and David Makovsky, *Myths, Illusions, and Peace: Finding a New Direction for America in the Middle East* (New York: Viking, 2009), p. 221.

48. Parag Khanna, *The Second World: Empires and Influence in the New Global Order* (New York: Random House, 2008).

49. Parsi, *Single Roll of the Dice*, pp. 172–93.

50. Ibid., p. 187.

51. Ibid., p. 192.

52. Julian Borger, "Text of Iran-Brazil-Turkey Deal," *Guardian*, May 17, 2010, http://www.guardian.co.uk/world/julian-borger-global-security -blog/2010/may/17/iran-brazil-turkey-nuclear.

53. Sanger, *Confront and Conceal*, pp. 186–87.

54. Mousavian, *Iran's Nuclear Crisis*, p. 18.

55. Roger Cohen, "Doctrine of Silence," *New York Times*, November 28, 2011, http://www.nytimes.com/2011/11/29/opinion/cohen-doctrine-of -silence.html.

56. Mark Perry, "False Flag," *Foreign Policy*, January 13, 2012, http://www.foreignpolicy.com/articles/2012/01/13/false_flag.

57. "Spymaster: Meir Dagan on Iran's Threat," *60 Minutes*, March 11, 2012, http://www.cbsnews.com/8301-18560_162-57394904/the-spymaster-meir -dagan-on-irans-threat/?tag=contentMain;cbsCarousel.

58. Roger Bergman, "Will Israel Attack Iran?" *New York Times*, January 29, 2012, p. MM22.

59. Vali Nasr, "Hard-Line U.S. Policy Tips Iran Towards Belligerence," *Bloomberg View*, January 4, 2012, http://www.bloomberg.com/news/ 2012-01-05/hard-line-u-s-policy-tips-iran-toward-belligerence-vali-nasr .html; "Council on Foreign Relations Foreign Affairs Focus: Vali Nasr on US-Iran Relations," YouTube, January 25, 2012, http://youtube/ NaFC9WFUPfc.

60. Fareed Zakaria, "To Deal With Iran's Nuclear Future, Go Back to 2008," *Washington Post*, October 26, 2011, http://www.washingtonpost.com/ opinions/to-deal-with-irans-nuclear-future-go-back-to-2008/2011/10/26/ gIQADQyEKM_story.html?hpid=z3.

61. William H. Luers and Thomas Pickering, "Military Action Isn't the Only Solution to Iran," *Washington Post*, December 30, 2011, http://www.washingtonpost.com/opinions/military-action-isnt-the-only-solution-to-iran/2011/12/29/gIQA69sNRP_story.html; William H. Luers and Thomas Pickering, "Envisioning a Deal with Iran," *New York Times*, February 2, 2012, http://www.nytimes.com/2012/02/03/opinion/envisioning-a-deal-with-iran.html.

62. Kateria Azarova and Anissa Naouai, "Step by Step: Russia's Plan to Bring Iran Back for Good," *RT News*, August 17, 2011, http://rt.com/politics/iran-approves-russian-nuclear/.

63. "Iran Will Consider Russia's Nuclear Plan," *Press TV*, January 28, 2012, http://presstv.com/detail/223505.html.

64. Joshua Hersh, "Iran Assassination Plot: Skeptics Question Motive and Method of an 'Amateur Hour' Scheme," *Huffington Post*, October 12, 2011, http://www.huffingtonpost.com/2011/10/12/iran-assassination-plot-skeptics_n_1008068.html.

65. Suzanne Maloney, "Obama's Counterproductive New Iran Sanctions," *Foreign Affairs*, January 5, 2012, http://www.foreignaffairs.com/articles/137011/suzanne-maloney/obamas-counterproductive-new-iran-sanctions.

66. Former Iranian diplomat Hossein Mousavian quoted in Steve Inskeep, "Iran's Decider: Supreme Leader Ayatollah Khamenei," *National Public Radio*, February 23, 2012, http://www.npr.org/2012/02/23/147277389/meet-irans-decider-supreme-leader-khamenei.

67. "Text of Obama's Speech to AIPAC," *Associated Press*, March 4, 2012, http://www.google.com/hostednews/ap/article/ALeqM5ioftJ0jiGfowjv-eLtNgGAVnxphA?docId=1d833bbc98324e338a99fbeccb38b763.

68. Ollie Heinonen, "The 20 Percent Solution," *Foreign Policy*, January 11, 2012, http://www.foreignpolicy.com/articles/2012/01/11/the_20_percent_solution.

69. Richard Haass, "Enough Is Enough," *Newsweek*, January 22, 2010, http://www.thedailybeast.com/newsweek/2010/01/21/enough-is-enough.html.

70. See Fareed Zakaria, "How History Could Deter Iranian Aggression," *Washington Post*, February 15, 2012, http://www.washingtonpost.com/opinions/history-could-be-a-deterrent-to-iranian-aggression/2012/02/15/gIQA6UVcGR_story.html, and "Deterring Iran Is the Best Option," *Washington Post*, March 14, 2012, http://www.washingtonpost.com/opinions/deterring-iran-is-the-best-option/2012/03/14/gIQA0Y9mCS_story.html; Bruce Riedel, "Iran Is Not an Existential Threat," thedailynewsegypt.com, January 20, 2012, http://thedailynewsegypt.com/global-views/iran-is-not-an-existential-threat.html; Maloney, "How to Contain a Nuclear Iran." Earlier iterations of this debate are covered

in David Sanger, "Debate Grows on Nuclear Containment of Iran," *New York Times*, March 13, 2010, http://www.nytimes.com/2010/03/14/weekinreview/14sanger.html. On what containment may look like see James Lindsay and Ray Takeyh, "After Iran Gets the Bomb: Containment and Its Complications," *Foreign Affairs*, March/April 2010, http://www.foreignaffairs.com/articles/66032/james-m-lindsay-and-ray-takeyh/after-iran-gets-the-bomb.

CHAPTER 5: IRAQ: THE SIGNAL DEMOCRACY

1. "Vice President Biden: Iraq Could Be One of the Great Achievements of This Administration," ABC News, February 11, 2011, http://abcnews.go.com/blogs/politics/2010/02/vice-president-biden-iraq-could-be-one-of-the-great-achievements-of-this-administration/.
2. Kenneth Pollock, "Maliki Dilemma," *National Interest*, February 1, 2012, http://nationalinterest.org/commentary/the-maliki-dilemma-6418.
3. Toby Dodge, "The Resistible Rise of Nuri Al-Maliki," *Opendemocracy*, March 22, 2012, http://www.opendemocracy.net/toby-dodge/resistible-rise-of-nuri-al-maliki.
4. Liz Sly, "U.S. Policy on Iraq Questioned as Influence Wanes, Maliki Consolidates Power," *Washington Post*, April 8, 2012, http://www.washingtonpost.com/world/us-policy-on-iraq-questioned-as-influence-wanes/2012/04/08/gIQAHEAU4S_story.html?hpid=z1.
5. Joseph R. Biden and Leslie H. Gelb, "Unity Through Autonomy in Iraq," *New York Times*, May 1, 2006, http://www.nytimes.com/2006/05/01/opinion/01biden.html?pagewanted=all.
6. Joseph R. Biden, "A Plan to Hold Iraq Together," *Washington Post*, August 24, 2006, http://www.washingtonpost.com/wp-dyn/content/article/2006/08/23/AR2006082301419.html; "Biden Vows to Fight Troop Surge in Iraq," CBS News, February 11, 2009, http://www.cbsnews.com/2100-250_162-2299237.html.
7. Michael R. Gordon and Bernard E. Trainor, *The Endgame: The Inside Story of the Struggle for Iraq, from George W. Bush to Barack Obama* (New York: Pantheon, 2012), pp. 628–50.
8. Michael R. Gordon, "Failed Efforts and Challenges of America's Last Months in Iraq," *New York Times*, September 23, 2012, p. A1.
9. Martin S. Indyk, Kenneth G. Lieberthal, and Michael E. O'Hanlon, *Bending History: Barack Obama's Foreign Policy* (Washington, DC: Brookings Institution, 2012).
10. Gordon and Trainor, *Endgame*, p. 657.
11. Sly, "U.S. Policy on Iraq Questioned."

12. Serena Chaudhry, "Feeling Marginalized, Some Iraq Sunnis Eye Autonomy," *Reuters*, January 1, 2012, http://www.reuters.com/article/2012/01/01/us-iraq-politics-sunnis-idUSTRE80005620120101.

13. "Kurdish Leader Accuses Iraqi PM of Leading Country to 'Dictatorship,'" *Al-Arabiya News*, March 21, 2012, http://english.alarabiya.net/articles/2012/03/21/202063.html.

14. Salah Nasrawi, "2011: Why Did Iraq Miss the Arab Spring?" *Ahram Online*, December 31, 2011, http://english.ahram.org.eg/NewsContent/2/8/30638/World/Region/-Why-did-Iraq-miss-the-Arab-Spring.aspx.

15. Vali Nasr, *The Shia Revival: How Conflicts Within Islam Will Shape the Future* (New York: Norton, 2006).

16. Vali Nasr, "When Shiites Rise," *Foreign Affairs*, July/August 2006, http://www.foreignaffairs.com/articles/61733/vali-nasr/when-the-shiites-rise.

17. David Laitin, *Hegemony and Culture: Politics and Religious Change Among the Yoruba* (Chicago: University of Chicago Press, 1986).

18. There is rich scholarship explaining the absence of communal violence when states can make a case for minority rule making rebellion difficult. Donald Horowitz, *Ethnic Groups in Conflict* (Berkeley: University of California Press, 1987); Roger Peterson, *Understanding Ethnic Violence* (New York: Cambridge University Press, 2002); Stuart Kaufman, *Modern Hatreds: The Symbolic Politics of Ethnic War* (Ithaca, NY: Cornell University Press, 2001).

19. Vali Nasr, "Regional Implications of Shi'a Revival in Iraq," *Washington Quarterly* 27, no. 3 (Summer 2004): 7–24.

20. Vali Nasr, "Syria After the Fall," *New York Times*, July 29, 2012, p. SR4; Fouad Ajami, *The Syrian Rebellion* (Stanford, CA: Hoover Institution Press, 2012), pp. 111–34.

21. On the importance of these civic ties see Ashutosh Varshney, *Ethnic Conflict and Civic Life: Hindus and Muslims in India* (New Haven, CT: Yale University Press, 2002).

22. On how political interest could entrench the politics of identity and turn it violent see Paul R. Brass, *The Production of Hindu-Muslim Violence in Contemporary India* (Seattle: University of Washington Press, 2011).

23. Steven Wilkinson, *Votes and Violence: Electoral Competition and Ethnic Riots in India* (New York: Cambridge University Press, 2004).

24. Benjamin Miller, *States, Nations, and Great Powers: The Sources of Regional War and Peace* (New York: Cambridge University Press, 2007).

25. Niall Ferguson, *The War of the World* (New York: Penguin, 2006), pp. 28–30, 255.

26. Vali Nasr, "If the Arab Spring Turns Ugly," *New York Times*, August 27, 2011, http://www.nytimes.com/2011/08/28/opinion/sunday/the-dangers -lurking-in-the-arab-spring.html?pagewanted=all.

27. Ayad Allawi, "How the U.S. and the World Can Help Iraq," *Washington Post*, August 31, 2011, http://www.washingtonpost.com/opinions/how -the-us-and-the-world-can-help-iraq/2011/08/30/gIQAIPZxsJ_story.html.

CHAPTER 6: THE FADING PROMISE OF THE ARAB SPRING

1. Fawaz Gerges, *Obama and the Middle East: The End of America's Moment?* (New York: Palgrave Macmillan, 2012).

2. Martin S. Indyk, Kenneth G. Lieberthal, and Michael E. O'Hanlon, *Bending History: Barack Obama's Foreign Policy* (Washington, DC: Brookings Institution, 2012), p. 112.

3. Ibid., p. 121.

4. Ibid., p. 122.

5. Ibid.

6. Dan Ephron, "The Wrath of Mahmoud Abbas," *Daily Beast*, April 24, 2011, http://www.thedailybeast.com/articles/2011/04/25/mahmoud -abbas-interview-palestinian-leaders-frustration-with-obama.html.

7. Jim Lobe, "US Standing Plunges Across the Arab World," *Al-Jazeera*, July 14, 2011, http://www.aljazeera.com/indepth/features/2011/07/ 2011714104413787827.html.

8. "President Barack Obama's Inaugural Address," *White House Blog*, http://www.whitehouse.gov/blog/inaugural-address.

9. "Obama Pledges Support for Tunisia," *Al-Arabiya*, October 8, 2011, http://english.alarabiya.net/articles/2011/10/08/170747.html.

10. Indyk, Lieberthal, and O'Hanlon, *Bending History*, pp. 146–48. Also see the president's comments, "Remarks by the President on the Situation in Egypt," http://www.whitehouse.gov/the-press-office/2011/02/01/ remarks-president-situation-egypt.

11. "Clinton Calls for 'Peaceful, Orderly Transition' in Egypt," *McClatchy*, January 30, 2012, http://www.mcclatchydc.com/2011/01/30/107726/ clinton-calls-for-peaceful-orderly.html.

12. Steven Cook, *The Struggle for Egypt: From Nasser to Tahrir Square* (New York: Oxford University Press, 2011), pp. 272–307.

13. James Mann, *The Obamians: The Struggle Inside the White House to Define American Power* (New York: Viking, 2012).

14. Ibid., p. 279.

15. Helene Cooper, Mark Landler, and David E. Sanger, "In U.S. Signals to Egypt, Obama Straddled a Rift," *New York Times*, February 12, 2011,

http://www.nytimes.com/2011/02/13/world/middleeast/13diplomacy
.html?pagewanted=all.

16. Robin Wright, *Rock the Casbah: Rage and Rebellion Across the Islamic World* (New York: Simon & Schuster, 2012); Marc Lynch, *The Arab Uprising: The Unfinished Revolutions of the New Middle East* (New York: Public Affairs, 2012), pp. 43–66.

17. Alaa Al Aswany, *On the State of Egypt: What Made the Revolution Inevitable* (New York: Vintage, 2011); Tarek Osman, *Egypt on the Brink* (New Haven, CT: Yale University Press, 2011).

18. Alexis de Tocqueville, *The Old Regime and the French Revolution* (New York: Anchor, 1955), p. 177.

19. The Muslim Brotherhood had a plurality win of 38 percent of the vote and 235 of 498 seats in the 508-member assembly (a token ten seats were filled by appointment). The Salafist al-Nour party, Islamists like the Brotherhood only more so, won 28 percent and 123 seats.

20. Martin Indyk, Kenneth G. Lieberthal, and Michael O'Hanlon, "Scoring Obama's Foreign Policy," *Foreign Affairs*, May/June 2012, p. 38.

21. Tony Smith, *America's Mission: The United States and the Worldwide Struggle for Democracy in the Twentieth Century* (Princeton, NJ: Princeton University Press, 1994).

22. Mary Elise Sarotte, *1989: The Struggle to Create Post–Cold War Europe* (Princeton, NJ: Princeton University Press, 2011).

23. Lynch, *Arab Uprising*.

24. Vali Nasr, "Economics Versus Extremism," *Newsweek International*, November 2, 2009, pp. 56–58.

25. Steven Cook, "On the Economy, Egypt's New Leaders Should Follow Mubarak," *Bloomberg View*, May 26, 2011, http://www.bloomberg.com/news/2011-05-26/on-the-economy-egypt-s-new-leaders-should-follow-mubarak.html.

26. Ari Paul, "Egypt's Labor Pains: For Workers the Revolution Has Just Begun," *Dissent*, Fall 2011, http://www.dissentmagazine.org/article/?article=4048.

27. Sinan Ülgen, "Supporting Arab Economies in Transition," *International Economic Bulletin*, July 5, 2012, http://carnegieendowment.org/2012/07/05/supporting-arab-economies-intransition/ck6p.

28. "Unfinished Business," *Economist*, February 4, 2012, p. 49.

29. Ülgen, "Supporting Arab Economies in Transition."

30. Ibrahim Saif, *Challenges of Egypt's Economic Transition* (Washington, DC: Carnegie Endowment for International Peace, 2011), p. 4, available at http://carnegieendowment.org/files/egypt_econ_transition.pdf.

31. Hafez Ghanem, "Two Economic Priorities for Post-Election Egypt: Macro-Stabilization and Corruption Control," Brookings Institution,

June 25, 2012, http://www.brookings.edu/research/opinions/2012/06/25
-post-election-egypt-ghanem.

32. Ibid.

33. Carrie Rosefsky Wickham, *Mobilizing Islam: Religion, Activism, and Political Change in Egypt* (New York: Columbia University Press, 2002).

34. Jean-Paul Carvalho, *A Theory of the Islamic Revival*, Department of Economics, University of Oxford, March 2009, p. 39, http://www .economics.ox.ac.uk/Research/wp/pdf/paper424.pdf.

35. Nathan J. Brown, *When Victory Becomes an Option: Egypt's Muslim Brotherhood Confronts Success* (Washington, DC: Carnegie Endowment for International Peace, 2012), available at http://carnegieendowment.org/files/brotherhood_success.pdf.

36. Zeinab Abul-Magd, "The Egyptian Republic of Retired Generals," *Foreign Policy*, May 8, 2012, http://mideast.foreignpolicy.com/posts/2012/ 05/08/the_egyptian_republic_of_retired_generals.

37. David Sanger, *Confront and Conceal: Obama's Secret Wars and Surprising Use of American Power* (New York: Crown, 2012), pp. 314–15.

38. "The Other Arab Spring," *Economist*, August 11, 2012, http://www .economist.com/node/21560243?fsrc=scn/tw_ec/the_other_arab_spring; Vali Nasr, *Forces of Fortune: The Rise of the New Muslim Middle Class and What It Will Mean for Our World* (New York: Free Press, 2009); Christopher M. Schroeder, "The Middle East Could Be a Cradle of Innovation," *Harvard Business Review*, October 12, 2012; http://blogs .hbr.org/cs/2012/10/the_middle_east_could_be_a_cra.html; Wright, *Rock the Casbah*.

39. Michael Mandelbaum, *Democracy's Good Name: The Rise and Risks of the World's Most Popular Form of Government* (New York: Public Affairs, 2007), pp. 91–92.

40. "Hillary Clinton Deserves Credit for U.S. Role in Libya: View," *Bloomberg View*, September 7, 2011, http://www.bloomberg.com/news/2011 -09-08/hillary-clinton-deserves-credit-for-the-positive-u-s-role-in-libya -view.html.

41. Mann, *The Obamians*, p. 279.

42. William Arkin and Dana Priest, *Top Secret America: The Rise of the New American Security State* (Boston: Little, Brown, 2011).

43. Sanger, *Confront and Conceal*, pp. 243–72.

44. Peter Bergen, "Warrior in Chief," *New York Times*, April 29, 2012, p. SR1.

45. David Rodhe, "The Obama Doctrine," *Foreign Policy*, March/April 2012, pp. 65–69.

46. Greg Miller, "U.S. Set to Keep Kill Lists for Years," *Washington Post*, October 24, 2012, p. A1.

47. Michael O'Hanlon thinks that the administration has lacked an effective strategy for dealing with failing states: "Obama's Weak and Failing States Agenda," *Washington Quarterly* 35, no. 4 (Fall 2012): 67–80.

CHAPTER 7: THE GATHERING STORM

1. Hassan Bin Talal, "U.S. Can't Abandon the Middle East," *Los Angeles Times*, April 17, 2012, http://articles.latimes.com/2012/apr/17/opinion/la-oe-hassan-middle-east-engagement-20120417.

2. Daniel Yergin, *The Prize: The Epic Quest for Oil, Money, and Power* (New York: Simon & Schuster, 1991), pp. 167–83.

3. Andrew Scott Cooper, *The Oil Kings: How the U.S., Iran, and Saudi Arabia Changed the Balance of Power in the Middle East* (New York: Simon & Schuster, 2011), pp. 137–98.

4. See Gene Whitney, Carl E. Behrens, and Carol Glover, "U.S. Fossil Fuel Resources: Terminology, Reporting, and Summary," U.S. Congressional Research Service, March 25, 2011, p. 22, Table 6, http://assets.opencrs.com/rpts/R40872_20110325.pdf.

5. Alex de Marban, "North Dakota Crude Elbows Alaska Oil Out of Washington Refinery," *Alaska Dispatch,* June 13, 2012, http://www.alaskadispatch.com/article/north-dakota-crude-elbows-alaska-oil-out-washington-refinery.

6. Thomas Friedman, "The Other Arab Spring," *New York Times*, April 8, 2012, p. SR1.

7. "Lights Out: Another Threat to a Fragile Country's Stability," *Economist*, October 8, 2011, http://www.economist.com/node/21531495.

8. Michael Kugelman, "Pakistan's Climate Change Challenge," *Foreign Policy*, May 9, 2012, http://afpak.foreignpolicy.com/posts/2012/05/09/pakistans_climate_change_challenge.

9. John Bongaarts, Zeba Sathar, and Arshad Mahmoud, "Seven Billion People, How Many Pakistanis?" *News*, November 1, 2011, http://www.thenews.com.pk/Todays-News-9-75429-Seven-billion-people-how-many-Pakistanis; "Pakistan to Become the World's 4th Largest Nation by 2050: Survey," *Pakistan Defence*, June 28, 2010, http://www.defence.pk/forums/economy-development/63702-pakistan-become-4th-largest-nation-population-2050-a.html.

10. Robert Worth, "Earth Is Parched Where Syrian Farms Thrived," *New York Times,* October 13, 2010, http://www.nytimes.com/2010/10/14/world/middleeast/14syria.html.

11. Ruchir Sharma, *Breakout Nations: In Pursuit of the Next Economic Miracles* (New York: Norton, 2012), p. 23.

12. Zuliu Hu and Mohsin S. Khan, *Why Is China Growing So Fast?* Economic Issues series, no. 8 (Washington, DC: International Monetary Fund, 1997), p. 1, http://www.imf.org/external/pubs/ft/issues8/issue8.pdf.

13. Niall Ferguson, "Mideast's Next Dilemma: With Turkey Flexing Its Muscles, We May Soon Face a Revived Ottoman Empire," *Newsweek*, June 19, 2011, http://www.thedailybeast.com/newsweek/2011/06/19/turkey-the-mideast-s-next-dilemma.html#.

14. Ahmet Davutoğlu, *Civilizational Transformation and the Muslim World* (Kuala Lumpur, Malaysia: Mahir Publications, 1994); "The Davutoglu Effect," *Economist*, October 21, 2010, http://www.economist.com/node/17276420.

15. Sharma, *Breakout Nations*, p. 119.

16. Vali Nasr, *The Shia Revival: How Conflicts Within Islam Will Shape the Future* (New York: Norton, 2006).

17. Halil Karaveli, "Why Does Turkey Want Regime Change in Syria?" *National Interest*, July 23, 2012, http://nationalinterest.org/commentary/why-does-turkey-want-regime-change-syria-7227.

18. "Alevis Fire at Government in Ongoing Cemevi Quarrel," *Hurriyet Daily News*, August 11, 2012, http://www.hurriyetdailynews.com/alevis-fire-at-government-in-ongoing-cemevi-quarrel.aspx?pageID=238&nID=25298&NewsCatID=339.

19. "Growing Less Mild," *Economist*, April 14, 2012, p. 61.

20. Halil M. Karaveli, "Why Turkey Is Not Going to Help Midwife a Pluralist Syria," *Turkey Analyst* 5, no. 15, Central Asia-Caucasus Institute, August 13, 2012, http://www.silkroadstudies.org/new/inside/turkey/2012/120813a.html.

21. Ibid.

22. "Erdoğan Lambasts Opposition, Says Syrian Crisis Not Sectarian," *Today's Zaman*, May 15, 2012, http://www.sundayszaman.com/sunday/newsDetail_getNewsById.action?newsId=280401.

23. Anthony Shadid, "Turkey Predicts Alliance with Egypt as Regional Anchors," *New York Times*, September 19, 2011, p. A4.

24. Matt Bradley, "Saudi Arabia Closes Embassy in Egypt," *Wall Street Journal*, April 28, 2012, http://online.wsj.com/article/SB10001424052702304723304577371912180606218.html?mod=WSJ_World_LEFTSecondNews.

25. Tony Karon, "Does Qatar Share the West's Agenda in Libya?" *Time*, October 5, 2011, http://globalspin.blogs.time.com/2011/10/05/does-qatar-share-the-wests-agenda-in-libya/; Rod Norland and David Kirkpatrick,

"Islamists' Growing Sway Raises Questions for Libya," *New York Times*, September 14, 2011, http://www.nytimes.com/2011/09/15/world/africa/in-libya-islamists-growing-sway-raises-questions.html?pagewanted=all.

26. Golnaz Esfandiari, "Qatar Conquers Iran's Airspace," *Radio Free Europe Radio Liberty*, November 5, 2011, http://www.rferl.org/content/qatar_conquers_irans_airspace/24382213.html.

27. Sharma, *Breakout Nations*, p. 213; Vali Nasr, "Will Saudis Kill the Arab Spring?" *Bloomberg View*, May 23, 2011, http://www.bloomberg.com/news/2011-05-23/will-the-saudis-kill-the-arab-spring-.html.

28. Sharma, *Breakout Nations*, p. 216.

29. Robert Kaplan, *The Revenge of Geography: What the Map Tells Us About Coming Conflicts and the Battle Against Fate* (New York: Random House, 2012), p. 258.

30. Kiren Aziz Chaudhry, *The Price of Wealth: Economies and Institutions in the Middle East* (Ithaca, NY: Cornell University Press, 1997); Thomas W. Lippman, *Saudi Arabia on the Edge: The Uncertain Future of an American Ally* (Washington, DC: Potomac Books, 2012).

31. Toby Jones, *Desert Kingdom: How Oil and Water Forged Modern Saudi Arabia* (Cambridge: Harvard University Press, 2010).

32. Nasr, *Shia Revival*, pp. 147–68.

33. Interview with a former Iranian official, July 2011.

CHAPTER 8: THE CHINA CHALLENGE

1. Jeffrey Bader, who worked on China at the Obama White House, writes of President Obama's belief that America had neglected Asia because of its focus on the Middle East and al-Qaeda in *Obama and China's Rise: An Insider's Account of America's Asia Strategy* (Washington, DC: Brookings Institution, 2012); also see David M. Lampton, "China and the United States: Beyond Balance," *Asia Policy* 14 (July 2012): 41.

2. Ibid.

3. Hillary Clinton, "America's Pacific Century," *Foreign Policy*, November 2011, http://www.foreignpolicy.com/articles/2011/10/11/americas_pacific_century.

4. Ibid.

5. Kenneth Lieberthal and Wang Jisi, *Addressing U.S.-China Strategic Distrust*, John L. Thornton China Center Monograph Series, no. 4 (Washington, DC: Brookings Institution, 2012).

6. Dale Copeland, "Economic Interdependence and the Future of U.S.-China Relations," in G. John Ikenberry and Michael Mastaduno, eds.,

International Relations Theory and the Asia-Pacific (New York: Columbia University Press, 2003), pp. 323–52.

7. Henry M. Kissinger, "The Future of U.S.-Chinese Relations: Conflict Is a Choice, Not a Necessity," *Foreign Affairs*, March/April 2012, http://www.foreignaffairs.com/articles/137245/henry-a-kissinger/the -future-of-us-chinese-relations.

8. David Smith, "Hillary Clinton Launches African Tour with Veiled Attack on China," *Guardian*, August 1, 2012, http://www.guardian.co .uk/world/2012/aug/01/hillary-clinton-africa-china.

9. Aaron Friedberg, *A Contest for Supremacy: China, America, and the Struggle for Mastery in Asia* (New York: Norton, 2011).

10. Arvind Subramanian, *Eclipse: Living in the Shadow of China's Economic Dominance* (Washington, DC: Institute of International Economics, 2012); Martin Jacques, *When China Rules the World: The End of the Western World and the Birth of a New Global Order*, 2nd ed. (New York: Penguin Press, 2012).

11. Zachary Karabell, *Superfusion: How China and America Became One Economy and Why the World's Prosperity Depends on It* (New York: Simon & Schuster, 2009); Robyn Meredith, *The Elephant and the Dragon: The Rise of India and China and What It Means for All of Us* (New York: Norton, 2007); Nicholas Lardy, *Sustaining China's Economic Growth After the Global Financial Crisis* (Washington, DC: Peterson Institute, 2012).

12. Kathrin Hille, "Clinton Struggles to Soothe Beijing's Fears," *Financial Times*, September 5, 2012, http://www.ft.com/intl/cms/s/0/9b296eec -f728-11e1-8e9e-00144feabdc0.html#axzz25abzfG2p.

13. Andrew J. Nathan and Andrew Scobell, "How China Sees America," *Foreign Affairs*, September/October 2012, http://www.foreignaffairs .com/articles/138009/andrew-j-nathan-and-andrew-scobell/how-china -sees-america?page=show; Robert Ross, "The Problem with the Pivot," *Foreign Affairs*, November/December 2012, pp. 70–82.

14. Thom Shanker, "Panetta Set to Discuss U.S. Shift in Asia Trip," *New York Times*, September 14, 2012, p. A4.

15. Kissinger, "Future of U.S.-Chinese Relations."

16. Henry M. Kissinger, *On China* (New York: Penguin Press, 2012), pp. 487–530; Zbigniew Brzezinski, *Strategic Vision: America and the Crisis of Global Power* (New York: Basic Books, 2012), pp. 155–82.

17. Daniel Yergin, *The Quest: Energy, Security, and the Making of the Modern World* (New York: Penguin Press, 2011), p. 222.

18. Rebecca M. Nelson, Mary Jane Bolle, and Shayerah Ilias, *U.S. Trade and Investment in the Middle East and North Africa: Overview and*

Issues for Congress, Congressional Research Service report, January 20, 2012, http://fpc.state.gov/documents/organization/183739.pdf.

19. *Direction of Trade Statistics Yearbook, 2011* (Washington, DC: International Monetary Fund, 2011), http://www.elibrary.imf.org/view/IMF042/11827-9781616351489/11827-9781616351489/11827-9781616351489 .xml?rskey=J2QZQv&result=1&q=Direction%20of%20Trade%20 Statistics%20Yearbook,%202011.

20. Qian Xuewen, "Sino-Arab Economic Trade and Cooperation: Situations, Tasks, Issues, and Strategies," *Journal of Middle Eastern and Islamic Studies* 5, no. 4 (2011): 68.

21. Kissinger, "Future of U.S.-Chinese Relations."

22. Bernard Gordon, "Trading Up in Asia," *Foreign Affairs*, July/August 2012, www.foreignaffairs.com/print/134960.

23. Jane Perlez, "Clinton Makes Effort to Rechannel the Rivalry with China," *New York Times*, July 8, 2012, p. A7.

24. Joseph Nye, "Energy Independence in an Interdependent World," *Project Syndicate*, July 11, 2012, http://www.project-syndicate.org/commentary/energy-independence-in-an-interdependent-world.

25. "China to Build $2bn Railway for Iran," *Telegraph*, September 7, 2010, http://www.telegraph.co.uk/finance/china-business/7985812/China-to -build-2bn-railway-for-Iran.html.

26. Myles Smith, "China-Kyrgyzstan-Uzbekistan Railway Project Brings Political Risks," *Central Asia Institute Analyst*, Johns Hopkins University, March 7, 2012, http://www.cacianalyst.org/?q=node/5731.

27. "Turkey, China Sign Two Nuclear Agreements During PM's Visit," *Daily Hurriyet*, April 10, 2012, http://www.hurriyetdailynews .com/turkey-china-sign-two-nuclear-agreements-during-pms-visit .aspx?pageID=238&nID=18032&NewsCatID=348. This article puts the 2010 trade figures at $19.5 billion; TUSIAD in Beijing puts the 2012 figures at $25 billion.

28. Interviews with oil executives investing in Iraq, and with Turkish Kurdish Regional Government officials, August and September 2012.

29. Kent Calder, *The New Continentalism: Energy and Twenty-First Century Eurasian Geopolitics* (New Haven, CT: Yale University Press, 2012), pp. xxxi–xxxii.

30. Yergin, *Quest*, p. 210.

31. James Fallows, *China Airborne* (New York: Pantheon, 2012), p. 98.

32. Yergin, *Quest*, p. 172.

33. Robert Kaplan, "Center Stage for the 21st Century: Power Plays in the Indian Ocean," *Foreign Affairs*, April/May 2009, http://www .foreignaffairs.com/print/64832.

34. *Preparing for China's Urban Billion* (San Francisco: McKinsey Global Institute, 2009), p. 18, cited in Fallows, *China Airborne*, p. 101.

35. John Lee, "China's Geostrategic Search for Oil," *Washington Quarterly* 35, no. 3 (Summer 2012): 75–92.

36. Steve Coll, *Private Empire: ExxonMobil and American Power* (New York: Penguin Press, 2012), p. 240.

37. Ibid., pp. 240–41.

38. Yergin, *Quest*, pp. 222–23.

39. Kalder, *The New Continentalism*, p. 3.

40. John Mearsheimer, *The Tragedy of Great Power Politics* (New York: Norton, 2001), pp. 360–402.

41. Coll, *Private Empire*, p. 243.

42. Robert Kaplan, *Monsoon: The Indian Ocean and the Future of American Power* (New York: Random House, 2010).

43. Kalder, *New Continentalism*, p. 36.

44. Farhan Bokhari and Kathrin Hille, "Pakistan in Talks to Hand Port to China," *Financial Times*, August 31, 2012, http://www.ft.com/intl/cms/s/0/5c58608c-f2a6-11e1-ac41-00144feabdc0.html#axzz25gV7a6Qn.

45. Kalder, *New Continentalism*, pp. xxxi–xxxiii.

46. Robert Kaplan, "The Geography of Chinese Power," *Foreign Affairs*, May/June, 2010, http://www.foreignaffairs.com/articles/66205/robert-d-kaplan/the-geography-of-chinese-power?page=4.

47. Kalder, *New Continentalism*, p. 8.

48. Susan Shirk, *China: Fragile Superpower* (New York: Oxford University Press, 2008), pp. 257–58.

49. Kalder, *New Continentalism*, p. 23.

50. Tony Smith, *The Pattern of Imperialism: The United States, Great Britain, and the Late-Industrializing World Since 1815* (New York: Cambridge University Press, 1981).

51. Coll, *Private Empire*, p. 241.

52. Kissinger, *On China*, pp. 513–30.

53. See Arthur S. Herman, *To Rule the Waves: How the British Navy Shaped the Modern World* (New York: HarperCollins, 2004).

54. Dambisa Mayo, *Winner Takes All: China's Race for Resources and What It Means for the World* (New York: Basic Books, 2012).

55. Debora Brautigam, *The Dragon's Gift: The Real Story of China in Africa* (New York: Oxford University Press, 2010).

56. Vali Nasr, "International Politics, Domestic Imperatives, and the Rise of Politics of Identity: Sectarianism in Pakistan, 1979–1997," *Comparative Politics* 32, no. 2 (January 2000): 171–90; Vali Nasr, "The Rise of Sunni Militancy in Pakistan: The Changing Role of Islamism and the Ulama

in Society and Politics," *Modern Asian Studies* 34, no. 1 (January 2000): 139–80.

57. Vali Nasr, *The Shia Revival: How Conflicts Within Islam Will Shape the Future* (New York: Norton, 2006), pp. 147–68.

58. James Lamont and Farhan Bokhari, "China-Pakistan Military Links Upset India," *Financial Times*, November 27, 2009, http://www.ft.com/intl/cms/s/0/9d5497f0-db8d-11de-9424-00144feabdc0.html.

59. Ibid.

60. "Pakistan, China Have Shared Interests in Peace Promotion: PM," *Nation*, May 15, 2012, http://www.nation.com.pk/pakistan-news-newspaper-daily-english-online/islamabad/15-May-2012/pakistan-china-have-shared-interests-in-peace-promotion-pm.

61. Dennis Kux, *The United States and Pakistan, 1947–2000: Disenchanted Allies* (Baltimore: Johns Hopkins University Press, 2001).

62. Harsh V. Pant, "The Pakistan Thorn in China-India-U.S. Relations," *Washington Quarterly* 35, no. 1 (Winter 2012): 83.

63. John W. Garver, "Sino-Indian Rapprochement and the Sino-Pakistan Entente," *Political Science Quarterly* 111, no. 2 (Summer 1996): 326–33.

64. Pant, "Pakistan Thorn," p. 86.

65. Ibid., p. 85.

66. R. Jeffrey Smith and Joby Warrick, "Pakistani Nuclear Scientist Accounts Tell of Chinese Proliferation," *Washington Post*, November 13, 2009, http://www.washingtonpost.com/wp-dyn/content/article/2009/11/12/AR2009111211060.html.

67. Kaplan, "Center Stage for the 21st Century."

68. Ibid.

69. John W. Garver, *China and Iran: Ancient Partners in a Post-Imperial World* (Seattle: University of Washington, 2006).

70. Scott Harold and Alireza Nader, *China and Iran: Economic, Political, and Military Relations* (Washington, DC: RAND Corporation, 2012).

71. John Garver, Flynt Leverett, and Hillary Mann Leverett, *Moving (Slightly) Closer to Iran: China's Shifting Calculus for Managing Its "Persian Gulf Dilemma"* (Washington, DC: Reischauer Center for East Asian Studies, Johns Hopkins School of Advanced International Studies, 2009).

72. John Garver, "Is China Playing a Dual Game with Iran?" *Washington Quarterly* 34, no. 1 (Winter 2011): 75–88; "The Iran Nuclear Issue: The View from Beijing," Asia Briefing no. 100 (overview), International Crisis Group, February 17, 2010, http://www.crisisgroup.org/en/regions/

asia/north-east-asia/china/B100-the-iran-nuclear-issue-the-view-from
-beijing.aspx.

73. Fallows, *China Airborne*, p. 190.

74. James Mann, *The Obamians: The Struggle Inside the White House to Redefine American Power* (New York: Viking, 2012), pp. 246–47.

CONCLUSION: AMERICA, THE PIVOTAL NATION

1. Gideon Rachman, *Zero-Sum Future: American Power in an Age of Anxiety* (New York: Simon & Schuster, 2011); Thomas L. Friedman and Michael Mandelbaum, *That Used to Be Us: How America Fell Behind in the World It Invented and How We Can Come Back* (New York: Farrar, Straus and Giroux, 2011); Edward Luce, *Time to Start Thinking: America in the Age of Descent* (New York: Atlantic Monthly Press, 2012); Robert J. Lieber, *Power and Willpower in the American Future* (New York: Cambridge University Press, 2012).

2. Roger C. Altman and Richard N. Haass, "American Profligacy and American Power: The Consequences of Fiscal Irresponsibility," *Foreign Affairs*, November/December 2010, http://www.foreignaffairs.com/articles/66778/roger-c-altman-and-richard-n-haass/american-profligacy-and-american-power. Brzezinski argues that restoring America's position in the world must start with putting its economic house in order. Zbigniew Brzezinski, *Strategic Vision: America and the Crisis of Global Power* (New York: Basic Books, 2012), pp. 37–74.

3. Fareed Zakaria, *The Post-American World, Release 2.0* (New York: Norton, 2011); Charles A. Kupchan, *No One's World: The West, the Rising Rest, and the Coming Global Turn* (New York: Oxford University Press, 2012).

4. Joseph Nye, *The Future of Power* (New York: Public Affairs, 2011).

5. Leslie H. Gelb provides an instructive examination of this issue in *Power Rules: How Common Sense Can Rescue American Foreign Policy* (New York: Harper, 2009).

6. Robert Kagan, "Not Fade Away: The Myth of American Decline," *New Republic*, January 11, 2012, http://www.tnr.com/article/politics/magazine/99521/america-world-power-declinism.

7. "Fact Sheet: 'A Moment of Opportunity' in the Middle East and North Africa," press release, May 19, 2011, http://www.whitehouse.gov/the-press-office/2011/05/19/fact-sheet-moment-opportunity-middle-east-and-north-africa.

8. Hassan Bin Talal, "U.S. Can't Abandon the Middle East," *Los Angeles*

Times, April 17, 2012, http://articles.latimes.com/2012/apr/17/opinion/la
-oe-hassan-middle-east-engagement-20120417.

9. Vali Nasr, *Forces of Fortune: The Rise of the New Muslim Middle Class
   and What It Will Mean for Our World* (New York: Free Press, 2009),
   pp. 252–63.
10. Brzezinski, *Strategic Vision*, p. 190.
11. G. John Ikenberry, *Liberal Leviathan: The Origins, Crisis, and Trans-
    formation of the American World Order* (Princeton, NJ: Princeton
    University Press, 2011).
12. Robert O. Keohane, "Hegemony and After," *Foreign Affairs*, July/
    August 2012, http://www.foreignaffairs.com/articles/137690/robert-o
    -keohane/hegemony-and-after.
13. G. John Ikenberry, "The Future of the Liberal World Order," *Foreign
    Affairs*, May/June 2011, http://www.foreignaffairs.com/articles/67730/g
    -john-ikenberry/the-future-of-the-liberal-world-order.

INDEX

A NOTE ABOUT THE AUTHOR

Vali Nasr is Dean of the Paul H. Nitze School of Advanced International Studies of Johns Hopkins University and the bestselling author of *The Shia Revival* and *Forces of Fortune*. From 2009 to 2011, he served as Senior Adviser to Special Representative for Afghanistan and Pakistan, Ambassador Richard Holbrooke. He is a Nonresident Fellow at the Brookings Institution and a contributor to Bloomberg View; he lives in Washington, DC.